ROAD
THROUGH
TIME

ROAD THROUGH TIME

The Story of Humanity on the Move

Mary Soderstrom

 University of Regina Press

Printed and bound in Canada at Marquis. The text of this book is printed on 100%
post-consumer recycled paper with earth-friendly vegetable-based inks.

Cover design: Duncan Campbell, University of Regina Press
Text design: John van der Woude, JVDW Designs
Copy editor: Elsa Johnston
Proofreader: Kristine Douaud
Indexer: Siusan Moffat
Map: Julia Siemer
Cover art: (*front cover*) Pleistocene human footprints from the Willandra Lakes,
southeastern Australia. / Istockphoto; (*back cover*) Buzz Aldrin's bootprint from the
Apollo 11 mission July 20, 1969. Image credit: NASA

Library and Archives Canada Cataloguing in Publication

Soderstrom, Mary, 1942-, author
Road through time : the story of humanity on the move / Mary Soderstrom.

Includes bibliographical references and index. Issued in print and electronic formats.
ISBN 978-0-88977-477-3 (softcover).—ISBN 978-0-88977-478-0 (PDF).—
ISBN 978-0-88977-479-7 (HTML)

1. Roads—History. 2. Roads—Social aspects—History. 3. Travel—History.
4. Human beings—Migrations. 5. Social change. 6. Civilization. I. Title.

TE145.S63 2017   388.109   C2016-907590-7   C2016-907591-5

10 9 8 7 6 5 4 3 2 1

University of Regina Press, University of Regina
Regina, Saskatchewan, Canada, S4S 0A2
tel: (306) 585-4758 fax: (306) 585-4699
U OF R PRESS   web: www.uofrpress.ca

We acknowledge the support of the Canada Council for the Arts for our publishing
program. We acknowledge the financial support of the Government of Canada. / Nous
reconnaissons l'appui financier du gouvernement du Canada. This publication was made
possible through Creative Saskatchewan's Creative Industries Production Grant Program.

This one's for Lukas.

Some of the travel described in this book was indirectly funded by the Conseil des arts et des lettres du Québec. I am very grateful for its support.

CONTENTS

Oregon Cave
C. 14 000 BCE

Clovis
C. 11 500 BCE

Monte Verde
C. 10 500 BCE

EARLY
HUMAN
MIGRATIONS

All dates are very approximate.
Paths are suggestions of routes.

Cartography: Julia Siemer, University of Regina, 2016.

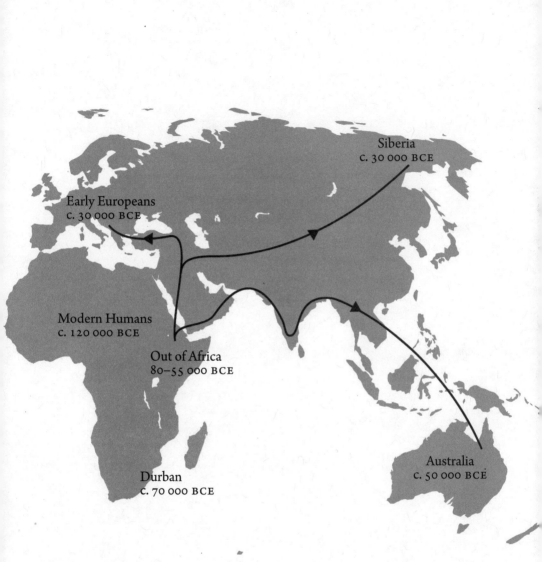

Chapter One

ON THE ROAD, I

P EOPLE'S EYES LIT UP WHEN I TOLD THEM I WANTED TO WRITE a book about roads. Ah, yes, nearly everyone said, you're going to do another *On the Road*! Since its publication in 1957, Jack Kerouac's beat generation classic has become emblematic of the romance of the road, of inviting paths taken or not taken.

Some of these people have known me since I was young in the San Francisco Bay Area and wore black stockings and turtlenecks, long hair, and political buttons. They may even have seen me once or twice when I ironed my frizzy red hair to make it hiply straight.

Others just knew that I've always read everything I could get my hands on, and that I followed my interests wherever they led me. Obviously, all of them expected a book that tried to be as edgy and adventurous as Kerouac's, with some facts thrown in.

I agreed that *On the Road* would have been a great name for my book, but I wanted to write something in a different register from Kerouac's sprawling chronicle of a hipster's wanderings. What interested me were the tracks that humans have made over time. I'd written two non-fiction books about cities and transportation, and become increasingly convinced that the roads we build determine our future.

Roads are vectors for change and exchange, the most enduring monuments we have built. In the last century and a half, their proliferation and transformation from simple routes for pedestrian or animal traffic to motorways have had disastrous effects on the environment, our consumption of resources, and our health.

But I'd never read *On the Road*, and I didn't put it on the reading list as I began my research. It was too light, too "fictional," too far away from the roads I wanted to talk about. My idea was to start with an account of a road trip I took when I was ten with my mother and sister, which opened my eyes to a world much larger than the familiar one where time is measured in minutes, seconds, and hours.[1] Then I'd go on, giving a virtual tour of the roads that humans have travelled since a small band left Africa thousands of years ago. The book would end with another bus trip, this time through South America where a new highway demonstrates many of the dangers of our obsession with roads.

However, the paths we take often have twists and turns. Certainly, mine has. Despite a childhood and youth on the West Coast where the car was king, at twenty-six I came east to another country, another culture. Since then you might say I've become a born-again pedestrian. For decades, I've lived in one of North America's most walkable cities, Montreal. On my travels, I've trudged down country roads in Tanzania, strolled through the streets of Paris, Lisbon, and Singapore, and backpacked in mountains on both sides of North America. Roads have become a passion, and to my surprise, once I began to read Kerouac's book, I discovered that it is far more relevant to serious reflection about roads than I expected. Same thing for Cormac McCarthy's dystopian novel *The Road*, while I learned much from Le Corbusier's *The City of To-morrow and Its Planning* and the ancient epic *Gilgamesh*. We'll get to them all in good time, but to begin, let us return to those two summer days in the mid-1950s when my mother, my sister, and I rode the Greyhound bus from the southwest corner of the United States almost to its northwest corner.

What I remember particularly was leaving Southern California as the bus crept along the Grapevine and crossed Tejon Pass. On the north side, the highway switched back and forth, but the name did not come from its vine-like circuitous route. Instead, it was inspired by the wild grapes found by Native Americans and Spanish explorers when they followed a cleft in the hills to the pass. By the time we travelled the road, grapes were few and far between, and the road's transformation into an eight-lane freeway clogged with traffic had just begun.

The moment that sticks in my mind occurred when we had been on the road for about ten hours. I was bored, and tired of sitting. My mother, in the seat in front of me next to my sister, who had already been carsick a couple of times, was not inclined to be sympathetic when I complained that the upholstery made the back of my legs itch. "Stop kicking the seat," was all she said.

Then the man next to me said: "Look out the window." It was half a command, and the first thing he'd said to me since we left Los Angeles. I stared at him. I wasn't supposed to talk to strangers, but did that include your seatmate on a long trip? I didn't know, but I did look out the window, because there was nothing much else to do.

I saw layers of rocks slanting upward like one side of a giant "A." They were purple, rusty brown, colours that balanced between the rich and the repellent, hinting of both royal robes and dried blood. They were beautiful and unsettlingly strange, unlike anything I have ever seen before.

I must have said something, but I have no recollection of what, just as I have no idea who the man was, no memory of what he looked like. What I do know with absolute certainty is that he introduced me to the first road through time I encountered.

Mary and Laurie, the girls who took the road trip in the 1950s.

Photo: Author's collection

"Pretty impressive, aren't they?" he said. "Each layer was laid down a long, long time ago at the bottom of some sea," he added.

I didn't believe him. At home in San Diego, we lived near a beach backed by cliffs where you could see layers of rock. Sedimentary rocks, my mother said. Climbing on them, she and I had found a few fossil shells in the horizontal bands.

But these rocks were almost standing straight up and down.

"No," I said to the man on the bus. "That can't be. Rocks like that are supposed to be flat."

"Ah," he said. "That's one of the wonders of the earth."

He talked about earthquakes—I'd felt three, but never anything very big—and the effect of small movements adding up over time, about mountains being thrust up, and how the earth was very, very old.

When the bus stopped next—at Bakersfield, a half-hour for supper in the scruffy Greyhound cafe—I asked my mother about what he'd said. She nodded, yes, that kind of thing happened, and then told me to take

"I saw layers of rocks slanting upward like one side of a giant "A." They were beautiful and unsettlingly strange, unlike anything I had ever seen before."

Photo: Karnak Ridge, Nevada / Timothy H. O'Sullivan, 1867 / Public Domain my sister and save places at one of the tables while she waited in line to place an order for coffee, milkshakes, and hot dogs.

Then we went back on the road, continuing north on Highway 99. But my life took a slightly different heading from then on, which has led me to this point where I want to talk about roads and time and change.

Ever since humans stood up and walked they have left tracks across the landscape. From the footprints that a trio of prehumans left in soft volcanic ash 3.6 million years ago in East Africa to a newly completed interoceanic highway in South America, we change things wherever we travel. These marks—be they dirt trails or concrete highways—frequently outlast the societies that built them. Even though we linger only a flicker of time in the history of this planet, the effects of our travel long outlive us.

Humans are engineered to think in short stretches of time, however, so the potential consequences of our actions in the long run almost always escape us. How can we reconcile our own sprints through time with the marathon we ought to consider? That is the double subject of *Road through Time.*

To explore this question, a map of where such an adventure might take us is necessary.

In "Bottleneck on the Road from Eden," this book will take a look at the way our ancestors travelled on foot for unbelievably long distances. Beginning with the tricky crossing from Africa to the Eurasian continent, we'll discover how humans were fruitful and multiplied, peopling most of the rest of the earth in perhaps twenty thousand years.

Humans' impact on the landscape was minimal for eons, until they mastered fire, tamed beasts of burden, began to grow crops, and defaced the forest that bordered the plains where they had prospered. "Into the Trees" tells this story.

As population centres grew and trade increased, the paths people took wore more deeply into the land. Because trade goods had to be transported by animals or humans, only the very precious were worth the effort. "The Things They Carried" tells the story of these trade routes, beginning with the Obsidian Roads and the Lapis Lazuli Road in Asia.

With increasing population and excess production, more complicated social organization meant greater inter-group conflict. "Warriors'

Roads" explores the routes built by emperors from Persia to the Andes, vestiges of which we can see today, and along whose tracks many of us still travel.

Although this is a book about roads, travel by water must not be ignored. It goes back as a far as those first steps out of Africa, but it came into its own as trade demand increased. Without help from machines, goods and people are easier to move on water than over land. "Across the Water" tells how sea and river trade routes developed, and how canals were built where rivers didn't run, until the great population crescendo that saw millions of people take to ships to exploit and settle new-found lands.

This New World wasn't uninhabited, despite what explorers from Europe thought. "Mystery Roads" follows the paths taken by adventurers out of Asia into the western hemisphere. This is a story that new scientific techniques are rewriting.

"The Revenge of the Road" chronicles the massive road building of the nineteenth and twentieth centuries, including the growth of cities, and dependence on, first, railroad and then internal combustion vehicles.

In "Speeding," we collide with the disaster wrought by our roads and the vehicles that run on them. Our sprawling cities designed—or redesigned—for the automobile are a big part of the problem. Two ways to deal with this challenge are explored in visits to Curitiba and Brasília in Brazil.

The book ends with "On the Road, 11," aboard a second trip by bus, this one across the Andes from Cusco, Peru, to Rio Branco, Brazil, on the new Interoceanic (or Transoceanic) Highway. From footpaths to roads opening up wilderness, the trip gives a front-row seat on massive changes taking place throughout the world. In the distance, we'll see the end of our collective travel on this fragile planet or, conversely, a future that will allow us to continue moving onward.

FIRST, THOUGH, A FEW THOUGHTS ABOUT TIME. In cities it is easy to forget the most basic signposts of time's passage. There is a difference between night and day, and in most places, the earth's progress around the sun is reflected in the length of day itself. But at night, the moon and stars are now swept away by artificial light radiating from millions of sources. Rarely does the full moon catch your attention, while the stars that you can see can be counted on one hand.

The night of our bus ride north, though, was an introduction to the glories of the night and the full moon. By then we'd worked our way to the front of the bus. My mother had persuaded other passengers that if they didn't want a car-sick child sitting near them, they should let her and my sister take the seats by the door where my sister could look out the windshield and hopefully not get sick again.

That left me on my own, two or three rows back, with a seat to myself where my mother told me to stretch out and sleep. We had hours and hours before us. It would be the early afternoon before my grandfather would come and pick us up at the small town bus stop that he and my mother had worked out was closest to where my grandparents lived.

The night was hot, the bus windows were open, and even though the windshield had been carefully cleaned at the last stop, it was already splattered with remains of dozens of flying insects that had collided with it as we sped along. The road itself was nearly empty, except for the long haul trucks and a few passenger vehicles driven by insomniacs or people in a great hurry to get some place. This was the northern end of the valley, the flat, fertile heart of California. Boring scenery, some would say.

The Sacramento River drains this part of the Central Valley and the northern Sierra Nevada mountains. As we'd driven north earlier in the day there had been a few places where we could see the mountains dimly to the east. Now in the darkness, they were invisible out my window.

My mother had said to be quiet if I couldn't sleep, and for awhile if I craned my neck I could see the red glow of her cigarette as she sat quietly with my sister. Then she quit smoking too, and the bus rolled along with its load of exhausted travelers. But enforced inactivity made me restless, and when all was silent, I crept forward until I was sitting on the top step of the stairs into the main level of the bus, almost next to the driver. Ahead I could see the road going straight for what seemed like forever.

Or so I thought.

The driver realized I was there, and he shot a quick look at me. "Come down here so you can get a better look," he said.

I remember hesitating: my mother was always after me to not get in the way, and certainly if I took the two steps down, I might be. Yet it was an invitation, and I had nothing else to do.

So I stepped down cautiously into the second revelation of the trip. When I looked up, the white dome of Mount Shasta faced me, completely lit by the full moon which had just about reached the zenith. It was the most beautiful thing I had ever seen, even more wonderful than the rocks.

I don't remember what happened next, perhaps I gasped, perhaps I exclaimed something. My mother heard me at some point and hissed for me to go back and sit down. The driver shot me a quick smile. I don't remember what else.

Except … except that the vision of the moonlit mountain comes to me at the oddest times—it has for years. It's the thing that I think of first whenever anyone mentions the moon and the stars, and how we are governed by them.

This vision and indeed that whole trip are examples of the elasticity of perceived time, an excellent point to reflect on humanity's place in

Mount Shasta, one of the volcanoes that have shaken the earth since well before humans began making roads.

Photo: Caia Cupito / Ore-Cal Rc&D / Released for Use in the Public Domain

the universe, which is seemingly timeless and yet is divided by us into discrete sections.

Years, months, weeks, days, hours, minutes, seconds—those were the divisions humans long ago agreed to use to consider time. However, two other kinds of time have become important in the last century. The first is the discovery of marvelously small units of time, which are measured by the vibration of atoms in certain elements. The second is the time that has passed since events took place tens of thousands or even millions of years ago. The two are linked because changes in atoms can be used to determine when events in the deep past happened. This in turn gives an idea of how long ago something took place—for example, when a volcano erupted, or a stone tool was made, or a piece of wood was burned into ashes—and so, of how far the world has travelled on the road of time since then. As this book proceeds, there will be many references to dating by these means.[2]

KEROUAC PROBABLY WOULDN'T HAVE CARED MUCH ABOUT THAT sort of dating, nor about the deep past. Dating women was more his thing, and his world was lived full tilt. He wrote the first draft of *On the Road* practically non-stop in three weeks on a 120-foot scroll of paper, and throughout his life he purported to live for the moment.

Too bad he used that title though, I thought, when I finished the plan for my book. It could describe what I wanted to do, although his story and mine had almost nothing in common, I was sure. No point even in reading it.

Then, in the summer of 2013, I chanced to see that one of Jack Kerouac's many women had just died. Bea Kozera was ninety-two, and, even though their romance lasted only a couple of weeks, they remained in contact for a time afterward. She had no idea of his renown, however, until a researcher found letters from her in the Kerouac archives and contacted her three years before her death. Her children and grandchildren were surprised to learn of the connection. They saw her as someone devoted to her family and her second husband, and who had worked hard to raise herself out of the poverty of a farm worker's life.

Yet, the obituaries said, she and Kerouac met in the same Bakersfield bus station where my mother, my sister, and I had our supper. He thought she was going in the other direction, and was delighted to find her across the aisle from him when he got on the bus that then climbed the Grapevine on a hot summer night. The two weeks of romance that followed was an emotional turning point in his life.[3] Just as importantly, what he wrote about it—called "the most heart-rending part" of *On the Road* by one critic[4]—was excerpted in *The Paris Review* and led directly to an offer from Viking Press to publish the whole novel.

Greyhound bus! Grapevine! His trip and mine must have occurred within a few years of each other. What a coincidence!

After resisting for so long, I decided I had to take a look at the book, if only to read what he'd written about that trip. There isn't much: a couple of pages, the bus "groaning up" the Grapevine, how "cute" she was. Then this: as they went down into the "great sprawls of light" on the Los Angeles side of the mountains, he saw "the whole mad thing, the ragged promised land, the fantastic end of America."[5]

What a picture! On the road where I learned about the past, Kerouac rushed forward toward a future where people don't smoke on buses but frequently can't breathe the air because of pollution. Where winding routes have been transformed into superhighways. Where everything is linked, and the information superhighway allows me to Google "Kerouac" and "Grapevine" and come up with a page reference in his book.

Where the detritus accumulated during the travels of our collective past may bring us to the End of Days.

Chapter Two

BOTTLENECK ON THE ROAD FROM EDEN

T HE BOYS, INDEED, MAY HAVE SHOWN THE WAY.
Even today, given the chance, boys of nine to twelve years of
age are explorers and testers of limits, and there's no reason to
think that was different in our deep past.[1] So if we want to consider how
humans have travelled over our long history, we could do worse than
begin by supposing that a trio of boys went scavenging one day along the
beach not far from what is now Eritrea on the Horn of Africa.

Let us suppose that they started out shortly after noon, slipping away
in the quiet time when all adults who could rested in the shade. The sky
was clear, a welcome change. A particularly intense storm front from
what we'd now call the South East monsoon had whipped the shoreline
for two days. The rain had been welcome—until now the season had
been unusually dry—but it was good not to have to huddle under the
dripping leaves.

Down on the beach, the boys may have skipped flat rocks against the
retreating waves, turned over bigger rocks to see what was underneath,
and kept a wary eye out for fish washed up by the storm surf. Ordinarily,
the women did most of the collecting along the seashore, harvesting
clams and mussels, but in the three weeks that their group had stopped

here, the haul had been much less than when they'd passed this way the year before. The grown-ups grumbled that the hunting was not good either. This was shaping up to be a hunger year.

The boys had heard that, and the anxiety about food had been communicated to them, so perhaps this afternoon they were more open to what they saw than they would have been otherwise. As they walked out toward the retreating tide, they checked the edges of the previously covered rocks. A few bivalves clung to them. Not much, but they agreed that on the way back they'd carry home what they could.

The other side of the channel was quite clearly visible. It looked to be greener than their side, but no one they knew had gone over to look. The men judged the distance too far to swim and, besides, why go to the effort of crossing when there was enough to hunt and gather on their side?

Certainly, there'd been no reason to do so until now, and the boys weren't tempted until they saw the turtle, a big one, lumbering across the sand. It must have been confused by the storm, carried by currents away from its usual territory, deposited by the waves high up on the beach.

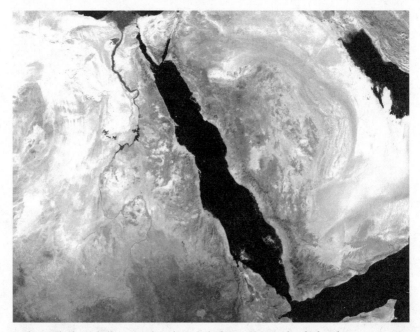

Red Sea: The long shallow sea where humans' adventures outside of Africa began.
Screenshot from Nasa World Wind

Without discussing it, the boys knew that if they could bring it home, there would be feasting and praise.

One of them had a stone knife in the skin bag he had slung across his shoulder. Turtles never moved very fast, but it wasn't easy to kill them because of the way they retreated into their shells when threatened. The best thing would be to get the beast to attack a stick, grasping the stick in its mouth. Then they could go in for the kill, smash its head, and cut its throat.[2]

The turtle wasn't interested at first in the branch one of the boys rescued from the pile of storm debris at the edge of the beach. It continued its slow progress, hissing each time the branch was waved in front of its face, but too bent on getting back to the sea to stop and fight. But then the boy with the knife had the bright idea of climbing on its back, ready to reach underneath the turtle's neck and slash it. He stretched out, clinging to the carapace with his left hand, the knife ready in his right. The other two boys were right beside them, as if they could stop the beast. But the turtle surged ahead, moving more quickly than they expected. The boy on its back struck, and then suddenly the beast was in the water with the knife protruding from the place where its neck joined its shoulder, and the boy was thrown off.

What to do? Not catching the turtle was one thing—it had been a long while since anyone had seen such a large one—but losing the knife was far more serious. Next to the shell amulet he wore on a thong around his neck, the knife was the boy's most valuable possession. He had spent days working on it with his father and uncle, learning how to shape a piece of obsidian, striking off flake after flake. He was proud of what he'd accomplished, and he didn't want to lose it. So he plunged in the water after the turtle, letting out a loud yell as he did.

For a few seconds, his friends stood immobilized. They all could swim, that was one thing they'd picked up during the seasons the group moved along the seacoast. But none of them had swum in these waters, which still looked riled up, as if somewhere in the far reaches of the sea the storm still lingered. Evidence of its strength lay piled at high water. In addition to skeins of seaweed, the trunk and part of the root system of a mangrove rested on the sand.

Despite the knife sticking out of its tough hide, the turtle was as graceful in the water as it had been awkward on land. The boy paddled after it, but the distance between him and the animal grew. He paused to take the measure of what was happening, and recognized that his chase was a lost cause. He turned and began paddling back toward the shore, but to his alarm and that of his friends', he continued to move away from them as the current from the outgoing tide caught him.

Without discussion, both boys on the shore ran to the mangrove driftwood and dragged it down to the water and into the surf. Just beyond the breakers, they were caught in the current too, but by kicking and paddling together, they were able to pull alongside their friend. He grabbed hold and for a few moments the three of them drifted with the current, not sure what to do next.

The water was not cold and was so saline that it wasn't a struggle to stay afloat. From their vantage point, the boys could see little but the undulating surface, as they bobbed up and down in the waves. The youngest one might have cried, had he not wanted to be brave in front of his friends, while the boy who had lost his knife was still furious. So the third one focused his attention on what was happening to them. Looking behind, he saw there was little chance they could kick their way back to the shore where their families were camped. But when the waves raised them up, he scanned where they were headed. There looked to be a point of land with a hill on it that they might reach if they paddled slantwise to the current.

It took all afternoon, but by sundown they were pulling themselves out of the surf. They saw mangroves clustering in the protected curve of the coast. An ibex watched for a long moment before it calmly continued to graze the short grass growing above the high-water line. The hill above was covered with grey-green bushes and low trees of the sort which made the boys wonder if there might be nuts lying on the ground underneath them. And most importantly, the cooling evening air carried with it the scent of fresh water. A spring had to be nearby. They scrambled out of the seawater and took their first steps in the new country.

Nevertheless, they were very tired and frightened that night. Toward morning, they thought they saw a flicker of light on the opposite shore, a signal fire lit by their families. Then they noticed that the current had reversed itself as the tide changed and that the rocks toward the mangroves on their right were covered with more bivalves than they'd ever seen in one place. By the end of the morning, they'd gouged out a cavity on one part of their mangrove float with flat rocks and filled it with mussels and clams. It took them until late afternoon to drift and kick their way back across the strait with that day's tide. The adults who greeted them first scolded about the danger the boys had put themselves in, and then were jubilant that a new source of food had been found. Before the season was over, a party of grown-ups also crossed to check things out, and, liking what they saw, ferried the others across on rafts made from driftwood. And so the first successful group of anatomically modern humans left Africa to people the rest of the world.

The rest, as they say, is history, or at least prehistory.

Well, maybe.

We don't know.

We'll never know for sure.[3] But it appears that sometime between 50,000 and 80,000 years ago, a relatively small number of humans, not unlike us, left what had been good hunting and gathering country in East Africa for, literally, a place where the grass was greener. Once across, they didn't know where they were going, except in the most limited sense, yet they travelled fast. By 25,000 BCE (before the common era) their descendants had colonized all of Europe, Asia, Australia, and much of Oceania. They crossed the Bering Strait to the Americas during the last Ice Age and, as conditions allowed, they pushed south, reaching the tip of South America in a thousand years or less.

This was not the first time that beings closely related to us went beyond Africa, but it was the first time that anatomically modern humans succeeded.

There have been periods when three or four species of what paleo-anthropologists call hominins walked the earth. Some of them survived for hundreds of thousands of years, but all are now extinct except us. At the moment, our nearest relatives are chimpanzees, with whom we share a good 98 per cent of our DNA, that genetic instruction manual which governs how we grow. But we parted ways, genetically speaking, six to eight million years ago. The first hominins—distinguished by two major characteristics: upright walking on two legs and smaller canine fangs in males—show up somewhere between four and seven million years ago. About 2.5 million years ago, there's evidence that they started using tools on a regular basis and eating meat in addition to the leaves, fruit, seeds, and tubers which are the staples of most primates' diet.

Their home base appears to have been East Africa, but tools and fossil bones categorized as coming from the prehuman *Homo erectus* show up elsewhere on that enormous continent and then in Eurasia. The earliest widely acknowledged finding outside of Africa—in a cave in the Republic of Georgia—has been dated to 1.8 million years ago. The type of hand axes found there are characteristic of the Acheulean "culture," a technique of making tools from stone. This "tool kit," as some paleoanthropologists call it, is found in many sites across Asia, as well as in Europe. The name comes from the village of Saint-Acheul, a suburb of Amiens in Northern France where a hand axe was uncovered in 1859. Objects there date to 800,000 years ago. The hominins who made them are characterized by their relatively long legs, larger brain case, and a pelvis that indicates they ate meat—eating meat doesn't require as long a gut for digestion—as well as vegetable products.

How do we know this? We can extrapolate this information from the fossils and tools that archeologists and paleontologists have been amassing for nearly two centuries, as well as the recent addition of game-changing advances in genetics and techniques used to date objects from the past. This is what anthropologists (and surveyors) call "triangulation": taking observations from at least three different points to get a fix on something.[4]

For sixty years, scientists have thought that the first anatomically modern humans—people fundamentally like us—developed in East Africa about 200,000 years ago.[5] Fossils of modern human skulls, found in the 1960s near the Omo River in Ethiopia, have been dated recently using new techniques to 195,000 BP. At that time, the Sahara was not the desert that it is today, but was green, with grasslands where now there is sand and scrub. (This kind of climate change has occurred several times in the last couple million years, the fossil record suggests. The reasons behind the fluctuations are only partly understood, and have to do with the track the Indian Ocean monsoon takes. The sort of climate change we are experiencing at the beginning of the twenty-first century appears to be of an entirely different order—but more about that later.)

To say this grassland landscape was inviting for these early humans is an understatement. It was precisely the kind of place that some might say was made for humans to hunt, gather, and shelter in. The truth is that the savannah was not made for humans; rather, humans were made for the savannah. Our ancestors were shaped by it. Those early humans who were best adapted to walking and running long distances to track game and gather nuts, fruit, and tubers, brought home more food for their offspring.[6] Well-watered plains provided access to springs and ponds in season. Open countryside allowed good visibility to spy out menace from predators, while widely spaced trees provided places of refuge and shelter. Cropped grass meant herbivores were present too. A number of studies have shown that humans today, all over the world, like this kind of landscape. It may be that our brains are hard-wired to prefer parkland and spreading trees, ponds and green grass just the way that some birds know at a glance from the air what landscape will be good to nest in.[7]

What makes scientists say that the fossils found near such formerly lovely places are those of anatomically modern human beings? The idea that paleontologists can take fragments of a skull and a few other bones and pronounce the individual a member of our family of *Homo sapiens* may seem far-fetched. But a skull tells volumes. One of the skull's most important elements is the place where the head is attached to the spinal column. The foramen magnum is the opening where the marvelous spinal cord composed of the body's neural wiring enters the skull. It indicates whether the individual walked upright or not. In chimpanzees and in several early hominin fossils, the foramen magnum is placed obliquely, so the head must be forced forward. In contrast, our heads are directly over shoulders. Take another feature of the skull and you get another snapshot of the life the individual lived. For example, the absence of a ridge on the top of the skull, where muscles that power chewing and biting would be attached, shows that the jaw was smaller than it was when individuals needed strength to chew lots of tough plant material. This lack of strong muscles strongly suggests, in fact, that the individual had begun to cook food on a regular basis. Fossils like these found near the remains of hearths suggest that hominins had some control over fire at least 800,000 years ago.[8]

But to get back to our three young friends, the channel they crossed was a version of the Red Sea, that legendary body of water that runs for about 2,000 kilometres (1,243 miles) more or less north to south between Africa and the Arabian Peninsula. The Red Sea was formed as the two land masses split apart in the eons-long waltz of continents over the earth's surface. Notwithstanding the Biblical story of God parting its waters so Moses could lead the Israelites to the Promised Land, the Red Sea has never been closed completely south of its northern portion

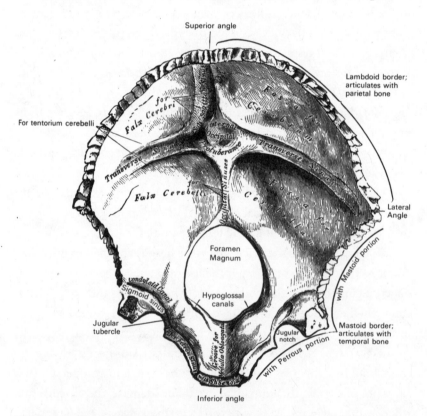

The Foramen Magnum, where the head is attached to the spinal column, indicates whether the individual walked upright or not.

Illustration by Henry Vandyke Carter, from Henry Gray, The Anatomy of the Human Body, *1918 / Public Domain*

where modern-day Egypt abuts Israel. Its water level and the vegetation on its banks have changed many times, however.[9] At least one attempt by anatomically modern humans to explore the northern end during a period of greater rainfall, about 180,000 to 150,000 years ago, succeeded for awhile, as evidenced by the bones and tools found at the Skhul and Tabon caves in Israel. A clutch of human teeth that have been dated to 80,000 to 120,000 years ago have also been found in China.[10] However, the absence of any evidence of modern humans for a good 50,000 to 75,000 years afterward anywhere outside of Africa, as well as the genetic makeup of everyone not recently descended from Africans, suggests strongly that these sorties ended sadly, perhaps because of worsening climatic conditions.

Two recent developments have turned the search for a crossing place out of Africa further south. The first is the growing recognition that there is an abundance of artifacts, seemingly made by people like us and very much like those found in East Africa, that are now lying on the surface on the Arabian Peninsula in terrain that is currently mostly desert but once was lush. The second is evidence from genetic analysis that humans ran into some kind of population bottleneck in their expansion. For a time that idea seemed rather far-fetched, but the body of evidence to support this idea now appears overwhelming: three papers and a commentary published in *Nature* in September 2016 all argue, in their own way, in favour of this idea, based on close study of the genetic heritage of people all over the world.[11]

We are, in large part, what our genes tell us to be: our cells contain 20,000 to 25,000 genes that give instructions on how we develop. They are packed into forty-six chromosomes, half of which we inherit from our mothers and half from our fathers at the time of conception. The information passed on is usually copied correctly as cells divide to make sperm and eggs, but inevitably errors get made. Some of these are dangerous to the person who carries them, but some, particularly when circumstances change, may turn out to be advantageous. That, in a nutshell, is how evolution works: a being that has some advantage due to a genetic change will be able to survive better, and therefore leave more offspring who will carry the change in his or her genes.

Most of the errors that occur as genes copy themselves don't seem to have any effect for good or ill. These errors, which are not unlike the static that shows up sometimes in radio transmissions, occur at a rate that is pretty standard. Therefore their number can be used to gauge when a specific characteristic developed. It is this kind of comparison of human and chimpanzee genes that suggests that the last time we had a common ancestor was more than six million years ago. Similarly, DNA analysis, performed on the genes that govern skin colour, suggests that modern humans lost their body hair approximately 1.2 million years ago. Before then our ancestors probably had pale skin and dark fur, similar to chimpanzees which are born with white faces and tan as they grow up. Just why not having fur was an advantage to our ancestors is unclear, but certainly, once the fur was gone, having dark skin protected them against the ravages of too much sun in tropical latitudes.[12]

The light skin colour of Europeans and northern Asians is a more recent development. Some analyses indicate that the mutations causing it occurred less than 20,000 years ago, as modern humans moved into places with short days in winter and put aside hunting and gathering for agriculture.[13] Exposure to sunshine allows us to synthesize vitamin D in our skin, which is essential for strong bones, and if skin is dark, less is made. Unless the lack of vitamin D is made up in diet—fatty fish and animal livers are good sources—the result can be debilitating bone deformities, such as rickets. Therefore, light skin was a definite advantage in some circumstances.

There are other genes that tell a story about human history. Among them are those that code for what's called mitochondrial DNA (mtDNA.) Mitochondria are tiny structures in our cells that are responsible for energy production. The genetic instructions for how they are made are transmitted only from mothers to their children. Studying mtDNA gives us a long look back at our evolution, as if a fiber optic cable (or virtual umbilical cord) stretched all the way to our oldest maternal ancestor.

What appears is this: today's native Africans have mtDNA that comes in several formulations, but everyone else has mtDNA that can be grouped into five categories corresponding to five "Eves," five maternal lines that seem to have been the only ones to have made it out of

Africa. According to the scientists doing this analysis, the results suggest that at some point during the last 100,000 years or so, the number of humans who left descendants plummeted. There is evidence of a population decline among present-day Africans, but nothing like what shows up elsewhere in the world. One study puts the size of the ancestral population that went on to people Europe, Asia, Oceania, and the Americas as low as a thousand or so.[14]

Scientists have proposed several explanations for this population bottleneck, including horrendous epidemics or mass destruction following the greatest volcanic eruption in the last two million years. The Mount Toba eruption on the Indonesian island of Sumatra can be dated pretty closely to about 74,000 years ago. It was followed by years, if not decades, of cold weather, according to counts of pollen dated from that time, which have been excavated throughout huge swaths of Asia and Europe. Thousands of people from the South China Sea to the borders of Europe might have died of starvation.

But there is also the possibility of a roadblock on the shores of the Red Sea so severe that only a relative handful of families made it across. To do that, these early humans would have had to use rafts or boats, or like our young friends, driftwood. There is no evidence of this kind of artifact, though. While scientists have found a plethora of stone tools, so far we have very few clues about what humans made from perishable material until about 30,000 years ago. The reason for this is easy to understand: while stones may lie in the back of caves or even on the surface of the ground for eons, practically unmarked, organic material usually rots quickly.

Hints of the domestic arrangements of these early modern humans are turning up, which could clarify the picture. Fossilized plant matter that may be sleeping mats has been identified recently in South Africa not far from Durban. Dated to between 60,000 and 77,000 years ago, these include the remains of aromatic bushes that are used even today to deter insects. This finding suggests just how sophisticated the makers of the mats were. Finds like these also hint at the long trails travelled by early humans in Africa itself. The distance from the parts of East Africa where modern humans evolved to Durban is nearly 7,000 kilometres (4,350 miles).[15]

There is also indirect evidence—by triangulation again—that people began wearing clothes long before then. DNA studies of human body or clothing lice show that they're different from human hair lice, and that the evolutionary split between these species came more than 100,000 ago. The implication is clear: even though the first needles found so far date to about 30,000 years ago, humans must have figured out how to arrange skins or plant fibers to cover their nakedness millennia before, and lice evolved to take advantage of the new niche afforded by clothing.[16]

This in turn suggests that people also had invented carrying devices—baskets, skin bags, perhaps even canteens—by the time they started on their journey out of Africa. One of the first carriers must have been a sling for transporting babies, says British anthropologist Timothy Taylor.[17] Most primate babies cling to their mother's fur, but human mothers are hairless across the arms, chest, and shoulders. Our babies are born with an instinct to grab and hold on, but they have nothing to cling to. Mothers or their helpers must have used their arms to schlep a baby around for more than a year until the child could walk. A woman had a tremendous advantage if she could free her hands by carrying her baby snuggled in a sling, perhaps made from the cleaned intestine of a large animal or a tangle of vines. Similar devices are used everywhere today, but when that practice began and what the sling was made of is knowledge lost in the great refuse pile of prehistory.

Similarly, the earliest boats rotted away thousands of years ago, but stone tools recently uncovered on the island of Crete in the middle of the Mediterranean, and dating to 800,000 years ago, indicate that *Homo erectus*, that proto-human, had gone sea voyaging to attain the island.[18] If they could do that, modern humans surely could figure out how to put logs together to ferry people and their possessions across the Red Sea. Nor was the distance necessarily very great. At its narrowest point, the Red Sea now is approximately 28 kilometres wide (about 17 miles), and the geologic record suggests that for thousands of years, sea level was about 50 feet lower. As a result, island- or channel-hopping would have been easier. Furthermore, there have been several periods in the last 200,000 years when a combination of relatively wet climate and low sea levels coincided for a brief time.

Most importantly, the period of time when all the conditions were exactly right for a successful crossing out of Africa needn't have been long. In fact, evidence about the roadblock in our collective past suggests that the opportunity for moving out of Africa was a window that was open for an extraordinarily brief period of time, perhaps just a generation or two.

So, let us assume the families of our young friends crossed to find very good living conditions in country where they truly had no idea what lay over the next hill or around the headland along the shore. How did they travel without a road, without a path?

"Have you ever seen a column of ants marching?" asks Michael Bisson, associate professor of anthropology at McGill University.

> Viewed from a distance, it looks like it's advancing steadily as a single mass. But look closely, and you'll see that there are always ants on the edges, scouting, going out and coming back, bringing information on what's out there. Well, humans did that too. Hunters would follow a big animal up a valley and come across a good place to settle. They'd come back with the news, and members of the group who were looking for their own space would go out to settle there.[19]

Anatomically modern humans evolved in savannah lands, like this one in Kenya.
Author Photo

They travelled through a landscape very much like the best of what they had known in East Africa.[20] In many places, the savannah stretched as far as the eye could see, crossed by streams, dotted by stands of trees, and inhabited by animals to be hunted. Beyond, grasslands continued almost without interruption as far as Central China, creating what some anthropologists have dubbed "Savannastan." The coastal plain around the Gulf of Aqaba, by the mouths of the Tigris and Euphrates rivers, and onward around the Indian Ocean to the Indian subcontinent was also rich in food, and for long periods was well watered. Sea levels at the beginning of this exodus were probably falling, as climate changed and an Ice Age began. This made island-hopping easy, with the result that as early as 50,000 years ago, modern humans made it to Australia.[21]

As noted earlier, our direct, modern human ancestors were not the first hominins to travel out of Africa. *Homo erectus*, who left those Acheulean tools from the tip of Africa to the British Isles and from Turkey to Java, died out in Africa and the rest of the world about 500,000 years ago.[22] Two other human relatives made beachheads in Asia. Fossils of Denisova hominins have been found in China, while fossils of the tiny "hobbits" (*Homo floresiensis*) were recently discovered on Flores Island in Indonesia. Not much is known about either group, other than the last of the Flores population appears to have died out only about 50,000 years ago.

Far more successful were the Neanderthals, who held sway for perhaps 300,000 years and were thriving when modern humans started their trek. Genetic analysis of Neanderthal remains suggests that they and modern humans shared an ancestor in Africa 350,000 to 400,000 years ago. Findings of Neanderthal fossils and tools stretch across Europe and into Asia, but have not been found south of the eastern Mediterranean. Neanderthals had large brains and muscular builds, and appear to have been adapted to do well in colder climates. They apparently lived in hunter-gatherer groups, and despite their reputation as "cave men," some groups of Neanderthals developed practices that must be characterized as a culture: they sometimes buried their dead with flowers and amulets, for example.

But Neanderthals, too, died out around 30,000 years ago. Their legacy lies in the artifacts they discarded, their fossilized bones, and a few genes that turn up in some native Europeans and Asians, but not in Africans. Despite their physical size and other traits that allowed them to thrive for so long, they apparently weren't up to competition with the new guys— that is, with people like us—setting out from the Red Sea.

Modern humans travelled light, but they carried with them rich cultural baggage and languages whose sophistication surely approached that of the ones we speak today. Recent linguistic research has applied some of the same tools of analysis used to unveil the story of mtDNA and our ancestral mothers. Just as genetic diversity is richer in sub-Saharan Africa today, the languages spoken there started off having more phonemes— little packets of sound that we use to make up words—than elsewhere. Some languages have as many as one hundred, but Hawaiian—spoken in the island group of the same name and one of the last places on earth to receive a wave of human settlers—has only twelve. (English, by way of comparison, has about forty-five.)[23] The implication is that our friends who left Africa did so with a fully developed language that was transformed subsequently into our present multitude of tongues.

But let us return to that season when the boys and their families stood poised on the brink of an adventure, the magnitude of which was far beyond their imagination. The trek those early humans began is staggering even to us, who know the map of the earth by heart, who have seen pictures taken from space of the land that lay before them.[24]

The longest journey begins with a single step, however, and they were about to take it.

Chapter Three

INTO THE WOODS

T HE AMULET THE BOY WORE ON A THONG AROUND HIS neck
was the small, perfect shell of a sea snail with a hole carefully
bored into it. His grandmother had given it to him to keep him
safe after he'd succeeded in snaring two hares on his own and was preparing for the first time to go hunting with the men. They would drive the
troop of oryx that came down this time of year toward a cliff edge on the
seacoast, where one or more would fall to their death on the rocks below.
The boy's task would be to charge with the others, when the leader gave
the signal. He'd be equipped with a spear and a knife, but his father had
said he was not to get in front, that he was learning this time, that in the
future he'd have a bigger role to play.

His heart pounded madly at the thought of being part of a real hunt.
He thought he was ready. He nodded as he listened to what was told him.
He watched the men prepare to honour the spirit of the oryx before they
set off.

But there was one more hurdle he had to cross.[1] He knelt before his
grandmother so she could easily paint designs on his forehead, cheeks,
and chin with a slurry of red ochre, reddish earth that contained iron
oxide.[2] Since they were near the seacoast, the shell she had prepared as

an amulet was not something exotic. But the ochre came from the highlands where their group used to pass part of the rainy season before they crossed the channel. His grandmother had carried a small quantity with her when they travelled down to the seacoast to forage, just as she took a small number of shells with her when they moved back inland.

He was his grandmother's oldest grandchild, and she'd helped his mother carry him about when he was a baby. She'd sung songs to him and chewed seeds into pap so he could eat when he was being weaned. She was as proud of him as his mother was at his first steps. She was also the oldest person in their group, and as such had a particular status. So, chanting special words, she coated the shell with the ochre, then slipped the leather string around his neck and brought the shell suspended from it to her lips.

He stood up and caught the eye of his father who had been watching intently.

The man nodded to the boy, who went to join the men as they set off first along the shore, and then turned inland where the game trail led into the hills.[3]

Again, the question has to be asked: how do we know that anything in this little tale actually might have happened? The answer must be: we don't. There is strong evidence that much about it did, however: evidence that explains what happened next as modern humans began traveling the paths that led to what some paleontologists call the Great Expansion.[4]

What lay before these pioneers was no "Kerouac-ian road trip," no "excellent adventure" of the sort that would lure millions later on in human history. Oh, there was high drama—a hunter's life can be dangerous. But having arrived at a very good place where there was little or no competition for water and food, they stayed put more or less, and were fruitful and multiplied.

How do we know this? Certainly, no footprints have showed up just on the other side of the Red Sea to show they passed that way. The first preserved impressions of modern human feet outside Africa were found half a world away, in Australia and Tibet.[5] Both sites date to about 20,000 years ago, tens of thousands of years after the crossing of the Red Sea. It takes a lot of travelling, one step after another, to get to either place.

Paleoarcheologists have spent considerable effort analyzing climate and geographic data in order to determine the paths these early humans might have taken, the corridors of settlement they followed. Unlike their descendants, these hunters and gatherers seem not to have initially left deep marks on the land they were travelling into.

What they are likely to have done, the thinking runs now, is look for a quartet of resources: water, grasslands where grazing animals could be hunted, nearby hills to take refuge in, and scattered clumps of trees, preferably nut-bearing, to be used as lookouts and also, in a pinch, safety.[6] They needed a fairly large territory. Extrapolating from modern hunter-gatherer populations, it looks like two square kilometres per person would provide a wide enough range if the territory was reasonably welcoming. If you calculate six families of five people each as the size of a band, you come up with an area of sixty square kilometres.[7] That's about the size of Manhattan, which, by way of comparison, now has a population of more than 27,000 people per square kilometre.

Back then, our ancestors had nothing but wide open spaces in front of them. The Romans called the part of the Arabian Peninsula where the ancestors of all non-Africans landed Arabia Felix (Happy or Lucky Arabia) because in their day it was so pleasant compared to the extremely dry and hot portion to the north that they called Arabia Deserta. The coastal plain in the south is hot and dry today but ends abruptly at an escarpment which rises up to 1,000 metres and, catching the seasonal monsoon rains, this coastal plain, even today, receives as much as 1,000 millimetres (39.3 inches) of rainfall in a year. In wetter eras, this countryside would have been quite inviting. Not only would grasslands have covered much of what is now scrub and sand, but when sea levels were lower, the streams rising in the hills would have watered a low coastal plain.

Take relief maps and factor in climate data from the past, then include information from fossil pollen and ancient bones, and a picture emerges of possible corridors of population expansion. One pathway would follow the more watered valleys of the Arabian Peninsula, where people could have turned north and east into the Levant, that area around the eastern edge of the Mediterranean. They could have gone up the Jordan Valley and continued further east to the shores of the Black Sea. Some people continued onward through what is now Turkey, Iraq, and Iran, while their descendants could have travelled still farther east until they reached what would become known as the Middle Kingdom of China. If drier climate prevailed by the time modern humans reached that far, the present tropical forests would instead have been grasslands, inviting people to turn south across the peninsula of Southeast Asia. More land would have been available in that region than today, because in times of low sea level, some islands would have been connected to the mainland, while others would have been a short hop away.

Two of the oldest modern human fossils found so far outside of Africa are probably those of the descendants of people who followed this corridor. A skull found in Borneo has been dated to about 40,000 years ago, while fossils buried ceremoniously in southern Australia appear to be somewhat older.

Another corridor might have led along the shoreline of the Gulf of Aden, across to the flood plains of the Tigris and Euphrates, and around into India. Much of this route is now underwater as sea levels have risen since the ending of the last Ice Age: it will take underwater exploration to determine what relics of early adventurers might be hiding there.

But it would be wrong to think that the Great Expansion was a relentless march into unknown territory. Rather, the movement was more like the way bees colonize when a hive has reached its size limits. When the number of people in a band reached a size that began to exceed the available food resources, a few families would go over the hills, or up the valley, or around a bend in the coast to find a place previously scouted by hunters and young adventurers where it seemed that resources were untouched. Looking at the bare bones of the movement—as recorded by archeological evidence or genes—humans appear to have travelled at least 25,000 kilometres (about 15,543 miles) in the first 20,000 years or so of the Great Expansion. Figuring a generation as about twenty years, that averages about 125 kilometres (approximately 78 miles) per generation. (Those humans who stayed behind in Africa also would have been on the move, probably going south through the African Great Lakes region and continuing down into what is now South Africa. Others would have gone across what is now the Maghreb.)[8]

Moving into fresh country set the stage for the next round of population increase since there would be more animals and plants to eat and, therefore, a greater chance that children would grow to well-nourished maturity. The piles of rubbish that collected at encampments—even seasonal ones—were breeding grounds for disease, but a new environment wouldn't have had them.

The health benefits of a new environment didn't only affect the young. Older generations also would probably have profited from more food and less disease, which in turn would have meant more help for young families from grandmothers and older aunts.[9] The wisdom of older hunters was probably invaluable, but the "Grandmother Effect" has been postulated as one of the reasons for the success of humans in general. Women who are no longer reproducing can help feed their children's children, giving them a better start in life. (This effect continues in current times. Jack Kerouac's girlfriend Bea was traveling to find work when he met her, but she wouldn't have been able to do so had her mother not been looking after her son. The effect also gave a happy ending to the trip my mother, my sister, and I took, but more about that later.) The help that older women provide also frees younger women to have children at shorter intervals. Among our nearest cousins the chimpanzees, females have babies every five years or so. Women, however, can have babies every twelve to eighteen months, with the interval being around three years in today's hunter-gatherer group.[10] If all went well—with Grandma's help of course—between the ages of fifteen and forty-five, a woman could give birth to ten children. (The advantage of becoming infertile in middle age—menopause, in other words—becomes evident, viewed in this light. Humans are among the few animals in which menopause occurs: others are chimpanzees and rhesus monkeys, and killer whales whose survival depends on old females who are aces at finding food.)[11]

When it came to our ancestors' survival, the greatest imponderable was climate. The gathering forces of the last Ice Age pushed humans back from northern latitudes about 30,000 years ago. Some of the oldest bone needles, found in Siberia, have been dated to that period. They tell a tale of people who could make clothes for themselves, but whose garments were not warm enough to allow them to survive the onslaught of glaciers, which would eventually cover northern latitudes except for a few ice-free regions.

The Neanderthals were better adapted physically for this kind of climate. With stocky bodies and big noses, their compact forms dissipated heat less rapidly than more spindly body types would. Many of them—perhaps all—also had light eyes, light hair and, most importantly for creatures who need sunshine to produce vitamin D, light skin. DNA sequencing shows a specific mutation on the gene that codes for these characteristics and which is different from the one that gives some Europeans and Asians light skin colour today. Some paleontologists also suggest that they might have been very hairy, even furry. But nothing of the Neanderthals lives on, except a small number of genes that some of us carry (which, to my disappointment, don't include the ones that produce red hair today: I'd always hoped that my carrot top was a link to cavemen.)

In other words, with almost no exception, modern humans had the world to themselves, and as the Great Expansion continued, they began to transform the landscape.

At first the effect was probably not very apparent. True, some big mammals in Australia (and later the Americas) that had not learned to shun human hunters went extinct, probably because of overhunting. But as long as there was free land for the taking just a little farther off, it appears that the human camps and settlements left little impression on the land. Most likely, there were tracks that people followed to trade in rare shells, ritual goods like ochre, and particularly good materials for making tools. It's highly probable also that people visited each other regularly, the way hunter-gatherers still do, to socialize and organize marriages. But no visible sign of these byways has been recognized to date, except in instances where later people used the same pass or ridgeline for their own purposes. But that is getting ahead of the story.

It took thousands of years, but eventually the limits of the vast Eurasian plains were reached and shorelines were explored as far as the Pacific Ocean. Yet, it would seem that several thousand more years passed before our ancestors throughout the world moved to a new level of society.

"Why did human beings not make civilization fifty thousand years ago?" J. P. Steffensen, a glaciologist, rhetorically asked *New Yorker* writer Elizabeth Kolbert.[12] He was a lead scientist in an attempt to lift ice cores from a glacier on Greenland which, it was hoped, would shed light on climate fluctuations. "Well, it was the Ice Age," Steffensen answered himself.

> And also this Ice Age was so climatically unstable that each time you had the beginning of a culture they had to move. Then comes the present interglacial—ten thousand years of very stable climate. The perfect conditions for agriculture. If you look at it, it's amazing. Civilizations in Persia, in China, and in India start at the same time.... They all developed writing and they all developed religion and they all built cities, all at the same time, because the climate was stable. I think that if the climate would have been stable fifty thousand years ago it would have started then.

Indeed, when conditions were right, changes came fast and furious, although formal agriculture—that is, planting crops intentionally and systematically—was not necessary in order for people to live more densely if they were able to use a wide variety of wild plants, as well as the game and food from rivers and seacoasts.[13] The First Nations settlements along the coast of the Pacific Northwest, until a century ago, were proof of this. While they gathered plant material for medicinal purposes and to make clothing and equipment, villagers counted on food from the sea, not agriculture, to support their way of life with its sophisticated art and elegant textiles.

This seems to have been the case also in one of the world's oldest permanent settlements, which was discovered in the 1980s when low water levels in the Sea of Galilee allowed digs at a previously inaccessible site. Three huts made from thick branches of tamarisks and oaks covered with thinner branches, grasses, and leaves were found there. They'd been burned, and the ashes, which included the remains of more than one hundred plant species that grew in all seasons, date to 17,500 BCE.

Other, even bigger, settlements have been found whose residents seem to have relied on wild plants and animals at the beginning of their history, although they subsequently switched to agriculture. One of the oldest settlements is Jericho in what is now Israel. Famous for the story of its destruction—its walls, you'll remember, fell when Joshua and his gang strutted around them, playing trumpets—the settlement may be the oldest continuously inhabited one in the world. Excavations place the lowest levels of its ruins at about 8000 BCE. Located at 830 feet below sea level, the first settlement was apparently on the shores of a lake. (Today, it is an oasis with plentiful water from springs.) The earliest inhabitants appear to have been sedentary hunter-gatherers who lived in large, circular, semi-subterranean stone structures.

A constant factor in these settlements is their access to water. No permanent town or village can be established without it. The Bible may say that Moses smote the rock with his rod and fountains of water burst from the ground,[14] but divine intervention isn't forthcoming often, if ever. Choosing a site close to a river, lake, reliable springs, or abundant groundwater was a far better bet. Well casings are among the oldest surviving wooden structures that people built: four well-preserved water wells have been uncovered in Eastern Germany dating from between 5469 and 5098 BCE.[15]

Jericho, in what is now Israel, is perhaps the oldest continuously inhabited settlement in the world. Its lowest levels of ruins are about 10,000 years old and predate agriculture.

Photo: Abraham Sobkowski / Released for Use in the Public Domain

People who lived in such early settlements transformed their landscape by changing the kinds of plants that grew around them. In his book *Guns, Germs, and Steel*, Jared Diamond says that probably the process was unconscious at the beginning.[16] Frequently, plant domestication depended on a genetic quirk that would otherwise be lethal to the plant. For example, take the case of wheat and barley. Wild versions had stalks that shattered when the grain was ripe, which meant the seeds fell on the ground where they could germinate and start the cycle over again. But a single mutation kept the stalk from breaking, leaving the seeds far above the ground, unable to fall and grow into new little plants the next season. The seeds were at the right height for humans to collect, though, and so they were the ones that were picked and brought back to camp. Most of them were eaten, but some seeds fell to the ground in the collection process or around the camp site, setting the scene for more easy-to-harvest grain the following year. The same thing happened with peas, which, in the wild, have seed pods that pop open. A mutation that kept the pods from opening produced peas that were easy for humans to gather. Then at some point, accidental sowing gave way to planting on purpose in Southwest Eurasia.

"Fertile Crescent" is often used to describe this geographic region which includes much of the vast savannah lands that curve north and east from the Mediterranean and down into the valleys of the Tigris and Euphrates rivers in what is now Iraq. Diamond argues that the people who lived here had much to gain from finding alternatives to hunting and gathering, because human activity—crossing and recrossing the grasslands for thousands of years—had depleted stocks of plants and animals. Vast herds of gazelle and their cousins had once roamed the plains, but intensive hunting took its toll. Digs at what appear to be campsites show a shift to smaller and smaller game as time passed. Furthermore, big rivers and coastlines were rare, so people could not easily supplement the game they hunted and the plants they foraged with fish and other aquatic resources.

So far, the earliest hard evidence of domesticated crops was discovered in what is now Turkey, dating from about 7200 BCE. Several sites contain seeds and chaff from einkorn and emmer wheat with distinctive modifications that set them off from wild varieties.[17] Ancestral barley and peas have been dated from slightly later, while during the following half-millennium, olives, sheep, and goats were domesticated. (The process of domesticating the olive demonstrates how sophisticated these early farmers were. Not only do olive trees take several years after planting to bear fruit, fresh olives aren't edible but have to be treated to remove toxic compounds. Amazingly, it appears that techniques to do so were developed independently several times.)[18]

During more or less the same period, people on the eastern side of the great Eurasian land mass were also finding that the plants they had been accidently sowing served well as food sources.[19] Bits of rice embedded in charred pot shards dated to 9000 BCE are the first evidence of rice in China, although it appears that the rice was wild, not cultivated. But by 7000 BCE, rice was being grown far beyond its original range and the plants reflected selection for larger grains, as people began to farm seriously. People in three other regions succeeded in domesticating plants and animals somewhat later: Southeast Asia, the Andes, and

Wheat, one of the first grains domesticated, grows well on what used to be grassland, as shown here in the Palouse Country of Washington State.

Author Photo

Meso-America. Settlers in New Guinea, the African Sahel, Ethiopia, and tropical West Africa also domesticated native plants and animals, but this came after the introduction of crops from other areas.

So by 6000 BCE or 8,000 years ago, a sizeable proportion of people were living in settlements, growing crops, and raising animals in order to provide food all year round. From our modern-day point of view, this makes tremendous sense, and it is hard to imagine that this fundamental change in how people lived could have a downside.

But more people, we are learning to our dismay as the earth's population balloons, can mean smaller and smaller portions of resources are available if the fine balance between supply and demand isn't maintained. Skeletons in many regions show that people actually were smaller and more diseased in early agricultural settlements than their hunter-gatherer ancestors had been. To get more food, the inviting grasslands where agriculture began were not going to be enough.

To some extent, these early people were lucky because country suitable for both hunting-gathering and agriculture was increasing. As noted earlier, this was the period in which the world was recovering from the last Ice Age, when glaciers were retreating, allowing forests and grasslands to move north into country that had been inhospitably cold. In Southeast Asia, savannah lands were also more extensive than today, since the dryer, cooler climate of the time did not favour the growth of tropical forests.[20]

But there was a limit to even this expanding savannah. Many communities of early agriculturalists, as well as more traditional hunter-gatherers, were eventually faced with the question: where do we go when the existing grasslands have been settled?

The answer was relatively simple, although it probably took much trial and error to discover: take land which wasn't savannah and make it grassland.

In many cases this meant going into the woods, which had and continues to have profound repercussions.

Growing cereals on grassland changes ecosystems and landscapes, but there are many similarities between fields of grass and fields of grain. It's no accident that one of the richest wheat producing areas in North

America, the Palouse Country of Idaho and Washington State, got its name from French explorers in the early 1800s who thought it looked like lawns—*pelouse*, in French. Even adding a few semi-domesticated grazing animals to the mix is a variation on an existing theme, since grasslands everywhere support herds of herbivores. In fact, remove the gazelles, bison, elephants, or what have you, and in many regions grasses will be replaced quickly by bushes and eventually trees.

Why is that? Because the grass was growing on land that was wrested from the forest as part of the great battle of humans against trees.

Battle? Yes, that may sound like an overstatement, but consider the evidence, and our attitudes toward the woods.

Undoubtedly, hunters living on the edge of forests have always followed the trails of animals into the trees, and gatherers have looked for berries and roots in their shade. But forested land is dark, frequently home to dangerous creatures, and difficult to traverse. Anyone who has tried to bushwhack their way through a forest in Eastern North America has an idea of just how hard that could have been. Whenever I think of the challenge, I remember one early June day when my husband and I tried to follow a trail in the White Mountains of Vermont where no one had passed since the previous fall. He carried our three-year-old daughter in a backpack and I, seven months pregnant, struggled to get over the logs that had fallen across the path during the winter. If it hadn't been for our dog who sniffed her way through the undergrowth, following scents left by hikers the season before, we would have been well and truly lost. At the time, I thought of Grimm's fairy tales and their subtext concerning the dangers that wait in the woods. Now I realize just how tough early woodland explorers must have been to enter woods for whatever reason, as well as how valiant were the women who followed them. (The incident demonstrated just how useful canine companions were too.)

Forests loomed everywhere at the edges of the grasslands.[21] After the last Ice Age, much of China north of the original savannah was covered with trees: herds of elephants roamed the cool and shady woods around Beijing in 3000 BCE. The hills and mountains of the Middle East were covered with vast forests, as was the vast plateau between the Indus and the Ganges rivers in India.[22] For a long time in central and West Africa, great rainforests formed a barrier until Bantu agriculturalists succeeded in moving into them and transforming the land. We have evidence of this struggle not only from archeological finds, but also from the oldest surviving written records.

The ancient *Epic of Gilgamesh*, dating from about 2600 BCE, is the first grand example. In it, the great king describes the forest, where the cedars of Lebanon grow, as being "ten thousand leagues in every direction," whose guardian spirit he sets out to destroy.[23] Gilgamesh is punished for this sacrilege in the epic, but in reality the forest was already being chopped down at the time the epic was written. The famous cedar logs were used to build cities from Babylon to Luxor over the next three thousand years until only remnants of the forest remain today.[24]

From elsewhere on the Eurasian land mass, no written stories of the great battle against the forest have come down to us, but palisades surrounding settlements on the Russian steppe are eloquent. They are made of logs as large as three metres in diameter, testifying to the size of the trees in the forests that once grew there.[25]

In China, no less than complete eradication of the forest began not long after the Gilgamesh story was written. The Chinese wood was used for buildings, agriculture, and military reasons, but beyond these practical ends, surviving texts triumphantly recount the destruction. One reads:

> We uprooted the trees then lugged trunks aside
> Those that, dead, still stood upright, and those that had toppled
> We pruned back the branches, or flattened entirely
> The stands in long lines and the thick tangled coppices.
>
> We cut clearings among them, we widened the openings
> Through tamarisk forests and knob-jointed cane-trees.
> We tore from the soil, or else lopped back, groves
> Of wild mulberry bushes and spiny Cuanias....
> We ripped out oaks whose leaves fall, and those green the year round.
> Clearing spacious expanses amid pine and cypress.
> Here God made our state, and our sovereign, His counterpart.[26]

Most of this deforestation was done with stone tools, but fire was an ally too.

As mentioned in chapter 2, there is evidence of hearths and fire that dates to the time of proto-humans, but it's hard to determine if those ashes came from a fire started by humans or lightning. To early humans, the conflagration that might follow a flash of light on the horizon and the crack and rumble of thunder must have seemed mysterious, beyond their control. How we came to tame fire is a question that has inspired speculation for millennia: there's a story about its conquest at the heart of many mythologies. The image of early people in awe of a wildfire racing across the savannah is found in more than one potboiler, too. It's usually followed by a scene where the intrepid hero gathers up embers to keep them safe for future fires, as in Jean-Jacques Annaud's 1981 film *Quest for Fire*.

Such drama probably didn't accompany humans' taming of flames, however, because ever since we started making tools we've had everything we needed to make fire. Strike two rocks together and you frequently get a spark. Conveniently, stones like chert and chalcedony, which are particularly good for making tools, also happen to be particularly good for making sparks.[27] Add a nearby pile of dry leaves or grass and it wouldn't take much for an anatomically modern human—or even an earlier hominin—to discover how to nurse a smouldering ember into a full-fledged flame. Flint, used in fire-starting with steel blades, is a kind of chert, and until the advent of readily available matches in the mid-nineteenth century, every well-equipped household had a tinderbox containing a flint, steel, and a dry, light material to catch the spark.[28] Even today, many woodsmen won't leave home without the combo, while the ubiquitous Bic lighter uses the same principle.

Once fire was tamed, our ancestors both in and outside Africa could use it to keep grasslands lush. That seems counterintuitive, but if a natural fire doesn't pass through a savannah every five to ten years, the prairie—even one grazed by big herbivores—may become choked with plants other than grass. Lighting a grass fire kept larger bushes and trees from getting a start and so created a more inviting landscape for grazing animals, large and small.[29] Native Americans of the Plains did this regularly; as a result, grasslands extended much farther east than they do now. Descriptions of the land in the 1820s around what is now St. Louis, Missouri, tell of tall grass prairie. Today, the landscape has been transformed not only by agriculture but also by the incursion of trees. Charles C. Mann writes:

> In the Northeast, Indians always carried a deerskin pouch full of flints,...which they used to set fire to the country....The flints ignited torches, which were as important to the hunt as bows and arrows. Deer in the Northeast; alligators in the everglades; buffalo in the prairies; grasshoppers in the Great Basin; rabbits in California; moose in Alaska; all were pursued by fire....Rather tha[n] domesticate animals for meat, Indians retooled the ecosystem to encourage elk, deer and bear.[30]

The fires rendered the land more fertile, too. Ashes enrich soil, which farmers have long recognized. In the early nineteenth century, the forests on the plain south of Montreal were burned in part to produce potash to

Humans have long used fires to clear grassland and to prepare fields for agriculture. On this morning, just before the planting season, smoke has settled in the hollows of the West Usambara Mountains of Tanzania.

Author Photo

enrich the farms along the Richelieu and St. Lawrence rivers.[31] Stubble in North American fields is still frequently burned, although smoke management and air pollution controls limit the use of post-harvest fires by farmers. In East Africa, where few if any such regulations exist, the air is heavy with the smoke from fires set to enrich the soil and destroy pests during planting season.

Fire also helped our ancestors attack the biggest trees in the forest that might not have fallen to stone axes unless weakened by flames.

Tales of huge forest fires show up in folklore, and even in one of the Hindu faith's major texts. Dating back to around 1170 BCE, the Mahabharata tells of the burning of the Khandava Forest on the southern edge of the Gangetic Plain, near modern-day New Delhi. To look at the countryside around the sprawling, densely populated Indian capital, you'd never think the banks of the Yamuna River were ever wooded. But according to the holy book, the gods Krishna and Arjuna once picnicked in the woods by the river when a poor Brahman came by, begging. They gave him alms, but as in so many stories of the magical and religious, the monk was not what he appeared to be. He revealed himself as Agni, the god of fire. No piddling alms would satisfy his hunger. What he needed was to consume the whole forest, and all the creatures that live there.

The pair agreed to this (well, does anyone ever argue with a god as powerful as the one of fire?), and so Agni gave them a chariot and bows and arrows to shoot fire into the heart of the woods. But setting fire to the forest was not enough: Agni told them to drive back all who tried to escape the fire until both the trees and the creatures that lived among them were consumed.

Some anthropologists say this story is a metaphorical description of what happened when a sophisticated, urbanized people who were dependent on agriculture moved from the Indus Valley onto the forested plain, pushing aside the hunters and gatherers who had roamed the territory earlier.[32] Indeed, there is evidence that actual fires were set again and again until the newcomers held sway over the land. Contemporary cultural, genetic, and linguistic evidence suggests strongly that the people who live there now are descended from those who brought agriculture to those forests, just as the ancient Hindu text suggests.[33]

The country whence they came is today the major agricultural region of Pakistan. Taken together, the provinces of Punjab and Sindh account for 90 per cent of all agricultural production in the country; most of it is on land artificially irrigated with water from the Indus River, which drains the highlands of South Asia toward the Arabian Sea.[34] Six thousand years ago, this land was home to a civilization as advanced as that of the great kingdoms of the Fertile Crescent, and actually may have extended over a wider area. But its cities—which featured sanitary sewers and piped water millennia before the Romans provided these amenities to their citizens—were abandoned around 1600 BCE.[35]

The food basket of these people included wheat, barley, cattle, goats, and sheep. The more of the latter, the bigger the impact on the land, since large herds exhausted grasslands near settlements quickly. Then the herdsman, his beasts, and possibly his family had to undertake a trek to find new pastures. Indeed, some researchers think that the desire to move flocks was responsible for the domestication of horses on the steppes of central Asia, as early as 3700 BCE.[36]

It's apparent from archeological records that horses weren't used to carry people at the beginning. Like other large herbivores—bison and aurochs, for example—horses were first hunted for food, and then raised to be eaten. But their suitability for other tasks became clear as soon as riding the beasts became widespread.

Just when this idea of riding horses occurred is unclear. But in contrast to the "Grandmother Effect," in another effect (call it the "Excellent Dude Effect" or even the "Kerouac Effect," since he would have understood it), foolhardy, adventurous young men or boys probably led the way, as they may have in crossing the Red Sea. This time, they climbed on more or less docile mares (stallions are much more difficult to break) and took off across the plain. Many must have fallen off, and some must have died or been seriously injured, since they would have had no bits, no reins, just the beast between their legs. But the joyrides they took would have suggested the possibility of using the animals for travel. That had an obvious practical side, since a mounted herdsman could lead his animals much farther afield than one on foot, thus increasing available forage.

This greatly increased mobility would not immediately lead to the kind of roads we think of today. Most travel continued on the same sort of trails that passing feet had worn over years and years, across grasslands and, increasingly, into the margins of forests. Even moving on horseback was at first more likely to wear wide swaths of trampled grass than produce anything new and different. Conscious construction of roads wider than what was needed for two travellers to pass each other came only when horses—and other draft animals like their cousins, donkeys—began hauling loads in wagons, and later pulling war chariots.

It took a millennium or so after the first horses were domesticated before some intrepid inventor discovered how wheels might be attached to a box so it could be easily pulled along. The first wheels show up about 3500 BCE, or about the same time as horses became companions to humans; however, these were potters' wheels, used by Mesopotamian artisans to make ceramics. If there's a connection between that kind of wheel and the one used for transport, it's not clear. As the late comedian Sid Caesar once said: "The guy who invented the first wheel was an idiot. The guy who invented the other three, he was a genius."[37]

When that brilliant idea finally surfaced, people had all the more reason to push back the forest. Wheeled vehicles could only be used easily on open terrain, unless paths were improved to allow them access to wooded land. One Chinese text heaps derision on a charioteer driving a powerful four-horse chariot who is overcome in battle and abandons his war machine to flee on foot into the woods. The implication is that "real" men faced each other on broad grasslands, either natural or created by human intervention.[38] Forests were the domain of superhuman forces, either for good or evil.

Around the world, attitudes toward forests are profoundly affected by that dynamic. Either we fear them, as attested to by Northern European folk tales full of evil waiting in the woods, or we try to appease the forces that we've upset in our battle with trees by providing sacred groves where powerful spirits can take refuge from our actions. The practice of safeguarding trees is found around the world—from Adonis' sacred grove at Afqa in Syria, and the Buoyem Sacred Grove in Ghana, to the more than 14,000 groves enumerated in modern-day India.

Between the two poles of veneration and mistrust, nearly all of us live in the open, even though many of the roads we travel may venture into the woods, or what was once woods. These latter roads have led to profound changes in the landscape, as the recently completed Interoceanic Highway in South America will illustrate.

In the meantime, however, the moment has come to consider what people have been carrying on all those roads.

Chapter Four

THE THINGS
THEY CARRIED

BACK ON THE SHORES OF THE RED SEA, OCHRE AND SHELLS were two things that the boy's grandmother made sure she brought with her as her family set out on the Great Expansion. The group also probably packed weapons and extra food in baskets or other carrying devices, but since they had no help from animals to do the carrying, anything else had to be considered very valuable to be included.

They also carried with them something which had no weight: ideas. Among them was the knowledge about how to make tools, what berries are ripe when and in what kind of terrain they might be growing, the proper relation to maintain with neighbours, how to comport oneself with kin, and what happens after death. This we can surmise from the remnants of culture they left behind, although doing that is difficult.

A few things, though, do seem certain. Several new ideas made the Great Expansion easier. We can date early evidence for some of these discoveries—for example, the needles that show up on the fringes of the growing glaciers from the Ice Age—but we have no idea if these objects represent a first, original invention or if the same brilliant idea occurred to others earlier or later.[1] What is clear is that frequently a good idea was passed along to neighbours, or carried to the next settlement, when people moved on.

Later, when people in more southerly regions began consciously planting crops, seeds figured prominently in their packsacks when they colonized new areas. But well before that, Stone Age people carried with them a number of tools made from various kinds of stone that equipped them to survive.

On my desk are four small rocks, all fitting nicely in my right hand. I had picked them up and put them in my pocket as my husband and I walked along a dirt road near Mono Lake in California on a summer trip. Today as I look at them, their shiny black surfaces catch the light, showing where bits have flaked off—and therein lies a tale.

These rocks are bits of obsidian, volcanic glass, produced when magma forced its way up from deep within the earth long ago and then cooled so quickly that it did not form crystals. My little stones aren't good for anything besides reminding me of a pleasant time spent on the shores of a lake that lies on the east side of the Sierra Nevada. But obsidian was among the most highly valued items in our ancestors' tool kit from the beginning: the first obsidian objects made by hominins have been dated to 700,000 years ago, well before anatomically modern humans developed. Obsidian remained the material of choice around the world for creating cutting tools, until the discovery of metal processing. Its capacity for holding an extremely sharp edge kept it in demand for certain surgical uses, until recently. A few surgeons still use obsidian scalpels for delicate cosmetic surgery.[2]

Clearly, good sources of obsidian were valued by many Stone Age societies, whose people were ready to trade for or travel to sources hundreds of kilometres away. In fact, what might be called the Obsidian Roads were probably the first trade routes in the world.

How do we know this? Well, obsidian has the interesting property of absorbing water at rates that can be measured. It also has chemical compositions that vary from place to place, leaving a recognizable signature. This combination means that with recently developed techniques, scientists can determine with great precision just how old an obsidian object is and where it came from.

My little stones' signature shows that they are from a vein of obsidian that Native Americans carried across the high Sierra Nevada, where the lowest passes are 3,000 metres high (about 9,800 feet), to settlements on the western edge of the Great Valley of California, where both Jack Kerouac and I took bus trips decades ago.

But that's getting ahead of the story.

On the other side of the world, evidence of the obsidian trade goes back much farther in time. Archeologists in Japan, Korea, and Russia have documented three major sources of obsidian from which stones made their way up to 800 kilometres (about 500 miles) from their sources during the depths of the last Ice Age. One of the sources was the Paektusan volcano in the northern part of the Korean peninsula. Objects made from this kind of obsidian are the most abundant so far studied, and they are also the oldest, dating back to 24,000 BCE.[3] Other objects that are considerably younger—dating between 11,000 and 15,000 BCE— show up in Primayre Province of maritime Russia and in Manchuria, nearly 1,000 kilometres (621 miles) as the crow flies from the volcano. The 10,000-year difference in the age of the findings could reflect a lack of intensive searching in the present day, or it could mean that populations retreated south while the North was bitterly cold during the Ice Age. Obsidian from various sites in the Japanese archipelago has been tracked, beginning about 18,000 BCE, on Sakhalin Island, the Russian territory north of the main Japanese islands. Although sea levels were historically lower at the time, transporting obsidian would have entailed a trip by boat across the water separating the two islands.

Researchers are on the lookout for signs that audacious adventurers leaving Northeast Asia beginning about then carried with them obsidian tools when they crossed over to the Americas.[4] So far, none have been found dating back that far, although it is possible some may yet turn up, particularly if undersea exploration is begun: many of the settlers' stopping points may now be under water. (The various ways the Americas were peopled will be discussed more thoroughly in chapter 7, "Mystery Roads.")

The first evidence of an obsidian road on the other side of the vast Eurasian continent goes back nearly as far as that found in the Far East. At the moment, the picture is more complete. The two major sources of obsidian in the Fertile Crescent are located in the Anatolian region of what is now Turkey: Cappadocia in central Anatolia and Bingöl further

east.[5] Looking at tools made from the two sources gives a kind of con-
nect-the-dots picture of an Obsidian Road dating back as far as 20,000
BCE and continuing for thousands of years. The earliest tools made from
Bingöl obsidian outside the immediate surroundings turn up in Iraqi
Kurdistan, apparently transported 500 kilometres (310 miles) or more
along the flanks of the hills that form the eastern boundaries of the Tigris
basin. Objects made from Cappadocia obsidian have been found south
of the Taurus Mountains that divide the Anatolian region from Syria and
the headwaters of the Euphrates River. As time passed, the use of obsidian from the two sources expanded, with Bingöl obsidian even occasionally making it over to the shores of the Mediterranean in what is now
Lebanon, more than 700 kilometres (443 miles) away.

But is it correct to call these routes "roads?" Excavations show that
several early towns near mountain passes were hubs of obsidian trade
and processing, and they must have been linked by paths.[6] Certainly,
the feet of those who carried the stone, as well as other valuables, had
an effect on the landscape. But even though the distances obsidian was
transported were frequently impressive, the obsidian trade was far more
local than the trade routes that followed like the Silk Road or, long before
that, the Lapis Lazuli Road.

The Silk Road, please note, is a more recent creation. While there is evidence that fabric was woven from the filaments excreted by the silkworm
as long ago as 4000 BCE, the fine garments made from it were reserved, at
first, for the Chinese Emperor and his closest associates. As production
grew, silk was used not only for garments, but also for fishing line, strings
for musical instruments, bow strings, and even fine papers made from silk
rags.[7] But its use was confined for centuries to its home territory, while
the secrets of silk production were jealously guarded. The earliest sign
of silk beyond the limits of what is now China was found adorning an
Egyptian female mummy dated from 1070 BCE in the Valley of the Kings.
A thousand years later, Chinese diplomats brought silk as gifts on official
visits to Persia and Mesopotamia, while the brightly coloured silk ban-
ners of enemy troops frightened Roman border contingents at the battle
of Carrhae on the Euphrates River in 53 BCE. Regular trade in silk from
China to the West did not start until several centuries later.

What we might call the Lapis Lazuli Route is much older.

My mother had a lapis lazuli ring. I'm not sure where it came from, or where it went, but I remember slipping it on my right index finger as a child. It was almost the right size to stay in place, or if it slipped around I could hold it with my thumb. The stone was a rectangle, about 2.5 centimetres long and not quite 2 centimetres wide, set in a silverish metal that tarnished. It always felt cool to the touch, and I would press it to my forehead or cheek on hot afternoons when, in order to keep me quiet so the littler children could nap, I was allowed to rustle through my mother's jewelry box. She wore the ring occasionally for dress-up affairs in the manner of post-World War II small towns. There must be a picture of her somewhere, a cigarette in her left hand with its modest etched-gold wedding band. The drink would be in her right and the lapis lazuli ring would appear startling and modern. (She had style, my mother. Even on that bus ride a few years later, she looked good despite the heat, despite our relatively reduced circumstances.)

She didn't prize the ring particularly, though. She certainly had little idea of just where the stone came from, or how highly prized it was long ago.[8]

Several sources of lapis lazuli are known now, in Canada, the Andes, and near Lake Baikal in Russia. But for millennia the coveted blue stone only came from one small area in the mountains of Afghanistan. Getting there was not easy, and trading the stone was far from simple. Yet, statues with blue eyes formed by bits of lapis lazuli set in bitumen show up in Mesopotamia as early as 2500 BCE,[9] while small objects made from the stone have been found in grave assemblages in Egypt as early as 3300 BCE.[10]

Even today, there is no quick way to get to the lapis lazuli mines in Afghanistan. A one-lane track crawls up the mountains, good enough for rugged four-wheel drive vehicles, but much of the stone is lugged out on the backs of the miners. Because of the long and difficult winters, work proceeds only for a few months; and each spring thaw reveals damage to the road, which has been the route of men seeking the blue stone for probably 6,000 years.[11] At the bottom of the gulch near the Sar-i-Sang mine unwanted rock lies where miners allowed it to tumble down, leaving a huge pile of white rock rubble. Images of the heap, shot by Al Jazeera in 2007, look not much different from photos taken by French archeologists in the 1970s when they investigated the source of the stone. The mining continues despite decades of conflict in Afghanistan, with much of the lapis lazuli apparently being sent out of the country through the mountains to Pakistan. Where the money received ends up is unclear.

Nor is it clear how the stone made its way so far from the source in those long-ago times. Some stones may have taken the route over the mountains and down to the south via the Indus valley, and from there to the sea where early traders carried it far away. Or, more likely, the stones were packed on the local trade routes which connected different settlements in Mesopotamia. There is evidence of at least three places where lapis was transformed from raw rock to finished objects, which suggests that it was a trade good that was crafted to meet local tastes.[12] What is more certain is that people in power, at a very early stage in the development of cities, valued the beautiful stone enough to transport it thousands of kilometres.

Other pretty things were carried long distances. Spondylus shells from the Aegean Sea show up in the Balkans by 6000 BCE, and amber from the Baltic region of Northern Europe made its way to the Mediterranean beginning about 2000 BCE.[13] Large amber beads adorn the breastplate of the

More than 4,500 years ago, lapis lazuli was carried hundreds of kilometres from the mountains of Afghanistan to Mesopotamia to provide the brilliant blue eyes of Ebih-Il, the Superintendent of Mari, now found in the Louvre.

Author Photo

Egyptian pharaoh Tutankhamun (about 1333–1324 BCE), and an amber lion has been found in Syria dating from around 1340 BCE. Shells and ochre were also carried by sojourners both in and out of Africa.

In short, aside from the trade in obsidian to make blades, and timber like the cedars of Lebanon, non-essential items, frequently sparkly objects or ones freighted with spiritual meaning, were the only things prized enough to be transported long distances.

Call it the bling factor, if you like. Certainly, the quest for flashiness had a role in the first metal worked by humans. Few people today would think of using anything other than steel to make tools and weapons because steel is so strong and versatile. But that wasn't evident at the beginning when people first began working metal. What they made, what they wanted were luxury items that were frequently very beautiful. Red copper, shiny lead, and yellow gold were the first metals humans worked. They are among the easiest metals to separate from the ore containing them, but they were prized in large part because they looked so nice. The oldest copper object so far uncovered is a bead found in what is now northern Iraq. It dates from 9500 BCE and is made from native copper ore which was hammered into a sheet and then rolled up.[14]

Getting from this stage of rudimentary bling to the development of copper alloys that could make something useful would take several thousand years. A suite of other ideas had to be developed first, such as how to make pottery. The connection doesn't seem obvious, but the skills needed to take clay and produce a pot for storage, or a bowl for eating, by firing it in an oven set the scene for smelting metal. Not that the first clay objects had much practical value either. The oldest known fired clay object is not a cooking pot or a cup, but the Venus of Dolni Vestonice, a zaftig little figure with

The bling factor in action: The flashy beauty of copper was prized long before the metal's usefulness in making tools and weapons was discovered.

Photo: Jonathan Zander / GNU Free Documentation License

pendulous breasts. Dating back to 27,000 BCE, it was found in a cave in Czechoslovakia and might have been the effigy of an Earth Goddess.

The first evidence of more utilitarian uses of fired clay shows up on the other side of the Eurasian continent several thousand years later. Ceramic containers found in China in the Yangtze River region have been dated to about 18,000 BCE, while ceramic vessels from between 13,000 to 15,000 BCE have turned up in central Europe. By the time people settled down in the first agricultural communities like Jericho and Çatalhöyük in central Turkey, they were making enough pottery to leave behind piles of shards, confirming what may seem obvious: growing food, storing it, and cooking it in pots of one sort or another go hand in hand.

At least one researcher speculates that the big gaps between the dates and locations of these early ceramics mean that the idea of baking clay was invented more than once. Certainly, it looks like pottery was independently developed in West Africa about 9000 BCE, while pottery shards dating from 7000 to 8000 BCE have been found in the Amazon basin.[15]

Once artisans figured out how to control fire well enough to bake a pot, copper ores could be smelted, and the lead in mixtures of lead and silver could be vaporized in ceramic vessels, leaving only silver behind. The tricky business of finding the right combination of temperature and manipulation took much trial and error. Initially, the discovery of copper alloys was probably accidental: smelted copper naturally "tainted" with arsenic shows up in the Balkans about 6000 to 7000 BCE. Deliberately working copper with other metals to produce materials that were both harder and easier to work came later. As three academics who've studied the development of metallurgy around the world comment: "People did not need copper tools; they wanted copper tools... [T]he earliest metal objects were not necessarily superior to wood, bone, flint, obsidian or ceramics for performing everyday tasks, and these other materials continued to be used for thousands of years alongside metal tools."[16]

Bronze, the alloy of tin and copper, is harder than copper, has a lower melting temperature, and gives better results when cast into moulds because the molten metal is more fluid and cools into a denser, more uniform material. Making spear points and axes was one of the early uses for bronze, but the result was frequently no better than tools made from other, easier-to-come-by material.

The idea that we can divide recent prehistory into a "Bronze Age" that comes after a "Stone Age" and before an "Iron Age" is far too simplistic, and even completely wrong. This concept of prehistory presupposes that any civilization had to progress in a measured way toward a cluster of cultural features that went hand in hand with bronze as the metal of choice—early writing, sophisticated social organization, and the development of cities. Now, however, it seems that bronze-making techniques probably were developed in only one region—Anatolia—over a relatively long period and spread both east and west by people trafficking ideas, as well as goods and raw materials. Bronze objects first show up about 4000 BCE as far west as Great Britain and Western Europe, and as far east as present-day Thailand and Vietnam. There is no evidence of earlier experimentation in these regions. Bronze production springs up apparently full-blown, like Athena from Zeus's head. The ingenuity of the Anatolian metalworkers is underscored also by the fact that, while copper, silver, and gold smelting developed independently in the western hemisphere several thousand years later, bronze was unknown before the arrival of Europeans, who carried with them the legacy of techniques developed in what is now Turkey.

To be sure, details of the bronze-smelting process varied from region to region as people adapted bronze-making techniques. In some places, bellows introduced air into the smelter in order to produce hotter temperatures, while in others vents channeled prevailing winds into the firebox. But it is certainly no accident that the route early humans took through the broad grasslands of what some call "Savannastan" became the one that spread new technology. The route corresponded more or less with the geological band of tin ore sources stretching from Europe to Southeast Asia, and also happened to be one of the easiest paths of travel in Eurasia—eastward from Anatolia across the steppes and grasslands of central Asia, and westward into Europe.

Sometime around the beginning of bronze-making, people began to invent a new way of living off the grasslands that involved horses. This development would have profound effects on the landscape, on what people carried with them, and, just as importantly, on how they got along with their neighbours.

As mentioned before, the use of horses for transportation and not just for food, coupled with the invention of the first carts increased the range of herding nomads. When this use of horses began is open to debate, but, at the end of the Cold War in the 1990s (perhaps ironically), the picture became clearer when vast amounts of research carried out by archeologists in the former Soviet Union became more accessible. Research done there was translated into English and other Western languages, and Western archeologists joined their Russian (and Ukrainian and Kazakhstani, etc.) colleagues in excavations. They unearthed a wealth of information about horses and the societies that depended on them.

Horses were well adapted to cold grasslands because, unlike sheep, goats, and cattle which must be supplied with hay and fodder, horses will use their hooves to break through snow to find grass underneath or water beneath ice. This made them a valued addition to a pastoral society's larder. David W. Anthony calls them "cheap winter meat" in his book *The Horse, the Wheel and Language*.[17]

By studying the wear on horse teeth found in graves and garbage heaps, Anthony and his fellow researchers have tried to determine when horses began to be ridden with bits between their teeth. The conclusion: at least by 3700 BCE on the Pontic-Caspian steppe. This steppe stretches north of the Black Sea as far east as the Caspian Sea, and from present-day Moldova and the western part of Ukraine to the Volga Federal District of Russia and western Kazakhstan.[18] The vast region of grasslands and savannahs, intercut by many large rivers, was inviting territory for herds of wild horses, and, Anthony argues, it's possible that bareback riding without reins may have begun there by 4200 BCE.

By 3400 BCE, horses and wagons were in widespread use, showing up as funerary offerings in the graves of notables throughout the region and even farther afield: wagon tracks at a gravesite in Germany date that far back. These were heavy vehicles, with solid wheels, and are sometimes depicted as being pulled by donkeys and onagers, a cousin of the horse. In addition, oxen also were used as draft animals. As well as allowing herding nomads to range widely and keep ahead of the damage done by grazing hordes of sheep and cattle, the wagons made it easier to haul heavier materials like metal ores.

As noted before, metal tools and weapons weren't any better than stone ones at first. While the sophisticated civilizations of Mesopotamia and the Indus River Valley prized bronze and copper luxury goods, they had little use for metal weapons. The steppe-based culture of nomads changed that when they began to mass-produce arms. The implications of this deep cultural mutation, that singularly dangerous set of ideas that people carried with them as they travelled the world's roads, are still with us today.

My husband has always joked that there were horse thieves in his family, but that no one ever admitted to their presence in the family tree. Given the fact that most of the Soderstroms and their collateral relatives were dirt farmers from Sweden who immigrated to the North American Plains in the 1870s and 1880s, I doubt very much that horse or cattle rustling was a career choice for any of them. But the idea that a horse thief was about the worst thing one could be permeated the society my husband grew up in, where the legacy of the Wild West lingered well into the twentieth century.

But the horse thief wasn't anathema only in the West. As Malcolm Gladwell, a great popularizer of arcane ideas, suggests, a good portion of America's Southern Appalachian mountains were settled by herders from the Scottish Highlands who brought with them a code of behaviour designed to protect their animals and their grazing territory from covetous others. "A herdsman has to worry," Gladwell writes. "He's under constant threat of ruin through the loss of his animals. So he has to be aggressive: he has to make it clear, through his word and deeds that he is not weak. He has to be willing to fight in response to even the slightest challenge to his reputation."[19]

Gladwell cites experiments on aggression conducted at the University of Michigan with students from the U.S. South and other parts of that country. The conclusion: even in a place far removed in time, space, and economic context, the Southerners were considerably more aggressive.

"Cultural legacies are powerful forces," Gladwell writes. "They have deep roots and long lives. They persist, generation after generation, virtually intact, even as the economic and social and demographic conditions that spawned them have vanished, and they play such a role in directing attitudes and behavior that we cannot make sense of our world without them."[20]

Hmm, you might say. That's interesting pop psychology with rather alarming implications for the American political and social context. But even if it's partially true, how does it relate to what ideas people in prehistoric times carried with them, or to the physical goods they lugged around, or to where they went? Anthropologist David Anthony might reply: even more than Appalachian mountain men, nomadic herders of the steppes were obsessed with guarding their animals from predators and, more importantly, from their neighbours. Their fear, he suggests, led to an escalation in the art of war, and to mass-production of weapons which made copper and bronze much more valuable for their clout than for their bling.

The evidence for this, Anthony writes, is found in objects considered important enough to accompany people beyond the grave. Men (and sometimes women) of stature have long been buried with jewelry and handcrafted arrowheads and javelin heads designed first and foremost for hunting and only incidentally for fighting. But when steppe people began herding livestock, something else started to show up in their burials: stone, and later copper, maces.

What the leaders are supposed to do with funereal wealth in the afterlife is never clear, but burying maces marks a break with a culture in which a hunter's heaven was what people hoped for. Unlike bows and arrows, maces have no use in hunting. Their only purpose is to bash in someone's head, Anthony notes. It's as if the notables were preparing to continue fighting over territory or guarding troops of animals from insurgents, even after death.

This emphasis on warfare is strikingly apparent at one amazing site in the eastern Urals on the northern steppes just inside present-day Russian borders. The fortification, now called Sintashta, was excavated between 1972 and 1987 CE (of the common era), and dates from 2900 to 2610 BCE. It was 140 metres (450 feet) in diameter and surrounded by timber-reinforced walls and a 1.5 metre-deep, "v"-shaped moat (nearly 5 feet.) Outside the protective perimeter, five funerary complexes have been found with remains of chariots, weapons, and whole horses that appear to have been sacrificed. What was notable about these graves, Anthony emphasizes, was that the accoutrements of conflict instead of crowns and jewelry had been buried there. Slag heaps, oven hearths, and copper itself attest to intensive metalworking, with much of the production going toward mass-producing weapons.

Excavations of Stone Age sites frequently turn up trash containing flint blanks and flakes leftover from making arrowheads, each of which was individually crafted with few weighing exactly the same. This meant that in addition to the effort that went into shaping the head, each one had to be adjusted to fit a shaft. It made sense to take care of them, to aim at prey with precision, and to recover the arrow or spear if possible afterward so it could be used again.

But once the trick of casting metal was mastered, it was much easier to make arrow- and spearheads. One mould could be used to cast tens, if not hundreds, of heads whose weight and size would vary only a little. The process of attaching them to shafts was less finicky, too, and losing one was therefore less of a big deal. One can almost hear cries equivalent to "Hey, Dude, this is cool!" as people started mass-producing weapons.

The resulting increased demand for copper and bronze meant an accompanying increase in long-distance trade. Copper ores are relatively common, but tin, the metal needed to make bronze and copper's most versatile alloy, is not. For perhaps the first time, a heavy material besides timber began to be transported over long distances on a regular basis. The tin mines of Anatolia were exploited as early as 7000 BCE, while by the end of the Roman Empire mines in Wales were nearly worked out. One text from the city of Ur (in present-day Iraq), that dates somewhere between 1822 and 1763 BCE, recorded the receipt of 18,333 kg or 20 tons of copper in a single shipment, most of it earmarked for only one merchant.

The new abundance of lethal weapons coupled with the invention of the chariot set the scene for a new sort of warfare: warfare on a larger scale. Wagons had been used in battles by the Mesopotamian kingdoms as early as 2900 BCE, but from illustrations of them, they appear to have been pulled by asses or onagers, not horses. This suggests that they might have been good for moving supplies but were cumbersome and slow.

Light, horse-drawn chariots (imagined here by a nineteenth-century artist) made war between groups more deadly, as in this attack by Persian scythed chariots against the forces of Alexander the Great in 331 BCE.

Drawing by André Castaigne, 1898-1899 / Public Domain

Chariots were something else. A few hundred years later (and well before the chariots of the Mycenanean civilization, long thought to be the chariot's inventor) the people of the Sintashta settlement had discovered how to build a more effective battle vehicle. Their two-wheeled chariots had wheels that weren't clunky circles of wood like the wagon wheels, but were elegantly crafted bent-wood structures held together by six to eight spokes. As a result, a chariot was much lighter and far more maneuverable, even when two men—the driver and an archer—rode in it. A charge by a group of Sintashta charioteers would have been a formidable sight.

The scene was being set for a new level of inter-group aggression, where archers riding in chariots could shower enemies with volleys of metal-tipped arrows, and charging horsemen armed with bronze maces could pummel men on the ground.

The roads these warriors travelled became the roads of empires, the thoroughfares along which raw materials for weapons were traded, as well as pretty shiny things.

Chapter Five

WARRIORS' ROADS

FLASH FORWARD SIX OR SEVEN THOUSAND YEARS. NOT FAR from where horses were first used in conflict, six hundred horsemen are ordered to charge up a valley on the edge of the Black Sea. The riders are gallant and brave, and they race forward without, it seems, a thought for their own safety:

> Half a league, half a league,
> Half a league onward,
> All in the valley of Death
> Rode the six hundred....
> Theirs not to reason why,
> Theirs but to do and die.
> Into the valley of Death
> Rode the six hundred.[1]

In the famous poem by Alfred, Lord Tennyson, you can hear the rhythm of the pounding hooves, almost see the wild eyes of the horses, and feel the surging movement of the horsemen on their mounts.

Conflicts have plagued the region on the shores of the Black Sea for thousands of years. In this particular mid-nineteenth-century conflict, the charge of the Light Brigade took place in what is now the Ukrainian city of Sebastopol. On October 25, 1854, the British officers blundered and sent their force up a valley guarded on three sides by Russian cannons and artillery. The outcome was not pretty. As Tennyson writes:

> Boldly they rode and well,…
> While horse and hero fell.
> They that had fought so well
> Came through the jaws of Death,
> Back from the mouth of Hell,
> All that was left of them,
> Left of six hundred.

The slaughter of the horsemen during the battle of Balaclava in the fall of 1854 (118 men were killed, 127 wounded, and 60 taken prisoner) marked the beginning of the end for cavalry, that storied partnership between horse and rider that moulded so many of the power games between groups of people over millennia.[2]

In this book about roads and the people who have made and followed them, there are two lessons to draw from this celebrated defeat. First, the thirst for conquest and control can lead people down paths that end in disaster. Second, the horses did not thunder along roads of the sort we are accustomed to in the twenty-first century.

Horses don't do well on paved roads. They evolved on the steppes, you'll remember, with hooves developed to carry them across dry surfaces with a bit of spring in them. As long as horses are given the chance to run regularly on variations of steppes, they don't need horseshoes, because their hooves grow hard and fast enough to make up for the wear and tear they receive. But once they are forced to travel across other terrain, particularly hard surfaces like rocks and paving, they need extra protection.

At Balaclava, drawings done by war artists depict rolling, grassy terrain, which probably meant that the horses had good conditions for their charge. But their battle formation was anything but a column that could be contained on a roadway. Instead, their formation spread across the valley.

This is not to say that by the time of the gallant—if foolish—cavalry charge roads were unimportant to the art of war. Conflict was as big an impetus for building roads as the desire for bling in encouraging trade—but more about that a little further on. Suffice to say, the idea of making the tracks of passing feet easier to follow did occur to people at least by the time of the first agricultural settlements, even though the evidence suggests that improved roads were rare for millennia.

Imagine this: In the late summer or early fall of 3807 BCE, perhaps about the time that the hazelnuts were ripe and began to fall to the ground, a group of farmers and herders, living far away from the steppes in present-day England, got together and decided that they should build a wooden walkway across the swamps. The people had been in the neighbourhood for more than one hundred years, probably arriving with barley to grow, and pigs, sheep, and goats to tend. Ash, oaks, elms, and other trees covered much of the land, and the newcomers chopped many of them down to clear fields and build structures. The winters were cooler and the summers were hotter than today. The sea level was lower, too, and there was game to kill and fish to catch: it would appear that the people were doing well. They also, it appears, had figured out a way to manage the woodlands, by coppicing some of the giant trees they felled, so they could get a sustained supply of wood from the shoots that grew up from stumps.[3]

But times were changing, as they always seem to be doing. For reasons that aren't quite clear, the people wanted to travel on a regular basis between high ground on the south to a hill on the north, which, for part of the year at least, was isolated by swamp waters. Perhaps thirty years before, they had built another track that led across the marshes, but the sea level seems to have begun to rise, as the world readjusted after the last Ice Age. The track was either now too short to connect the two points of high ground, or suffering from exposure to the elements, or both. What to do?[4]

The decision—it would be interesting to hear what kind of discussions went on—was to salvage some of the early structure, and cut down enough trees from the margins of the marshes to build another, nearly two-kilometre-long track. Oak planks were used for the walkway, fitted into a cradle of alder poles (probably from the coppiced wood) that were forced into the soil to make an "x" shape. In all, 4,000 metres of heavy planks, 2,000 metres of heavy rails, and 6,000 pieces of logs or split pegs were used. Perhaps 200,000 kilograms of wood was transported to the site, much of it already cut to size, although scrap wood found along the track suggests that fitting was done as the work progressed. Probably much of the felling and transporting was done during the winter of 3607–3606 BCE, but archeologists who examined the track's remains, and then tried to imitate the work, think that assembly must have been done quickly. Once construction of the pathway was started, each additional element rested on ones already in place, meaning that work had to proceed as rapidly as possible. The archeologists think that a team of ten or so men could have completed construction in the space of several days in the spring of 3806 BCE.

The exactness of that date—which is several centuries before the building of Stonehenge and around the time the first wheel tracks show up in Germany—sounds suspicious. How could anyone pinpoint the precise time that anything was built so long ago? But this was a wooden structure, which eventually became covered with swamp, setting the stage for the area's transformation into a peat bog. The muck was both acidic and devoid of oxygen, which preserved many of the planks in excellent condition. Then in 1970, Ray Sweet (after whom the Sweet Track is named) unearthed the first timbers when he was cutting peat. Because of the long-buried wood's excellent state of preservation, scientists were able to determine exactly when the trees were cut based on the pattern of tree ring growth. Some of the posts salvaged from the causeway the Sweet Track replaced were dated to thirty or so years before. Other poles and planks from trees felled within ten years of the track's construction appear to have been used for repairs.

And after that, there is no new wood, no evidence of repairs. It looks as if the rising waters of the swamp engulfed the track, and it was forgotten under layers of reed and marsh plants, slowly decomposing into peat. The people who lived there might well have built other tracks nearby, but they have not been discovered. We know for certain, though, that the

Sweet Track was not unique. Remnants of another plank roadway, perhaps one hundred years older, were found in 2009 in London 4.7 metres (15.4 feet) below ground level, during the construction of a new wing to the Belmarsh prison. In other parts of the world, similar tracks may be waiting buried in swamps or beneath volcanic ash or the trash of people who came to live there later.[5] We just don't know what further excavation might turn up.

Evidence of roads paved with stone doesn't show up for a thousand years after the Sweet Track, and when it does, it's in Egypt, far away from both cold, damp northern Europe and the drier grasslands where horses were domesticated. Made from slabs of black basalt, sandstone, limestone, and even some logs of petrified wood, the road measures nearly 2 metres wide (6.5 feet.) It runs about 11 kilometres (6.8 miles) from a basalt quarry in the hills southwest of Cairo, near the shores of a now-dry lake that connected with the Nile at high water. It appears that giant blocks of basalt were dragged down the roadway, apparently with big logs used as rollers. Then they floated on barges to pyramid construction

The Sweet Track is among the oldest known remnants of a road. Study of the logs from which it was constructed dates the track to 3807 BCE, more than 5,800 years ago.

Photo: Geoff Sheppard / Creative Commons Attribution-Sharealike 3.0 Unported License

at Giza, sometime between 2200 and 2600 BCE.[6] The black stone was used extensively also for paving inside mortuary structures and for royal sarcophagi: Egyptologists suggest that the colour symbolized the mud of the dark, life-giving Nile.

The road, no matter how well engineered and seemingly inviting for wheeled transport, was not designed to have wagons travel it, though. The first wheeled vehicles were introduced to Egypt much later, about 1700 BCE, when rulers from the East held sway along the Nile, bringing with them lightweight, horse-drawn chariots. Wagons didn't become common until even later.

The second-oldest paved roads show up on the island of Crete during the period of Minoan civilization about 2000 BCE. Although Minoans were a seafaring people, they went to considerable effort to connect settlements on the island by well-surfaced and engineered roads.

But most paved roads, until a millennia and a half later, were mostly ceremonial, and not designed to make getting from place to place easier. Take, for example, the Processional Way leading to Ishtar Gate in the Babylon of Nebuchadnezzar. Lined with magnificent tiles depicting aurochs, lions, and dragons, and decorated with borders of flower images, it was about 25 metres (82 feet) wide. Large crowds could assemble there for state occasions, such as the Babylonian new year, which was celebrated at the spring equinox when the king would leave the city to bless and review the crops growing outside. While it's likely that a road extended into the countryside, there is no evidence of the construction of the kind of broad, paved thoroughfare that we associate with roads today.

Why? Well, just as we can only guess at a lot of things about the past, we can only surmise that unless an early ruler wanted to impress his subjects, he had no reason to build one. In settlements, a certain amount of paving might be undertaken. Paved streets show up in Harappa and Ur about the time that ceremonial roads began to be built elsewhere. But streets, paved or unpaved, clearly weren't necessary for town living: the people who lived 9,000 years ago in Çatalhöyük, the extensively excavated early town in what is now Turkey, didn't have them. For the thousand years that the settlement thrived, houses were clustered closely together without lanes to separate them, and with access through openings in the roofs.[7]

On routes between settlements, bridges might be constructed and pathways through mountains improved, but getting from place to place on foot or with pack animals rarely required grand public works projects. Even travel with wagons did not mean much more road improvement, although the first Chinese emperor (259–210 BCE) standardized the width of wagon axles and roads to make travel easier.[8]

Communication, though, was essential in early civilizations: how to get a message from one place to another quickly for administrative reasons, or in time of war. The first integrated system of mail transport was established by the Persian king Darius the Great (550–486 BCE) to strengthen communications along what has been called the Royal Road.[9]

Among the first written documents we have are those related to trade: what appear to be bills of lading, letters ordering shipment of copper and other metals, and receipts of merchandise. They show up in the excavations and archives of all the early literate civilizations, and give us a window into ordinary lives. They probably were sent along with the trade goods, by pack animal or wagon, no faster than a serious walk along trails that were, at best, only minimally improved.

How fast was that? Listen to the "On the Trail" section of Ferde Grofé's colourful work for symphony orchestra *The Grand Canyon Suite* to get some idea of how unhurried that gait is. The music begins with violin and horns protesting like whinnying horses and donkeys not keen on being saddled up. Then it settles into a comfortable, rolling rhythm— doot, ta doot, ta doot, ta doot—neither the music nor the animals are going any faster than is absolutely necessary.

But when desire for power is pushed to the forefront, that ambling pace won't do. Just contrast the Grofé piece with the "Cavalry Charge" from Rossini's *William Tell Overture*. The trumpets blare out notes twice, three times as fast, and the warhorses blaze past. To run empires, a system of better roadways was needed, with posts where riders could change exhausted horses for fresh ones so that vital messages could be galloped forward.

This push for better communications over long distance comes at the point in time when prehistory becomes history, when surmises from archeology can be corroborated by the written record. As it happens, there exists a very clear description of the Royal Road, which Herodotus, a Greek who chronicled conflict between Greek states and the Persian Empire in his *Histories*, may have travelled and with which he was clearly impressed, despite the fact that Darius was Greece's enemy.

The Persian king did not build his Royal Road from scratch, nor was his capital at Susa his original creation. (Susa is now known as Shush in southwestern Iran, about 200 kilometres (150 miles) north of the Persian Gulf.) Indeed, the history of Susa reflects just how old and full of incident this part of the world is. There is archeological evidence that humans settled here at least 7,500 years ago; the Biblical books of Nehemiah, Daniel, and Esther take place in large part here; and it has been continually inhabited since its beginnings, except for a short inter-regnum after the Mongol invasions of the thirteenth century CE.[10]

Today, Shush is a town of about 60,000, and is served by Iran Highway 37, part of a modern highway system running from Tehran (Iran's largest city and capital) in the North to Bandar Imam on the Gulf. For part of the way, the highway is two lanes, but at Shush it becomes four lanes, and plans call for expanding the remaining two-lane segments into four lanes for the entire distance. Despite its small size, Shush is frequently plagued by air pollution. That's due partly to dust storms and partly to horrific pollutants coming from inadequately regulated industry and vehicle emissions in the region: nearby Ahvaz was named the world's most polluted city in 2011 by the World Health Organization.[11]

The Greek historian Herodotus left a detailed description of the first grand road network, the Royal Road of Darius the Great.

Photo: Marie-Lan Nguyen / Wikimedia Commons, Creative Commons Attribution 2.5 License

Darius the Great wouldn't recognize the place, in other words. Set between the Karkheh and Dez rivers, by all accounts Ahvaz was noted for its good climate (Darius found his other capital Persepolis in the mountains too cold in winter), fertile fields, and strategic location. The plains of Mesopotamia open up to the west, while the passes of the Zagros Mountains to the north and east lead to the Iranian Plateau. These two regions have nurtured great civilizations for thousands of years, civilizations whose influence has seemingly alternated in importance. The twentieth-century conflicts between Iran and Iraq can be seen as just the most recent manifestation.

People living in the northern regions of the land between the Tigris and Euphrates rivers (the name "Mesopotamia" comes from the Ancient Greek meaning "land between rivers") were among the first in the world to transform the rich savannahs, which so attracted our early ancestors out of Africa, into croplands. Later, extensive irrigation systems relying on the bountiful waters of the rivers transformed the southern part of the land between the rivers into rich fields. A succession of powerful city states and kingdoms—among them, Uruk dating from 4000 to 3100 BCE; Akkad from 2334 to 2193 BCE; the Assyrian cities of Assur and Nineveh, from 2500 to 650 BCE; and Babylon, from 2300 to 620 BCE—ruled the region and made themselves felt on the surrounding peoples.

The Elam civilization, in contrast, was centered on the Iranian plateau to the east. Its written records date almost as far back as those in Mesopotamia, but the language has been only imperfectly deciphered. This means that its history is less understood than that of Mesopotamia. Clearly, however, the people who lived and prospered there matched the Mesopotamians in cultural sophistication, techniques of warfare, and wealth. The balance of power between the inter-river region and the highlands changed many times over 3,000 years, with Median and Achaemenid empires succeeding the Elamite. Susa, lying between the two poles of civilization, profited for the most part from its location.

Darius the Great's father had been governor of one of the highland provinces, Bactria, in what is now Afghanistan.[12] As a young man, Darius served with the Persian king Cambyses in a successful expedition to conquer Egypt (528–525 BCE)—Cambyses is known also as the mastermind behind the construction of a canal leading from the Nile to the Red Sea. When Darius gained power after a rebellion, he continued his predecessor's drive to enlarge the Persian Empire. Under him it became the largest empire the world would see until the Roman Empire at its height several hundred years later. At its greatest extent, the Persian Empire ran east to Afghanistan, south into India, nearly circled the Black Sea, embraced all of what is called the Middle East today, and hesitated on the doorstep of Europe. (Alexander the Great of Macedonia conquered somewhat more territory in his brief campaign of glory, but his empire had already begun to dissolve even before his death in Babylon in 323 BCE.)

Darius evidently loved Susa, because there he built his palace whose ruins are a major reason to visit the modern city today. (Another reason is a building supposedly housing the tomb of the Biblical Daniel, who ended his life there—the edifice itself is only about five hundred years old.) Darius boasted in an inscription written in three languages that the materials and the labour required to build the city came from all over his empire. It says that Babylonians made sun-dried bricks, and Assyrians and Greeks brought cedar from Lebanon to build the palace. To decorate it, silver and ebony worked by the finest artisans were brought from Egypt and India. The inscription goes on to state, "Darius the King says: At Susa a very excellent work was ordered, a very excellent work was brought to completion."[13]

Excavations led by the French archeologist Jacques de Morgan at the end of the nineteenth century uncovered layers and layers of artifacts in Susa. Among the objects discovered were a wealth of plunder from Babylon, including gorgeous funeral offerings and a column bearing the code of Babylonian king Hammurabi, the first written law extant.[14] A visitor won't find the latter on the site, though: it's a must-visit exhibit at the Louvre Museum in Paris. De Morgan, whose work was financed by French sources, signed an agreement in 1900 with local authorities giving France the right to what was found, so the Louvre is filled with treasures from Susa.

Back at Shush today, perhaps the most striking building is a castle reminiscent of the Château de Vincennes in the French capital. Now housing a museum containing some artifacts from the excavation, the castle was built by de Morgan to protect his team from attacks by plunderers because, at the time, the region did not have a government effective enough to safeguard the site. To walk around the castle's ramparts today is to get an idea of de Morgan's conflicted and outdated ideas about archeology. For example, he ordered the use of bricks unearthed during the excavations to make the walls.[15] Some bearing cuneiform inscriptions and others decorated with glaze that once were part of mosaics can now easily be seen. Near-Eastern specialists shake their heads over the opportunities lost to know even more about Darius and his times.

Indeed, a lot of water has flowed down the two rivers in Shush since Darius took control. In addition to the expressway passing through, a railroad serves the town, but tourist guides suggest that visitors would do better to stay in Ahvaz, a few hours away by car, because of the difficulty of getting to Shush and its lack of accommodations. This is a far cry from the time when Susa was Darius's capital, and his Royal Road connected it with the four corners of his empire.

Not that his road bore much resemblance to the high-speed thoroughfares we know today, or even to the widespread network of roads the Romans constructed half a millennium later. It seems the road incorporated many existing established routes, but with refinements. The distance involved is impressive—nearly 2,900 kilometres (1,700 miles) on its main branch, running from Susa to the shores of the Mediterranean. Branches led to Persepolis, and north to Rayy, the city sacred to Zoroastrianism which is now part of greater Tehran.

Herodotus gives a detailed description of the Royal Road's main sections. "At intervals all along the road are recognized stations, with excellent inns, and the road itself is safe to travel by as it never leaves inhabited country," he writes.[16] Travelling at "150 furlongs a day" (about 30 kilometres or 18.75 miles, a pace entirely possible with or without pack animals), Herodotus says it would take ninety days to make it from Sardis (the home of the fabulously wealthy Croesus), at the eastern edge of the Mediterranean coastal plain, to Susa. In all, 111 stations were on the trajectory which, like a string of pearls, went through nearly every city or monument of any consequence from the preceding three thousand years of Eurasian history.

From Susa the route went west to Babylon, near what is now Baghdad on the Euphrates. After that it turned north, passing through the old Assyrian capital of Nineveh (near present-day Mosul.) Then it headed north-west, apparently on the eastern side of the Tigris River before turning west to cross the Euphrates and the Cilician lowland that extends eastward from the Mediterranean Coast. But rather than head for the sea, it turned north through the Taurus Mountains by way of a carefully guarded pass called the Cilician Gates that led to the much higher Anatolian Plateau. Traffic on the road would have been constricted here because until the twentieth century the roadway was no wider than a wagon track. Once through the pass, the road turned west to cross the plateau toward the coast, where it ended. In several places, there were guardhouses controlling traffic, as well as bridges over watercourses that could not be easily forded.

According to Herodotus, the distance could be covered in less than fifteen days, when the system of post horses was used. The road was divided into sections that could be covered in a day by a man on horseback. At each station, a rider would hand off his dispatch to a fresh rider and horse: "No mortal thing travels faster than these Persian couriers," Herodotus writes. Nothing stops them "from covering their allotted stage in the quickest possible time—neither snow, rain, heat nor dark of night," he adds in a phrase that was adopted by the United States Postal Service to vaunt its mail service at the beginning of the twentieth century.[17]

The Persian relay system appears to have been faster than any other until the thirteenth century, when Genghis Khan's couriers carried messages from his headquarters near the Yellow River in China to the western side of the Black Sea, a distance of more than 8,000 kilometres (5,000 miles.)[18] Khan's system was somewhat different from the Persian one: each of the great Mongol leader's riders was responsible for the message he carried, and so one courier travelled the whole distance, strapping himself to his mounts so he would not fall off. (At the same time on the other side of the world, it should be noted, the Incas who did not have fast, load-bearing animals, were using fleet human runners to carry messages, as well as perishable items like fish, hundreds of kilometres in the Andes and its foothills.)

For warrior empires, sending dispatches quickly across a far-flung empire was important, but moving troops was even more essential in time of conflict. Doing that frequently required routes more developed than the post road. Darius's aim was to conquer the known world, and he set his engineers to work overcoming natural obstacles that stood in the way of his battle plans, accomplishing feats that were not equalled until modern times. One of them was a bridge across the Bosporus, the strait that separates Asia from Europe at the western end of the Black Sea where Istanbul is now located. It wasn't until the middle of the twentieth century that the strait was bridged permanently.[19] For the battle of the Bosporus, Darius assembled six hundred ships and 700,000 men drawn from all over the empire, Herodotus writes.

Most of these troops travelled on foot. They and the cavalry units were accompanied by wagon trains carrying considerable baggage. In addition to the usual supplies, tools, and weapons, the Persian elite troops (the Ten Thousand) brought along their women and servants. Without a doubt, all those marching feet must have had an effect on the landscape. Herodotus does not comment on the state of the Royal Road after Darius's forces passed, but he does remark that north of the Black Sea, where the roads were far from the Royal thoroughfare, the army's footsteps destroyed the grasslands where it passed.

But try looking for remnants of the Royal Road today, and you'll not find many. Ancient Susa itself was burnt and rebuilt four times after Darius's death as waves of empires rolled over it, most recently after invading Mongols destroyed it in 1218 CE. Today, roads near the modern town run mostly north and south, connecting it to cities in Iran. Going west, as the Royal Road did, is possible, but it means crossing into Iraq over a border that, to put it mildly, has seen considerable conflict in recent years.[20]

Farther afield, parts of Darius's route lie beneath roads built by later powers. In 1961, researchers from the University of Pennsylvania tried to follow the Royal Road from Gordion in Anatolia eastward to the Euphrates: they found that over long distances the course of the road could be discerned by, among other things, the placement of bridges. A few years later, stretches of a hard-packed, gravelled road were unearthed

near Gordion itself, which may well have been part of the Royal Road. At
6.5 metres in width (more than 20 feet wide) with curbing of flat stones,
it appears to be "a great trunk route, rather than a mere country lane."
Other geographers suggest that much of the Roman road system in Asia
Minor and beyond was based on the Royal Road.[21] They say that the
major Roman contribution in the region, after they took control in 133
BCE, was to pave roads that had not been paved until then.

Elsewhere in the empire, Romans also used and improved roads
already in place: In his *Commentaries*, Julius Caesar notes that when the
Romans marched into Gaul, they found that the locals already had a
network of roads capable of carrying supply wagons for warriors as well
as goods. These roads, it would seem, are the descendants of the roads
begun 3,000 years before by people like those who built the Sweet Track
in England, and who, even then, had established long-distance trade.

Witness to that traffic is a smooth, carefully worked axe head without
a haft or handle, which has been found about halfway along the Sweet
Track. Made from jade, the axe's chemical composition indicates that it
was made from volcanic stone coming from Monte Viso in the Italian
Alps. This hard evidence of pre-Roman trade is far from unique. More
than one hundred axe heads manufactured from stone quarried in the
same region between 5500 and 3700 BCE have been found in England
and Ireland.[22] Hundreds of others have been found throughout Europe,
suggesting a grand movement of the objects, most of which appear not to
be used as tools, but as items of cultural or spiritual value. Interestingly,
about the same time in China, jade was beginning to be used to make
objects whose purpose is unclear, but which also seem to have been
valued for something beyond the ordinary. Perhaps it was jade's green
colour that had symbolic importance; perhaps it was the way the stone
took a marvelous sheen. We do not know, and we may never, just as we
don't know exactly along which routes they were transported.

But we do know that as the Romans began perfecting their network
of roads, a sophisticated road system in China was under construction.
The first Chinese emperor Qin Shi Huang, who united the country
and famously left eight thousand terracotta warriors to guard his tomb,
was responsible. He ordered the standardization of a number of things,

notably characters for writing Chinese which previously had varied from region to region, as well as the width of wagon wheel axles. The latter sounds like almost a piddling consideration, but it meant that a wagon could go anywhere in the empire because roads would be built to the same width. The effect is dramatically visible along the Jingxing Path, one of eight ancient trails in the Taihang Mountains which form a 250 kilometre north-to-south barrier west of Beijing. Over centuries, wagons wore away the stone surface of the road in places so that ruts were created that are visible today.[23]

As in the Persian Royal Road, in China existing roads were integrated into an interregional highway system. The Chinese twist on the idea of a highway fit for kings was to reserve a special lane on the roads which could only be used by the emperor. Also impressive was the Direct Road, a 600 kilometre road (about 400 miles) linking major cities. The emperor decreed the road should be 50 paces wide and lined with pines at intervals of about 9 metres (29.5 feet). It began in his capital city and went westward across the great Loess Plateau in northern China and into Mongolia.[24] One of the other major roads is the recently rediscovered "Ancient Road of Mules and Horses," which was paved with slate slabs 2 to 3 metres wide (6.5 to 9.8 feet). The road began, old records suggest, when a horde of 500,000 people, including 150,000 soldiers, trampled everything in its path as it followed the emperor's advance south, during the wars that led to unification of the seven Chinese kingdoms.

Moving troops was, without a doubt, a major reason for constructing the Roman road system. At its height, the system included 88,500 kilometres (55,000 miles) of roads, which now underlie the road systems of many countries in Europe, North Africa, and Eurasia.[25] The first road, the Via Appia, was built expressly to move Roman troops 212 kilometres (132 miles) south of Rome to combat enemies near what is now Naples.[26] Built largely by Roman legionnaires when they were not actively fighting, the roads were usually about 7 metres wide (23 feet), broad enough for the passage of columns six men abreast. They were made with three layers of material about a metre deep: a foundation of large stones and sand, a middle layer of pebbles and gravel, and a top layer of paving stones. Drainage ditches ran down either side of the road, and the centre was somewhat higher than the two sides to allow for run-off. Whenever possible, the roads were straight and avoided going up and down mountains and valleys. Riders on horses might be able to traverse mountain trails or make their way along a stream bed, but troops travelled best across open country. Roman legions regularly marched 25 kilometres (15.5 miles) a day with full pack—about 25 kilograms (55 pounds)—and could go faster when required to do a forced march. Such speed would be impossible if the road surface was not firm, even, and well maintained.

As time passed, the roads were used for transporting goods as well as troops, but as we saw when discussing what early humans carried with them, among the most important things were the intangible ones, including the idea of what constituted Roman civilization. The roads were vectors for transmitting it, providing communication among administrative units and the integration of new territories into the empire. At first, Roman citizens—male, freeborn, residents in the home territories—had

At its height, the Roman road system included 88,500 kilometres (55,000 miles) of roads in Europe, North Africa, and Eurasia. The excavated Roman Road at Conímbriga in Portugal was one of its westernmost portions.

Author Photo

privileges that others in the empire did not. But that changed with time, particularly as the weight of the population shifted away from the centre and toward the provinces. Even before then, some of the advantages of being ruled by Rome became widespread. Among them was the construction of communal baths. Today, accustomed as we are to a quick shower in the morning at home, that might seem of minor importance. Nor was it a complete innovation. The Greeks, at times, had public baths, while citizens of one of the earliest cities, Mohenjo Daro in what is now Pakistan, could also bathe in a specially built structure. But the Romans policy of providing public baths wherever their influence ruled had important implications for public health as well as social structure.

Large public bathing facilities called thermae required a good water supply plus readily available wood to heat it, so aqueducts were built, drainage systems were engineered, and transport of fuel was arranged, bringing collateral benefits that went beyond just providing a place to wash. As importantly, the baths were open to all, including women and slaves (who may have had special hours reserved for them, but were welcome nonetheless). Visiting a public bath was a chance to mingle with others, to chat, and to swim, on a more or less equal footing.

You can see evidence of this throughout the empire. Ruins of aqueducts cross the countryside in Spain, France, Tunis, Croatia, and Portugal. One aqueduct in Turkey that supplied Constantinople was used until the eighteenth century, and remains a striking part of the city's landscape, since six lanes of a broad urban boulevard pass between the arches.[27] But the ruins of Roman baths are more common and widespread. Outside of Italy, excavated baths, some of which are well-preserved, can be found from Libya to Scotland, from the eastern Mediterranean shores of Syria to nearly the edge of the Atlantic.[28]

A good example is found at Conímbriga in central Portugal which not only has the vestiges of an aqueduct that carried water 4 kilometres (2.5 miles) to the little city of 10,000 or so, but also contains the ruins of at last three thermae, as well as a stretch of the original Roman road. There had already been a settlement on the plateau for centuries when advancing Roman frontier forces under Decimus Junius Brutus took it in 138 BCE.[29] The water delivery system was one of the first constructions of the new regime, it seems, but within a short time the system was followed by a low defensive wall that encircled the settlement and the fields around it.

The location of the town was strategic: on the edge of a steep canyon of a stream that runs into the Mondego River and alongside the Roman road between Olisipo (Lisbon) and Bracara Augusta (Braga). Conímbriga—a town as far from Rome as Susa was from the western end of the Royal Road or the end of China's Direct Road was from the Qin Emperor's capital—apparently benefited from trade along the Roman road system.[30] The small museum near the excavated ruins—now a Portuguese national monument—displays domestic equipment found on the site, including beautiful red terra sigillata dishes that must have come from southern Gaul and North Africa since nothing similar was made near Conímbriga. Likewise, coins dating back to 210–211 BCE from all over the empire have turned up during excavations.

There is an abrupt end to the dates of coins about 407 CE. By then Conímbriga had passed through difficult times. The excavations—begun in earnest in the 1940s and now estimated to have explored about 15 per cent of the town—show that around 235 CE a decision was made to retrench, probably in the face of increasing threat from Swabian Visigoths who coveted the territory. Part of the city was sacrificed, with buildings torn down and the amphitheatre abandoned, so that a much larger wall—six metres high and an average of three metres wide—could be built to protect residents. Among the buildings destroyed was a bath complex, as well as several houses with glittering mosaic floors that are treasures of Roman art, as wonderful as those at Pompeii.

Inside the wall, at least two other bath complexes were built, along with a grand forum for assemblies and religious celebrations as the people seemed to prepare themselves to tough it out.

But even this was not enough. As the Roman Empire crumbled in the fifth century CE, the Romans at Conímbriga left the settlement completely. After the city was attacked and partially destroyed in 468 CE, they relocated to a hilltop village about 15 kilometres (9.3 miles) away called Aimonimum. The combined settlement was called Coimbra, an abridged form of Conímbriga. Remnants of the aqueduct which served the village, as well as the warehouses underneath its forum, still can be seen, but the only vestige of the Roman roads that linked this corner of the empire with the centre is the road unearthed at Conímbriga.

Visit the site on a summer day and the air will be fragrant with the scent rising from low bushes that grow beside the cultivated fields now covering much of the plateau. An asphalted road leads from the nearby town of Condeixa-a-Velha, and a dirt road climbs behind the museum and administration buildings into the hills above the ancient town. A stretch of the old Roman road approaches the walled town from the south. Sedges cover the spaces between the paving stones, suggesting that the road is used little nowadays. Ahead is the wall that guarded the town, swooping in a big semicircle to keep out the restless descendants of the people who were there before the Romans. The ghosts of the engineers who built the town, the men who marched to it, and the families who lived in it seem as present as the high clouds that filter the sun this day.

Who were they? A folk who spoke a Latin that would be slowly trans-formed into Portuguese.[31] Records show that local inhabitants such as the Turrania, Valeria, Alios, and Maelo families mixed over the decades with families from Italy like the Lucanus, Murrius, Vitellius, and Aponia fam-ilies. That fact bears witness to the lasting attraction of the Roman rule, of the perceived wisdom of choosing an alliance with rich and powerful representatives of the greatest empire created until then. The policy of allowing soldiers—who often were sent on missions for years—to marry local women went a long way toward encouraging assimilation, too.

So when push came to shove, the people of Conímbriga —many of whom had already become Christian, as attested to by the ruins of a small church recently excavated in the town—decamped for some place safer.

The expressway that leads into Coimbra these days is a fine, wide, well-engineered road. But anyone who travels the new road, after seeing what is left of the Romans' road into Conímbriga 1,800 years after it was built, must wonder how long the new road will remain if our elaborate sys-tem of maintenance is impaired. Certainly, after the fall of Rome, Roman roads began to decline even though maintenance did continue for awhile. Remnants of the roads show up when work is done on the infrastructure of cities like Paris, London, and Rome, and the modern highway network in much of Europe frequently follows what the Romans had designed. But after a couple of hundred years of what some call the Dark Ages, the system had deteriorated to the point where overland travel anywhere was a nightmare of muddy trails and pothole-pitted tracks. When European warriors encountered the excellent 23,300 kilometre (14,292 mile) Inca road system in the sixteenth century, they were awed: nowhere, their chroniclers wrote, had they seen anything like it in Europe.

This is why those gallant horses, which we heard thundering by at the beginning of this chapter in the doomed charge of the Light Brigade, were relatively fresh. At the height of the Roman Empire, it would have been possible to journey from England to the Black Sea overland, except for the jump across the English Channel. The 4,400 kilometre (2,734 mile) trip would have taken about two and a half months, according to the ORBIS simulator (the Stanford Geospatial Network Model of the Roman World developed at Stanford University), but there's no way of guessing what shape the cavalry units would have been in when they arrived.

No one would have thought of trying to do that in the mid-nineteenth century. The British units went by ship all the way to Crimea, a sea journey that was not easy, but there was no alternative. Things would change over the following seventy-five years, but during the next Great Expansion of humans around the globe, waterways would be the system of choice.

That traffic changed the world in a very short time, making it both smaller and more homogeneous, which is why the countryside at Conímbriga looks so familiar to anyone who has spent time in North American temperate zones. The flowers nodding in the early afternoon breeze—poppies, Queen Anne's lace, and chicory—are now found along roads all over the world, even though they are native to Europe, unintentional passengers on the next great wave of human expansion.

Chapter Six

ACROSS THE WATER

IN A BOOK ABOUT ROADS, WHY DEVOTE A CHAPTER TO WATER routes? Seems not to be on topic, a trail that leads away from where we want to go. Yet, the story of roads and their impact on the world can't be told without an aquatic detour.

As we've seen, humans' conquest of rivers and seas goes back as far as our extinct cousin *Homo erectus,* who made it from the mainland to the Mediterranean island of Crete 800,000 years ago.[1] Tools made by this prehuman also show up on islands on the other side of the world, such as Flores in the Pacific Ocean.[2]

The call of the sea is powerful: even such a fanatic of the road as Jack Kerouac went sailing before he started roaming the land. After quitting Columbia University at the beginning of World War II, he shipped out with the U.S. Merchant Marine and later enlisted in the U.S. Navy. (The latter was not a good experience—he lasted only about ten days in the Navy before he was discharged for "unfitness"—but the period was the subject of his first novel *The Sea Is My Brother,* unpublished, with reason it seems, until after his death.)[3]

But while travel by water is ancient, the traces of the conquest of the waves are even harder to find than those of early roads. Sea routes don't leave the same kind of tracks that feet do. Ruined port installations remain in some places, and lost ships litter the bottom of seas, but only by triangulation can we deduce what paths voyagers on water followed, at least until people started to bend waterways to their will by building channels and canals.

Not far away from the ruins at Conímbriga, you can see the kind of things we do to rivers now. On a summer evening, the quiet waters of the Mondego River now slip under the bridge at Coimbra. More than 1,600 years after the Visigoths took control of Conímbriga and the Romans left for the heights above the river, a man in a single-man shell sculls in the shadows of the setting sun. His trajectory is for pleasure; his aim is of no great importance in the grand scheme of things. But his silhouette on the calm waters of a river that has been channelled and controlled recalls the story of how people conquered the water, just as they conquered the land. The river, which rises in the highest mountains in Portugal, once flooded coastal lowlands regularly. Now, it is dammed and channelled so that its waters irrigate some of Europe's largest rice plantations. At its mouth, shipbuilding thrived in the eighteenth and nineteenth centuries, but now the outside world notes its Atlantic beaches mainly for the surfing they afford, and for the big casino located there.[4]

A couple of hundred kilometres south, the Tagus River, much larger than the Montego, enters the ocean. It was from there that Portuguese explorers set out in the fifteenth century, looking for spices and gold. Other European adventurers followed, including Christopher Columbus who, as a young man, learned navigation on Portuguese ships. What they found at the other end of their voyages will be the subject of the next chapter, but in this one we're going to look at why and how people travelled by water. The simple answer is: because frequently it was easier to go down rivers, across lakes, and along seacoasts than it was to travel overland, particularly with heavy and bulky objects. That sort of cargo had to be very valuable—like obsidian in a region where none was present—for it to be transported any distance, as we've seen. It takes less energy to paddle a canoe full of goods, even when going upstream, than it would be to carry the same amount of cargo in packsacks. After the invention of wheeled vehicles, boats still offered many advantages, since they can slip across water with less resistance than wheels can roll along roads that are sometimes bumpy, bouncing up and down to boot. Introduce sails to a boat and you've got the added force of the wind to help you move.

Visit the well-lit Mesopotamian gallery in the Louvre Museum and you'll come face to face with an example: a series of friezes from the palace of Assyrian king Sargon II (721–705 BCE.) The alabaster bas-reliefs were found near what is now Mosul in Iraq and show men in boats— some being rowed, others under sail—behind which logs are attached. The logs are assumed to be the coveted cedars of Lebanon that once covered much of the high ground east of the Mediterranean Coast, and which the rulers of Mesopotamia and Egypt rightly prized. Just where this log drive took place isn't clear. Some archeologists think it shows logs being assembled off the Mediterranean coast for shipment up the Orontes River and inland. But the distance from the highest point on that river to Sargon II's palace would be a long drag on the other side of the mountains. Others think it's likely that the logs were cut nearer to the catchment basin of the Euphrates, floated down the river, and then dragged up the Tigris to the construction site. We might know more had we the rest of the frieze, but two shipments of treasures were lost—one to pirates, and another in a river accident—after a French expedition excavated the palace in the nineteenth century.[5]

These incidents were just two of many in the long history of seafaring, where danger has always been present. In *The Odyssey*, Homer's description of a storm at sea brings in the gods to whip up the waves, but he conveys well the fury that ordinary seafarers frequently faced from more prosaic sources than the gods:

> The son of Saturn raised a black cloud over our ship, and the sea grew dark beneath it. We did not get on much further, for in another moment we were caught by a terrific squall from the West that snapped the forestays of the mast so that it fell aft, while all the ship's gear tumbled about at the bottom of the vessel. . . .
>
> Then Jove let fly with his thunderbolts, and the ship went round and round, and was filled with fire and brimstone as the lightning

struck it. The men all fell into the sea; they were carried about in the water round the ship, looking like so many sea-gulls, but the god presently deprived them of all chance of getting home again.[6]

Yet, despite the possible dangers, people have thought for thousands of years that the advantages of travel over water outweighed the risks. Although watercraft of some sort must have existed long before, the oldest known boat dates back to about 8000 BCE. It turned up, somewhat ironically, during construction of a highway in the summer of 1955 in the Netherlands as road workers dug out a peat bog.[7] The plan was to replace the road with sand and thus give better footing for Route A28 which crosses the country from north to south between Groningen and Utrecht. About two metres down, the machine operator mucking out peat came across what he thought was just a big, old tree trunk. Workers struggled to bring it up to the surface and were planning to cart it away as they continued building the roadway.

This detail of an image from a bowl dating from 480–470 BCE gives a taste of the dangers of traveling by water. It shows Odysseus lashed to the mast to avoid being lured into shipwreck.
Photo: Marie-Lan Nguyen / Wikimedia Commons, Creative Commons Attribution 2.5 License

But the "log" accidently rolled off the wagon. For several days, it lay by the side of the construction site until a farmer who lived nearby took a closer look. Clearly, he saw, this was not an ordinary snag. He hauled it back to his house in a wheelbarrow and contacted people at a local museum. They said it couldn't be left to simply dry out because the waterlogged wood would crack and deteriorate. In the end, the log was dried out in a specially built airtight cylinder, but until that could be constructed, it was stored in the cold room of the municipal slaughterhouse in Groningen.

The boat measured 2.98 metres (9.75 feet) by .44 metres (1.44 feet) with a pointed bow that looked like it had been worked with tools made from bones or animals. Very old, was the verdict of all who first saw it, but the scientific dating report was astounding: it must have been made sometime between 8040 BCE and 7510 BCE. Skeptics who suggested that might be a trough for feeding animals, given its rough shape, had to back down because there is no evidence that anyone had yet domesticated either animals or plants at that time.

More recent findings corroborate the long history of humans and boats. One dugout found upstream from Paris along the Seine in 1984 dates from between 7190 to 6450 BCE,[8] while one found in Nigeria in 1987 near Lake Mali has been dated to around 6000 BCE.[9] On the other side of the world, remains of a dugout dating back to 5500 BCE were discovered in 2002 in China.[10] Still more recently, the rock paintings at Gobustan near the Black Sea in what is now Azerbaijan became a UNESCO World Heritage Site in 2007. The petroglyphs include ones depicting reed boats that appear to have been made sometime around 10,000 BCE.[11]

None of these crafts were designed for long-distance travel or for venturing far from shore, but they and others like them were good for using rivers as highways. As Joseph Conrad wrote about the Congo, rivers may lead to places where overland traffic would be nearly impossible:

Going up that river was like traveling back to the earliest beginnings of the world, when vegetation rioted on the earth and the big trees were kings. An empty stream, a great silence, an impenetrable forest. The air was warm, thick, heavy, sluggish. There was no

joy in the brilliance of sunshine. The long stretches of the water-
way ran on, deserted, into the gloom of overshadowed distances.[12]

But rivers also run into the heart of continents less hostile to men on
foot. Take Mark Twain's Huck Finn floating down the Mississippi at a
time when the biggest population movement in North America was by
wagon or on foot across the prairies:

> The second night we run between seven and eight hours, with the
> current that was making over four mile an hour. We catched fish,
> and talked, and we took a swim now and then to keep off sleepi-
> ness. It was kind of solemn, drifting down the big still river, laying
> on our backs looking up at the stars, and we didn't ever feel like
> talking loud, and it warn't often that we laughed, only a little kind
> of a low chuckle.[13]

Sounds idyllic, and Jack Kerouac agreed: he said that he thought of
himself as Huck Finn, lighting out for the territory, fleeing constraints,

Humans have made boats of various kinds for tens, if not hundreds, of thousands of years.
Among the earliest records are these images of reed boats found in Azerbaijan, dating from
10,000 BCE.

Photo: Aleksander Dragnes / Creative Commons Attribution 2.0 License

headed for liberty. But rivers more often than not have been routes along which civilization has spread. It's no accident that several of the oldest civilizations occur on the banks of major ones: the Indus, the Nile, the Yangtze and Yellow in China, and of course between the Tigris and Euphrates.

Herodotus praised the potential of the great rivers that provide routes north from the Black and Caspian seas. One of them, now called the Dnieper, he said had no equal but the Nile, providing "the finest and most abundant pasture, by the far the richest supply of the best sorts of fish, and the most excellent water for drinking. ... No better crops grow anywhere than along its banks, and where grain is not sown the grass is the most luxuriant in the world."[14] Not surprisingly, the country through which it flows became among the most productive agricultural land anywhere: the Ukrainian breadbasket.

On the other side of the Eurasian land mass, the great Chinese rivers run from west to east, unlike those of Eurasia which run mostly north to south. The Yangtze is the third longest river in the world, rising in the glaciers of Tibet and flowing 6,300 kilometres (3,915 miles) before it enters the East China Sea at Shanghai. To the north, the Yellow River runs 5,464 kilometres (3,395 miles) from the mountains of western China through great loess grasslands and valleys before entering the Bohai Sea. Called "yellow" because of the great load of silt it carries, the Yellow River has flooded and changed course hundreds of times throughout recorded history. In 1931, a flood killed between one and four million people, while in the nineteenth century it dramatically shifted its channel by about 300 kilometres (186 miles).

The two Chinese rivers were early avenues for travel, but getting from one drainage system to the other was complicated by the fact that their basins are separated by mountains and hills. This meant that travel between the two axes of civilization on the major rivers was not easy. But not long after Darius I successfully constructed a canal from the Nile to the Red Sea, the Chinese began one of the biggest engineering projects the world has ever known in order to unite the two river basins: the Grand Canal. Today, the world's longest canal system runs from Beijing in the north to Hangzhou south of Shanghai.[15]

It's no accident, by the way, that the two civilizations that had experience in channelling water for agriculture also were among the first to undertake ambitious projects to create artificial water routes for transport and travel. Without the techniques developed in the construction of the many small irrigation channels that led water away from the rivers of Mesopotamia and China into fields, engineering an integrated system would have been impossible.

The Chinese first attempt seems to have involved using existing waterways, marshes, and lakes to link newly conquered regions in the north with seats of power in the south, during a period when China was ruled by warring kingdoms. By the sixth century CE, when construction on the Grand Canal was intensified, the purpose included making sure that the capital could receive grain from the south. When completed, the canal had 24 locks and stretched 1,776 kilometres (1,104 miles). Although it periodically went into decline when political conflict drained resources away from maintenance, the canal was China's major transportation route, until the twentieth century and the building of railroads.

According to one commentator, the long history of canal building in China was a good "thermometer of the health of the dynasties that participated in its construction, unlike the Great Wall which was a better gauge of the pathology of its builders."[16] And certainly, even though millions of men and women were conscripted to work on it over centuries, the manner in which it allowed goods to be sent from one part of the country to another had a positive impact on ordinary lives. Yet, the Grand Canal had its military uses, because troops could not be posted in the northern reaches unless a way was found to supply them with grain. As Napoleon is supposed to have said, an army marches on its stomach.[17]

Similarly, cities only grow when their people can eat. Feeding large population centres required large agricultural hinterlands. When a population centre grew so large that its demands outstripped the products growing nearby, leaders had to look farther afield for food. By the third century CE when Conímbriga was flowering, the countryside around Rome provided only about 10 per cent of the city's needs. Between two and three thousand shiploads of wheat a year had to be imported from Egypt and North Africa. As Tacitus quotes Emperor Tiberius, the very existence of the people of Rome was "daily at the mercy of uncertain waves and storms."[18]

When local food was lacking and imports waned, trouble waxed. Famine appears to lie behind one of the greatest episodes of sea warfare the ancient world had known, long before Darius I or Rome began their days of glory. The Sea Peoples ravaged Egypt and much of the eastern Mediterranean at the beginning of the twelfth century BCE. Just where they came from is not clear, but driven by drought, famine, and possibly natural disasters, they attacked and destroyed.

The period before these invasions was a time of much interregional trade and travel. A shipwreck off the coast of Turkey that has been dated to about 1300 BCE gives a taste of that. About 17 metres (50 feet) long, designed primarily to travel under sail, and made of Lebanese cedar, the ship carried nearly a ton of raw tin probably from Afghanistan, 10 tons of raw copper from Cyprus, as well as gold objects from Egypt, and a dozen ebony logs from Nubia.[19] We do not know where it was headed, but the possibilities of markets for these goods were great on Greek islands, the Turkish mainland, Mesopotamia, Egypt, and the Levant in empires variously called Mycenaean, Hittite, Kassite, and the Egyptian New Kingdom.

But all of these centres of civilization faltered within a decade or so of each other near the turn of the eleventh century BCE. In this cultural decline and disorganization, the Greeks even lost the ability to write. During the previous period, including the time of the Trojan Wars that provided the subject matter for Homer's great epics, Greeks used a notation system based on the use of symbols for syllables, with some ideograms representing words. Called Linear B by linguists and archeologists, the system disappeared abruptly about the end of the twelfth century BCE and was not replaced until five hundred years later by a variation on the alphabet invented, it appears, by the Phoenicians. The epics of Homer, who lived in the eighth century BCE, were originally oral works, and not written down until much later.

The Sea Peoples attacked Egypt in 1207 BCE and again in 1177 BCE. Both times they were defeated, although the victories were hollow. The second time, the Egyptian win was immortalized by the Pharaoh Ramses III in his funerary temple at Medinet Habu, with images of Egyptians combating men in ships powered by oarsmen and sail. But this success was short-lived, because Egypt's influence was broken. Subsequent pharaohs ruled over much less territory until the valley of the Nile rebounded in the days of the twenty-second dynasty (approximately 945 BCE.)

Elsewhere the Sea Peoples wreaked havoc, too. One letter from a small-time ruler in what is now northern Syria to a higher ranking king of Cyprus reads:

> My father, now the ships of the enemy have come. They have been setting fire to my cities and have done harm to the land....
> May my father be aware of this matter. Now the seven ships of the enemy which have been coming have done harm to us. Now if other ships of the enemy turn up, send me a report somehow, so that I will know.[20]

Rulers throughout the eastern Mediterranean in a host of letters decry failed crops and famine in the decades before the decisive battle between the Sea Peoples and the Egyptians.[21] Significantly, several of these letters speak of hoped-for shipments of grain, which lends credence to the hypothesis that famine and climate change lay behind the Sea Peoples' attacks.

The ships they sailed in were probably not fundamentally different from the ships used for trade. Both were propelled by sails and oarsmen, who in the popular imagination were slaves forced to row for hours at an infernal cadence. Jack Kerouac, inspired by the famous scene in *Ben-Hur* where Charlton Heston is rowing along with ranks of slaves, evokes the rhythm in his book *Desolation Angels*: "and everything is going to the beat – It's the beat generation, it's *béat*, it's the beat to keep, it's the beat of the heart, it's being beat and down in the world and like oldtime lowdown and like in ancient civilizations the slave boatmen rowing galleys to a beat."[22] In fact, however, both Greeks and Romans relied mainly on freemen to row their galleys, in part because the great ships carrying as many as 170 men put in to shore at night as there was no place on board for the crews to sleep. Controlling slaves under those circumstances would have been hard.[23]

In time, ships designed for trade were built wider than warships, in order to make more room for cargo. In some cases the wood to build them came, as we've seen, from the mountains of what is now Lebanon; but forests elsewhere were pillaged to build fleets. There's evidence that mangrove forests on the coasts of the Arabian Peninsula, as well as around the Indian subcontinent, were cut down to build ships. Much later, in the fifteenth century CE, the Chinese sacked forests in Vietnam for timber to build their Treasure Fleet, while the Portuguese, a couple of hundred years later, traded for wood from Russian old-growth forest. The Russian term for the kind of pine used is *karabel'nie sosni*, after the Portuguese caravels (the major class of ships during the first years of European exploration).

That is getting a bit ahead of the story, however. The Sea Peoples were not the only seafarers who brought destruction on ships. Any list of raiders called pirates by some group or other must include Greeks, Romans and that other great seafaring nation, Phoenicians. Cargos were captured, crews enslaved, and towns on the shores sacked repeatedly. Among the famous captives were Julius Caesar, held briefly on an island in the Aegean Sea, and St. Patrick, who probably would never have gone to Ireland had he not been captured and enslaved by Irish pirates.

The distances travelled by these adventurers were often long. The Vikings, based in the North Sea and the Scandinavian Peninsula, were the scourge of European ports for a couple of hundred years. Beginning in the late eighth century, they sailed down the Atlantic Coast, through the Strait of Gibraltar, and into the Mediterranean where they captured Sicily. Farther south, fleets of Arab ships plied the Indian Ocean, developing masterful techniques for navigating and understanding currents and weather patterns. Pushed by religious zeal after the arrival of Islam in the eighth century CE, they increased the danger of sailing in the Mediterranean as they attacked and conquered the Iberian Peninsula and North Africa. This increased danger meant that for several hundred years Europeans had to have very good reasons, such as trading for valuables or defending religion, to go down to the sea in ships.

The desire to trade took the upper hand during the early fifteenth century when overland trade routes with the Far East—the Silk Roads—were disrupted by turmoil on the steppes of Asia. As we've seen, trade routes to the East had been in existence for millennia, going back to times before agriculture when luxury goods like lapis lazuli were transported thousands of kilometres from the mountains of Afghanistan to both Egypt and China. The broad corridor of plains north of the Aral, Caspian, and Black seas and the rivers that cut across it were vectors for the transmission of ideas, seeds, and ways of life.[24]

The collective name—the Silk Roads—was invented in the late nineteenth century by the German anthropologist Baron Ferdinand von Richthofen to describe the complex set of routes across the Eurasian continent taken by traders. The modern name evokes the image of one road along which caravans and traders passed, a sort of superhighway for camels and horses. But that is far from the case.

Two large trajectories appear to have existed from the beginning. Both start on the Chinese plain between the Yangtze and Yellow rivers, running west through what is called the Hexi Corridor. The routes separated and ran either north or south of the Tian Shan mountain range (sometimes translated as "Mountain of Heaven") and the great interior deserts, in what is now the extreme west of China. At that point, a branch went north of the Aral and Caspian seas and ended on the Black Sea. Other branches either turned south following the Indus River to the Arabian Sea or continued past Darius's capital city Susa toward Babylon and onward to the west coast of the Mediterranean in the Levant, following at times Darius's old Royal Road.

In places, the paths taken were far more than simple tracks. The Chinese monk Faxian who travelled to India between 399 and 414 CE in search of better texts of the Buddha's writing, says:

> The way was difficult and rugged, running along a bank exceedingly precipitous which rose up there, a hill-like wall of rock....When one approached the edge of it, his eyes became unsteady; and if he wished to go forward in the same direction, there was no place on which he could place his foot; and beneath were the waters of a river called the Indus. In former times men had chiseled paths along the rocks and distributed ladders on the face of them...at the bottom of which there was a suspension bridge of ropes.[25]

But in other places, particularly when skirting or crossing deserts, the way was less evident. Swirling sandstorms could obscure the path, and traders relied on their own years of experience or that of their guides to get them safely across. For these sections, camels were the beast of burden of choice, because they could go nearly as fast as horses, carry heavier loads, and travel for longer periods without water.

For several hundred years few, if any, traders made the long trek from beginning to end. One Chinese official, Gan Ying, was sent to Rome in 97 CE from the northwestern Chinese province of Xinjiang, but he made it no farther than a large trading centre (probably in Mesopotamia) near a "great sea." There local officials who had a trade monopoly with Rome convinced him to turn back since, they said, many had died of homesickness on the journey that might take months or years.[26]

This changed dramatically in the early thirteenth century when Genghis Khan led his nomads on a mission of world conquest. They were people whose way of life was well adapted to the harsh, cold, open lands. They did some hunting, and probably a little gathering, but the basis of their society was the horse from which they drew food, clothing, and housing.

The larger-than-life Mongolian Emperor Genghis Khan is memorialized in this 40-metre statue. He and his sons controlled the largest contiguous empire in history.

Photo: Steffen Wurzel / Creative Commons Attribution-Share Alike 3.0 Unported License

Initially, the Great Khan's mission was to unite the tribes around their home territory (now Mongolia, wedged between Northern China and Siberia) and, incidentally, to bring in goods from elsewhere as tribute. But after consultation with the Great Blue Sky, the Mongols' deity, he led his people and his sons south, east, and west. Within twenty-five years, they had subjugated more land and people than even the Romans had done. Cities that surrendered were relatively well treated, but those that resisted were annihilated. From the captive population, anyone with skills—doctors, engineers, tradesmen, artisans—was co-opted, while the aristocracies were usually eliminated. Tribute was distributed among the Mongol leaders, but ordinary subjects also shared in the booty. The captives' religions were, by and large, allowed to be practiced without hindrance. Several of Khan's daughters-in-law were practicing Christians, for example, although it must be added that sexual conquest obviously was an arm of foreign policy either through arranged marriages or rape. Across Eurasia today, up to 20 per cent of all men share a particular genetic configuration on their Y chromosome that can be traced directly back to Genghis Khan and his sons.[27]

Trade—peaceful trade—was the key to the success of the empire, however, so the Mongols both built bridges to make long-distance travel easier for goods-laden horses and camels (the Khan's co-optation of subject Chinese engineers was famous), and expanded the messenger system to make theirs better than the one that Darius had. Actual roads, however, were not much improved. Khan's armies preferred to travel over open plains rather than follow roads, and with five horses per warrior, they cut a swath that no road would contain.[28]

But trade routes were safe. Repeatedly, guides to travellers during the period were awed by how secure travel was: "a maiden bearing a nugget of gold on her head could wander safely throughout the realm," or so the saying went.[29] Marco Polo, who with his father and uncle spent several years trading in Mongol territory at the end of the thirteenth century, comments on how well-run and comfortable the post houses along the route were: Kublai Khan, who received them, was one of Genghis Khan's grandsons. This Pax Mongolica stretched from the western edge of the Hungarian plain, eastward to Manchuria and the Indochinese Peninsula, south as far as India's mountains, and over much of the Middle East. The rich civilizations of the centre and south of the Indian subcontinent were tempting, but their heat and humidity suited neither Mongol horsemen nor their mounts, so the force stopped short. Nor did the western army continue into the European heartland: its forests were difficult for their cavalry forces to negotiate, and its cities were poor compared to cities elsewhere. But the Mongol reputation was widely recognized, as evidenced in Chaucer's *Canterbury Tales*:

> This noble king was called Genghis Khan,
> Who in his time was of so great renown
> That there was nowhere in no region
> So excellent a lord in all things.[30]

And in 1348, when Edward III of England ordered 150 garters made for the knights of his newly founded Order of the Garter, they were to be made of blue silk, called Tartar blue. The fabric originated in the Mongols' territory and had been brought all that long distance along the secure trade routes maintained by them.

By that time, however, the routes were becoming less and less secure for two reasons. One was the spread of the plague, the Black Death, which swept out of China beginning in the 1330s. Carried by fleas on rats which apparently hitched rides in cargo carried on the Silk Roads, the disease left millions dead over the next fifteen years. Some estimates put mortality at 30 per cent of the population in much of Europe and across Eurasia, with double this mortality rate in parts of China. The devastation profoundly shook the societies where it occurred, just as seven hundred years later AIDS swept along the trucking routes in East Africa, frequently spread by truck drivers on the Tanzam Highway, the paved road running through Tanzania to Zambia.[31]

At the time that the Black Death raced along trade routes, the Great Khan's offspring, who had divided the empire into four large regions (the Golden Horde in Russia, the Mughal Empire in India, the Ilkhanate in Persia and Iraq, and the Yuan Dynasty in China), suffered a crisis in leadership. Petty banditry and civil wars broke out. In his biography of the Great Khan, Jack Weatherford writes:

For nearly a century the Mongols had exploited their mutual material interests to overcome the political fault lines dividing them. Even while sacrificing political unity, they had maintained a unified cultural and commercial empire. With the onslaught of plague, the center could not hold, and the complex system collapsed. The Mongol Empire depended on the quick and constant movement of people, goods and information throughout its massive empire. Without those connections, there was no empire.[32]

Nor was there nearly as much silk, gold, and spices making their way west. For ordinary Europeans, that probably was no great disaster, since the continent struggled with its own population loss and disorder. But in the next century, as things recovered, leaders and adventurers began to think of ways to resume trade and enjoy the bounty from the East. Given the difficulty of traversing the overland trade routes, they searched for other paths. The Portuguese began sending out explorers in the 1430s, and Christopher Columbus, you'll remember, set out at the end of that century to find Kublai Khan's China by sailing west.

Now, however, let us return to that rower on the Mondego River in central Portugal, whom we glimpsed earlier when we considered the warrior roads of the Romans and others. As the twilight deepens, he is now too far away to discern the colour of his hair or his skin, the sort of clothes he's wearing, or any other clue as to just who he is or where his ancestors came from. Suffice to say that he is a member of the privileged classes of the twenty-first century, an inheritor of a world order that would change drastically when Europeans, led by the Portuguese, went out to find riches and, incidentally, to claim more territory.[33]

Chapter Seven

MYSTERY ROADS

T HE EUROPEANS, OF COURSE, DIDN'T SET OUT TO EXPLORE.
They had no real desire to find new lands. What they wanted
was the riches from old ones. What they found was a fully populated New World that eventually did provide much wealth for the
old one, although the extent of the riches wasn't evident immediately.
Columbus's exploits were overshadowed at first by those of Portuguese
navigators like Vasco da Gama, who opened seaways to the Far East
just as Columbus was returning to Spain from his trip to the Caribbean
islands. Discovery of the riches of the Aztec and Inca empires on the
mainland of the western hemisphere came decades later. By the time
Europeans arrived in numbers with the intention of settling, and saw
forests and plains nearly free of inhabitants, they were wrong to think
that the western hemisphere was up for grabs. Diseases introduced by
the first wave of explorers and conquistadors sent shock waves of death
throughout the hemisphere, wreaking destruction worse than the Black
Death had earlier in Eurasia. The accounts by the first visitors and those
a hundred or so years later are dramatically, tragically different.

Based on records from the first years of Spanish conquest, it looks as
if the native population of Central Mexico plummeted from something

like 25.2 million in 1518 to 700,000 in 1623.[1] The chronicle of the first European voyage down the Amazon reported many settlements in its upper reaches, and several very large towns farther down (evaluation of the chronicles suggests a population of around five million.) The contrast with the empty shores that later explorers found cast doubt on the accuracy of first reports, but recent archeological discoveries indicate they were right on the money. In Canada, population estimates at the time of contact range from 200,000 to two million: when Samuel de Champlain sailed up the St. Lawrence, he found no sign of the prosperous villages along the great river's valley that Jacques Cartier had reported sixty years before. Part of that population displacement may have been due to inter-tribal warfare, but the dramatic depopulation points to epidemics raging through the tribes. On the other side of the continent, where California hosted a dense population leading a comfortable life, the indigenous population in 1800 is estimated at about 700,000, but a hundred years later, it dropped to less than 15,000.[2]

Where did the ancestors of these people come from, when did they arrive, and how did they get to the point where they had mastered a hemisphere?

The short answer is: they came from somewhere in northeastern Asia thousands of years before and had successfully colonized the Americas, creating civilizations no less sophisticated than those in Eurasia and more or less contemporaneous with them. Genetic analysis shows that, without exception, indigenous populations throughout the hemisphere share a very similar genetic heritage. This argues for descent from a rather small population following a population bottleneck like the one we talked about earlier that occurred when humans first tried to walk out of Africa. The result is that it seems that all the people here when Europeans arrived were descended from a very small population.[3]

In a book about the roads humans have taken to get from one place to another, it would be fitting to say that these stalwart hunters and their families walked out of Asia and into North America through a corridor between two huge ice sheets after the last great Ice Age, about 14,000 BCE. That would be a grand pedestrian adventure equal to the epic trek which started so long ago on the shores of the Red Sea.

This scenario, which held the number one spot on the archeology charts during most of the twentieth century, is based on the premise that for a short period during the Last Glacial Maximum, the final period of the Ice Ages, an ice-free corridor existed between two ice sheets that covered much of North America. One, the Laurentide Ice Sheet, covered the eastern part of the North Americas as far south as New York and Illinois. The other one, the Cordilleran Ice Sheet, originated in the high mountains of the continent's western regions. At least twice, the sheets merged to make the northern part of the continent completely inhospitable. But sometime around 14,000 BCE, there was enough warming to melt a passage through which stalwart hunters and their families (because a population is never established without mothers, fathers and, of course, grandmothers nurturing children) could follow big game south.

Big game is the right term, indeed. The Americas were home to huge beasts, including giant sloths, turtles the size of small cars, Hummer-sized bison, elephant cousins of various sorts, camels, and horses. Their bones are found at sites widely strewn around the western hemisphere. Then, after about 12,000 BCE and following the arrival of hunters from Asia in the Americas, they seem to have suddenly disappeared from the landscape.

Elegant spearheads and tools made by these people were discovered a little south of the railroad junction point at Clovis, New Mexico, in the late 1920s.[4] It can be cold there in January. Even though Black Water Draw—the place where the oldest traces of these hunters were first found—lies on about the same latitude as Los Angeles and Charlotte, North Carolina, winds frequently sweep south, seemingly directly from the North Pole. To stand there on the high, nearly level plateau (called Llano Estacado or Staked Plain), shivering as a little snow blows across the landscape, gives an idea of what those families were up against. Being an early American was not for wimps. Making the trek between the ice sheets would have been a formidable challenge.

These people were skilled hunters, definitely, as well as master tool-makers. The distinctive technique they used required carefully flaking away chips along both edges of a spear point, making a sharp, frequently beautiful object. This kind of point came to be called Clovis, after the place they were first found. By extension, the people who made them were also called Clovis. (The points were not arrowheads, by the way: the first incontrovertible evidence of arrows shows up in the Arctic no earlier than 3000 BCE. Their dispersal afterward, some archeologists suggest, is due as much to the effectiveness of bows and arrows in fighting among groups, as any improvement in hunting efficiency.)[5]

At the time of the first Clovis discoveries in the 1920s, there was no way of knowing just how old the objects were. Because they were found in conjunction with animals long extinct, however, anthropologists and paleontologists were sure they were very old, possibly much older than the 3,000 years then given as the length of time native populations had lived in the Americas.[5]

Radioactive carbon dating threw the whole time line into question when it was introduced in the 1950s. Based on the known, rather slow rate of decay of one slightly radioactive form of carbon into a more stable form (half of all carbon-14 atoms in an object are transformed every 5,730 years), the method was first tested on objects whose age was known from other sources—an Egyptian mummy coffin for example. Then scientists began to apply the method to the Clovis sites. Because the stone from which the spears were created is not organic, radioactive carbon dating relies on organic objects found in conjunction with the spears, such as plant residue and animal bones. To their amazement, they found that objects from more than eighty sites where Clovis points were

For decades, the people who made distinctive blades called Clovis points were thought to have colonized the Americas from Asia by walking down an ice-free corridor as the Ice Age ended.

Photo: Bill Whittacker / Creative Commons Attribution-Share Alike 3.0 Unported License

discovered all dated between 11,500 and 10,900 BCE. Coincidently or not, these dates cover the period when the big beasts went missing.

Aha, said some. Look what we have here.

With a little more rainfall as the ice sheets melted, the landscape, now so stark and dry, would have been considerably lusher, more like the inviting savannahs where humans originally evolved and where we have seen that people coming out of Africa prospered. What probably happened here was that those enterprising hunters—faced with beasts that had never before come into contact with wily, armed humans—went wild. Within a few hundred years, the hunters advanced southward, killing as they went, until the limits of the land and the stock of prey were reached. The result was a hemisphere nearly completely settled and the big beasts dead.

This narrative was so plausible that it became the background for all considerations of early man in the Americas for half a century. The doctrine was: Clovis hunters led the way, everyone came afterwards, and the rest is history.

Only it wasn't quite that simple. If you'd been paying attention to what was being reported, you would have seen that early on. As soon as radioactive carbon dating was applied to other sites, dates older than Clovis by thousands of years turned up. This can't be, was a frequent response from scientists who'd invested much in the 'Clovis First' idea. The controversy grew. Some paleontologists stormed out of meetings, characterized those who disagreed with them as incompetent, and generally fought with vehemence, which can seem out of place with academic pursuits until one has spent some time around academics and sees just how aggressive they—like people in other occupations—can be when defending their turf.[7]

BUT THE TIDE OF THOUGHT HAD TURNED. Some of the evidence which accomplished this shift comes not far from the road my mother, sister, and I were following as we sat on that bus all those years ago—and at about the same time.

At the end of the Great Valley of California, we travelled through the Cascade Mountains until the highway broke out onto the plateau past Mount Shasta. We stopped for breakfast in the old logging town of Klamath Falls and then pushed on toward a landscape that I remember as being so boring—with scrubby pine trees, brown grass, and rolling hills—that the only thing to do was fight with my sister. Yet, the country-side has seen more than its share of drama. To the west, Mount Mazama once rose, taller and broader than Mount Shasta is now. It slumbered through the millennia under the weight of glaciers during the Ice Ages, but about 7600 BCE it began to wake. It sputtered and shed magma for perhaps a couple hundred years until in one enormous explosion—forty-two times the force of the one that blew the top of Mount St. Helens in 1980—it shed about a mile of its height, and sent volcanic material all over the region. When it was over, the cavity which had been the centre of the mountain remained, and became the deep blue body of water now called Crater Lake. Witnessing the explosion must have been awe-inspiring, and it is very likely people did. Artifacts made by humans have been discovered under layers of ash from the explosion, just to the east of where our bus travelled, on the other side of the easternmost range of the Cascade Range in the Northern Great Basin.

Shortly before World War II, University of Oregon paleontologist Luther Cressman (Margaret Mead's first husband) and his crew went exploring there. They uncovered the remains of horse, bison, and camel, in association with objects that appeared to be man-made, underneath a thick layer of ash from the volcano. He had no way of determining how old the artifacts were, of course, because this was well before the advent of radioactive carbon dating, but he asserted that they were thousands of years old.[8] He was strongly criticized for those claims, but he and his students continued to explore. Over nearly thirty years, they investigated more than one hundred sites. Among their finds was a cache of sandals woven from grasses that were dated to 7000 BCE when radiocarbon dating became possible in the 1950s.[9]

That's not as old as the Clovis finds, but it is pretty old, and on face value corroborates the evidence of a long history of humans in the Americas. But it is now clear that people were in this part of Oregon well before they were in New Mexico. After Cressman retired, the caves he explored were not investigated seriously for a few decades, although amateur artifact seekers combed the sites, and undoubtedly removed much of archeological interest. Beginning in the twenty-first century, however, University of Oregon researchers returned with new tools for dating objects, and a renewed desire to see what might be lurking in the bottoms of caves. They reported the definitive results of their most spectacular finds in 2014: human coprolites—ancient dried poop—calibrating to more than 14,000 BCE, a time before agriculture anywhere, before anyone in the world had settled down in permanent settlements, and, significantly, well before the Clovis people.

Like the area where Clovis artifacts were first found, these sites lie in a large currently arid region that, as the last great Ice Age was ending, was considerably more hospitable than it is now. Some of the sandals uncovered by Cressman are encrusted with mud, as if the person who once wore them had walked across marshes or through pools of standing water. But the cave where they were found, as well as the caves from which the coprolites came, are now miles from any water source. It's the extreme dryness of this high desert region that preserved the ancient hints of human occupation. As noted earlier, very few things made of organic substances survive for millennia unless they are protected by dryness or, conversely and almost perversely, by burial in acidic, extremely wet conditions, such as the peat swamps where the Sweet Track was discovered.

For thousands of years as the Ice Ages ended, meltwater filled low spots of the Great Basin region, forming what paleontologists call Lake Chewaucan.[10] Wave action in the vast lake—which was over 1,244 square kilometres (480 square miles) at its greatest extent—ground out the caves where the ancient human artifacts were found. It appears that the caves were used as seasonal campgrounds, possibly in winter. People took shelter in them from cold weather. In most of the caves, the greatest concentration of tools and bones from butchered animals—huge bison, camels, and horses among them—lie below the layer of volcanic ash from Mount Mazama, indicating that after the eruption people found the area less attractive until the devastated landscape revived itself.

The region, however, continued to be home for millennia to hunters and gatherers who developed sophisticated techniques for making tools and baskets. (In the latter Cressman saw the logical flowering of the skills behind the woven sandals.) Despite the increasingly arid conditions as the climate changed after the Ice Ages, they found ample food sources. Until the nineteenth century when their way of life was shaken by encroaching white settlers from the East, Native Americans in the Great Basin appear to have lived comfortably on the land. Their harvest began in the spring with the tubers of bitterroot, biscuit root, yampa, and wild onions. They took hordes of salmon coming upstream to spawn, caught crickets which they dried and pounded into flour to use in winter, and baked the white bulbs of camas lilies for cold season use. Berries, grass seeds, and pine nuts also made up part of the diet, along with big mammals like elk and little ones like rabbits.[11]

It was a bountiful land, say the current local Native American tribe, the Klamath, country that was given to them at the beginning of time. There is no place in their creation story for a migration from anywhere else by their ancestors.

Scientific evidence, as already noted, suggests that the ancestors of everyone who peopled the western hemisphere before Europeans arrived came out of Asia. The question that looms increasingly large is: what highway did they travel?

True, the famous 2,500 kilometre (1,553 mile) long ice-free corridor—first postulated without much evidence in the 1930s—did indeed exist at least twice: once before the Last Glacial Maximum and then again after the massive ice sheets began to melt.[12] But during the window of time that would allow for the Clovis people's migration, the great Laurentide Ice Sheet had coalesced with the Western glaciers to make a continuous field of ice. It's taken decades to determine this because the corridor's path lies along the eastern edge of the Mackenzie Mountains and down the Mackenzie River in Canada's Northwest Territories. The region is nearly without roads so residue from the glaciations could not be studied until the 1980s and 1990s, when geologists using airplanes and helicopters could take a closer look. Since then, more research has determined that the way was blocked by ice from about 19,000 BCE until around 11,000 BCE. After that, many of the valleys would have been filled by meltwater lakes. The verdict: for thousands of years it would have been difficult, if not impossible, for early North Americans to use the corridor as a highway.

But it appears that north and west of the ice sheets, conditions were favourable enough, even during the height of the Last Glacial Maximum, for people to thrive on hunting, fishing, and gathering north of the Arctic Circle.[13]

Two climatic features allowed this. The first was the fact that because so much water was captured in ice sheets and glaciers, the level of seas and oceans was dramatically lower. This meant that much of the shallow Bering Sea was dry land. Named Beringia by scientists, it stretched 1,000 kilometres (about 620 miles) from north to south in places, connected North America with Asia, and was home to a wealth of big prey to hunt.

The second climatic bonus was also an effect of all that water frozen in ice and so removed from circulation: the air was very dry over a large part of Siberia and western North America north of the Arctic Circle. Temperatures in winter were terribly cold, the growing season was very short, but little snow fell. Hence the country was not ice-covered as was territory at similar latitudes in Europe and the rest of North America.

Recent finds near the mouth of the Yana River, five hundred miles above the Arctic Circle in Siberia, show that people were doing quite well there, thank you very much, circa 28,000 BCE. The bones at the Yana sites—1,103 from at least 31 mammoths accumulated over 2,000 years have been found—lie closely associated with human artifacts. Two right mammoth shoulder blades, for example, have stone spear points embedded in them. Also found were personal ornaments and a sewing kit with implements made from bone or ivory.[14]

On the other side of what is now the Bering Strait, evidence of very early human presence is thinner on the ground, but still present. Research in the Bluefish Caves not far from the Old Crow River in the Yukon have turned up bone implements that suggest humans were around up to 35,000 years ago.[15] The finds are controversial—questions have been raised as to whether the bone was broken by carnivores or perhaps worked by humans millennia after the animal died—but research goes on. In Alaska, so far, the relics found date from considerably later.

So it is unclear just how widely people ranged through Beringia, but it looks quite possible that they were there for up to 20,000 years before they could venture farther south. That is ample time for small changes to take place in the genetic composition of the population, studies suggest. However, what is more important to our understanding of the peopling of the Americas is the fact that every Native American throughout the western hemisphere shows common kinship with people who now live or who did live in parts of Northern Siberia.[16] This is true both of existing populations as well as those of the remains of all prehistoric Americans whose genomes have been analyzed so far.[17]

The latest and perhaps most spectacular corroboration concerns a little boy who died in what is now Montana sometime around 10,600 BCE. Just a toddler—his age at death is estimated to be a year or a year and half—his family mourned him deeply, burying him with ritual. His small skull was covered with red ochre, the same pigment used by people in ceremonies since long before humans left Africa. Nearby was a cache of tools made from stone and animal bone, also covered with ochre and clearly made by people of the Clovis culture. The child's body is one of the oldest found in the western hemisphere, and his grave is the oldest evidence of respectful burial so far uncovered.

At the time of his discovery in 1968, the date of his burial could be determined through radiocarbon dating, but little could be learned about who he was, except in the context of the objects found with him. That all changed dramatically in February 2014, when scientists reported sequencing his complete genome from samples of his bone. They found that, without a doubt, he was related to the ancestors of all the native populations in the Americas. Somewhat surprisingly, natives of Central and South America seem more closely related to him than Native Americans now living in the northern parts of North America, but his relationship to them is also "very close," researchers say.

While that analysis doesn't answer completely the question of where the people came from who were in the western hemisphere when Europeans arrived, it more or less rules out the possibility of an early successful migration from continents other than Asia to the western hemisphere. Previously, some researchers had posited a European origin:

Clovis tools bear certain similarities with those made by a group in east-central France between 20,000 and 15,000 BCE. These led archeologists Dennis Stanford and Bruce Bradley to propose in 2004 that people from the Solutrean culture (named after the Rock of Solutré in France near which their artifacts were first found) might have followed pack ice around the North Atlantic to colonize North America.[18]

Other researchers have pointed to reconstructions of some early skulls with facial features that don't look like those of today's Native Americans. Perhaps the most publicized case is that of a skeleton found in 1996 by two young men—spiritual sons of Kerouac and his friends, surely—at a speedboat race along the Columbia River near the town of Kennewick, Washington. They were wading offshore when one of them stumbled over something round, which turned out to be a human skull. Because the final race was about to begin, they stashed it in some bushes until it was over. Then they got a bucket to transport the mud-covered head and went looking for police, who promised an investigation in a newspaper story recounting the find shortly afterward. The article ends with the laconic note: "So far, police have no idea of the age or origin of the skull."[19]

Unravelling that mystery took nearly twenty years. The U.S. Army Corps of Engineers, which maintains the stretch of river where the skull and the skeleton it was attached to were found, took custody of the bones. Local Native American groups were reluctant to have it studied, arguing that it was one of their ancestors and should be reburied with respect. After a court battle, scientists were eventually allowed an opportunity to study the bones carefully for a short period.

The results of that study have been published recently.[20] The findings suggest that he was probably a seal hunter from a coastal region who, despite a spear point lodged in his hip, badly healed injuries to five ribs, and a shoulder injured from repeatedly throwing spears, had travelled a long way from his origins. It was clear from the beginning of examination that the skeleton was very old, because the spear point was made of stone, not metal. More specific radiocarbon dating indicates that he died about 7000 BCE, at a time when the native population along the Columbia had already started harvesting the bountiful salmon that mount the river every year. But initially some researchers thought he probably wasn't an ancestor of living Native Americans because he exhibited supposedly European traits or because of his resemblance to the Ainu people of Japan, both of which showed up in a clay reconstruction of his face made by forensic experts. That idea wasn't laid to rest until 2015, when scientists were able to complete a DNA analysis of his remains. The results confirmed that he has genetic signatures that make him a relative of all Native Americans, except the Inuit. It seems he also is closely related to the Colville people, who live near where his body was found, and who hope to bury him with proper respect sometime in the future.[21]

His case is not unlike that of a young girl found in Mexico in 2007. Dated to between 11,000 and 10,000 BCE, she appears to have drowned in an accident on the Yucatán Peninsula. She has a small, projecting face with narrow cheekbones, wide-set eyes, and a prominent forehead, unlike most Native Americans of later times who tend to have longer, flatter faces, and rounder skulls.[22] Named Naia (Greek for water nymph), she was found in a submerged cave by divers, and in 2014 scientists announced that she has a genetic marker in her mitochondrial DNA common today across the Americas. In an article in *Science*, they suggested that the difference in physiognomy between her and present-day Native Americans is due to small changes that evolved over millennia, and not because they came from dramatically different places.[23]

But if the way south from Beringia was blocked for thousands of years by icefields, how did Naia's ancestors get to Yucatán even before ancestors of the little boy got to Montana? The question becomes even more puzzling when you consider other early human relics found in South America. The discovery of Monte Verde in Chile in the 1990s set the stage for a major challenge to the idea that early Americans walked south to Clovis and continued beyond. Home to twenty to thirty individuals near the coast of Chile, the Monte Verde settlement has been dated to around 10,500 BCE. The radiocarbon dating figures seem strong, although some critics have vigorously questioned the care with which the excavation was done.[24] But there are other cases. One of them is at Taima-Taima, on the west coast of Venezuela, where human artifacts associated with the bones of huge, slaughtered mammals have been found dating from

12,000 BCE. In fact, there are at least twenty widely separated sites which predate the Clovis find.

ANOTHER SUMMER, ANOTHER ROAD TRIP. We had driven the spectacular Highway 4 from Nanaimo on the east coast of Vancouver Island to the Pacific Coast. This is a land of long lakes and peaks that rise more than 2,000 metres (6,200 feet) from sea level. Located near major seismic faults where plates of the earth's crust move against each other, the island bears the marks of great upheavals clothed now in lush growth made possible by current moderate temperatures and abundant rainfall. First Nations people (what Native Americans are called in Canada) have lived a rich life here for thousands of years, which is clear from their traditions as well as archeological evidence. They fished, hunted seals and other sea mammals, gathered berries and roots, made handsome waterproof clothing from the bark of trees, sustained populations as dense as agricultural societies, and lived with a certain respect for the land.

From up on the ridge, we can see Long Beach stretch seemingly forever, the zone where the ocean meets the land. In the early morning fog, the rocks offshore where seals sun themselves are hidden. Seabirds—oystercatchers, my bird guide says—dip their way over the packed-down sand left by the retreating tide. Logs cluster at the edge of the high-water mark, tossed onto the land by winter storms.

There's a handsome visitor centre with exhibits about the Nuu-chah-nulth First Nations (the name means "along the mountains and sea"), whose traditional territories lie within the Pacific Rim National Park Reserve. After much discussion, the Canadian government and the First Nations have worked out a cooperative plan for governing the shoreline park, which contains fabulous views, pristine beaches, good surfing, and so far rather little commercial development.

It also has coves that give an idea of the kind of places where adventurers from Beringia might have stopped, long before any overland trek from the north was possible. That's what increasingly appears to have happened: many scientists now think that the first wave of people who went out to settle the Americas did so by boat, hugging the shoreline, following the migration of sea mammals, coming ashore at likely places. Glaciers clung to the tops of mountains—on Vancouver Island, one still lingers at the summit of Comox Glacier, a mountain fifty kilometres east and north of the visitor centre—but the coastline would have been much more inviting.

To take the trail toward South Beach from the visitor centre today is to cross high ground made up of debris—what geologists call unconsolidated material—left by glaciers as they melted. The sandy beach at the water's edge is punctuated by harder rocks, scraped clean first by ice and then pounded by the surf. A headland protects a cove, where millions of mollusk shells are piled, partially covered by sand. The midden is rather recent, testimony to the seacoast's largesse enjoyed by the First Nations who lived in the vicinity. Researchers would love to find similar, much older evidence of human presence along the coast.

Their quest is complicated by the way sea level has fluctuated over time. Not only was the sea level much lower during the Last Glacial Maximum all over the world, but also the great geologic instability of

Recent findings suggest Native Americans travelled along the Pacific Coast 16,000 years ago or more, stopping in coves like this and living off the largesse of the sea. Note the large collection of mollusk shells left by present-day First Nations people.
Author Photo

the west coast of the Americas has played a role. The tectonic plates of the earth's crust have moved in relation to each other, north and south, and up and down. As well, in northern latitudes the earth's crust had been weighed down by ice sheets, and has rebounded in places as the ice melted. As a result, the sites in many places where early adventurers paused are likely to be underwater today. Some suggestive finds have been made, however.

One of the most exciting discoveries was reported at the end of the 2014 summer research season by two University of Victoria scientists, Quentin Mackie and Daryl Fedje. They used an unmanned submarine to "fly" over underwater terrain off the east coast of Haida Gwaii (the Queen Charlotte Islands) in Juan Perez Sound, taking sonar images. At depths of up to 120 metres (about 320 feet), they found what looks like a settlement and the remains of a fishing weir, that they date to 11,700 BCE.[25] Mackie told the *Globe and Mail*: "You know people have been there, not just passing through, but that was their homeland." More research with remote-controlled equipment—the site is too deep for scuba diving—will be required to take photographs, and to scoop up any artifacts and bones in order to date them definitively.

No one knows at this point how many settlements like this might lurk beneath the sea. But, pausing near a patch of berries at the top of the ridge in the Pacific Rim Reserve today, it's not difficult to imagine that country like this would have been welcoming places for early adventurers. The story that they went from headland to headland, cove to cove, exploring rivers rising in the hinterland as they progressed south is not at all hard to believe.

This narrative can explain most of the discoveries of human activity that predate Clovis, but not all. Take, for example, the mammoth bones found elsewhere in the Great Plains that were apparently hacked up by humans and date from around 17,000 BCE. Other finds, near rivers far away from the Pacific Coast or a possible end to the trail through an ice-free corridor in Florida, South Carolina, and Virginia, are younger and equally puzzling.[26] Their proponents propose that, well before the two great continental ice sheets coalesced, some people ventured south overland from Beringia.[27] Citing similarities between artifacts found at the

Old Crow River and Bluefish Caves in the Yukon, as well as at the Yana Rhinoceros Horn site in Siberia, they suggest that the number of these adventurers need not have been big, but they could have roamed into the centre of North America before the routes south were cut off by ice. Later migrations from Asia might have encountered these people. But it's highly probable that their genetic profile would not have been too different from that of later migrants. This means that if human remains turn up at these sites, genetic differences might be hard to discern.

Other sites where vestiges of human activity have been found, particularly in Brazil, can't be explained by even that narrative. Perhaps the most perplexing is a complex of caves south of the Amazon in northeastern Brazil that is filled with rock paintings and which was apparently used for thousands of years.[28] The Pedra Furada archeological site, now a Brazilian national park, was first described by the French-Brazilian anthropologist Nière Guidon in the 1960s, but scientists in North America have not paid much attention, or have criticized the excavation and dating techniques. In an attempt to counter this, teams have recently reported carefully undertaken work that makes the case for human occupation at one of the sites at least as far back as 18,000 BCE, if not earlier.[29]

If the finds are valid, the next question is: where did these people come from?[30] A dash down an early version of an ice-free corridor, followed by a hop across the Caribbean seems most unlikely. So does a crossing of the Andes from a Pacific Coast beachhead by very early adventurers. Another possibility is that the art and the caves were made by people from Africa, even though genome analysis of current indigenous populations shows that they are part of the great genetic kinship of the Americas, with roots in Asia. (Admixtures of African genes show up in many Brazilians, but they represent recent contributions. Even an analysis of the skulls of one native group dating from the nineteenth century, the Botocudo, indicates that while some African haplogroups are part of their genetic composition, the tests used indicate that the infusion of African genes came afterwards, when African slaves worked alongside the native population.)[31]

The idea of another "Out of Africa" scenario seems less improbable when the New World history of pottery, bottle gourds, and certain human intestinal parasites is considered. The earliest pottery so far discovered anywhere dates from about 18,000 BCE and was found in the Yangtze valley in China.[32] (Earlier experiments in the Balkans with firing clay, mentioned earlier, appear to have been confined to making symbolic figurines, not pots.) Pottery shows up in the Mesopotamian region about 7000 BCE, while in North America the first evidence dates to about 4500 years ago, chiefly in South Carolina.

In South America, however, the making of ceramics has a much longer history. Pottery shards have been found not far from the Amazon in Taperinha dating from 5671 BCE, while within a few hundred years people south of the Amazon were making ceramics in enormous quantities, enough, in fact, to smash and burn. The first evidence of *terra preta*—made up of small bits of pottery, organic waste, and charred material—dates from 5400 BCE. This remarkably fertile soil (whose name means "dark earth" in Portuguese) appears to have made possible dense populations and large towns in the lower Amazon basin in the centuries before the arrival of Europeans.[33]

As might be expected, if the people who lived there were the first in the western hemisphere to make ceramics, the dates of pottery finds should get younger farther away from the *terra preta* zone. The next oldest finds come from northern Columbia—4530 BCE in San Jacinto and 3794 BCE in Puerto Horminea. In North America, the earliest shards so far were found along the Savannah River in Georgia, and date from around 2880 BCE.[34] Amerindians in Canada and the northern United States appear to have had no pottery before the Common Era, when the technology spread north from Mesoamerica. Until then, they used baskets or sacks made from animal hides to carry things.

So, did the folks in Brazil independently come up with the idea of firing clay to make ceramics? Maybe. Or maybe they were influenced by another civilization that appears to have invented pottery even earlier. People in the Nile Valley and part of Sub-Saharan Africa were making pots well before pots were common in most of Eurasia and Asia: the oldest shards have been found in Mali and date to about 9400 BCE.[35] Perhaps the skill required to make ceramics was an idea that was carried somehow across the Atlantic from central Africa to Brazil.

But how would the pot makers get to Brazil? There are some interesting simulations that suggest it would be possible to drift or paddle from the western bulge of Africa to northern Brazil within forty to ninety days. [36] The success rate would not be great—only one or two times out of ten attempts—and once in Brazil the adventurers would have to go back and tell the folks at home about what transpired in order to set up a colony. And even if this migration were possible, would the newcomers bring with them the knowledge necessary to make pots? The answers are unknown, but the simulations are suggestive.

So, too, is a simulation of the ways that the tropical bottle gourd could have been spread. The plant has been used extensively all over the world to make light, durable containers, floats for fishnets, and musical instruments. [37] A native to Africa, the gourd shows up as early as 8000 BCE in South America (well before pottery, it should be noted.) It's been proposed that early sojourners in the Arctic brought the gourd with them when they left Asia, since some studies show a genetic relation with Asian bottle gourd varieties. But how could they bring with them a tropical plant? They grew no crops, and paused in the Far North for generations, where the gourd could not grow. Not surprisingly perhaps, subsequent studies have shown the New World varieties to be more closely related to the African ones than to Asian ones.

Similar questions must be asked about intestinal parasites, such as hookworms (*Necator* and *Ancylostoma*), whipworms (*Trichuris trichiura*), and other helminths that are specific to humans and are found in

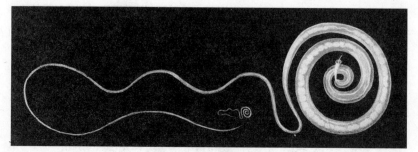

One of the unsolved mysteries of the peopling of the Americas is how tropical parasites like this whipworm *Trichuris trichiura* survived if Native Americans spent several hundred years or more in the Far North.

Illustration by Alfred Delorieux for Johann Gottfried Bremser, 1831 / Public Domain

Old World populations. They also turn up in pre-1492 mummies and coprolites in North and South America, but since these tropical organisms have stages of development that take place outside their human hosts—hookworm eggs require a temperature no lower than twenty-two degrees Celsius—they are not likely to have survived generations of life in the Arctic.[38] Human hosts must have brought them more directly to the western hemisphere, but just when and how, we don't know. The roads they travelled remain mysterious.

What is certain, however, is that by the time Europeans arrived, there were many roads. Some of the pathways were no more apparent than the early trade routes in Eurasia, where foot traffic over centuries beat down paths. An example is the trail across the Sierra Nevada Mountains, mentioned earlier, that led from the obsidian beds on Mono Lake to the Central Valley of California. Other established trails linked hunting grounds and settlements, as well as one watershed to another where rivers and lakes allowed travel by canoe. Native Americans made travel on footpaths easier when they set fire to the understorey of many eastern forests in order to encourage deer, buffalo, and small game, as mentioned earlier. In the seventeenth century, Captain John Smith wrote that he could ride at a gallop for miles in Virginia, but after the native population plummeted, the forest reasserted itself and the back country became a tangle of low brush and trees.[39]

Elsewhere, roads were far more developed. When Hernán Cortés landed at what is now Veracruz in Mexico in 1519, he found a well-established roadway extending from the coast to the Montezuma's capital in the great Valley of Mexico. The road was somewhat difficult for Cortés's forces because it was not designed for draft animals, horses, or wheeled vehicles—the Native cultures had none. But it was laid out with stopping places every fifteen to twenty miles, where travelers could find food and water. Nor was it the only road. Cortés writes that some of the natives tried to persuade him and his forces to take one route that was long and circuitous, but his men found a more direct route when they tried to climb a volcano to see why it spewed out smoke.

The towns along the way impressed Cortés with their size and wealth. Toluca, he says, was bigger than the Spanish city of Granada and had a market where 30,000 people were buying and selling. As for the settlement in the Valley of Mexico, he writes that it was composed of several smaller cities connected by causeways "one or two spears wide," with houses "as fine as those in Spanish cities."[40]

The roads that Cortés travelled were new roads compared to those built by the Mayas on the Yucatán Peninsula. This civilization had passed its height when the Spaniards arrived, and it wasn't until a few centuries later that archeologists uncovered its extent, from the glories of Chichen Itza to the other rich Mayan urban areas. The fact that they were linked by roads only became apparent in the twentieth century with the development of new means of studying the jungle-covered terrain through aerial photographs and satellite.

Farther north, carefully constructed road systems were not as extensive, but did exist. The roads radiating from Chaco Canyon in New Mexico are perhaps the most notable.[41] The town existed for more than three hundred years, and consisted of massive buildings now called Great Houses that were constructed of stone and contained hundreds of rooms. Other settlements with similar large houses are found kilometres away, linked with the main settlement by straight roads as wide as 9 metres (about 30 feet) that usually do not follow the contours of the land. At one point, the Great North Road reaches a canyon wall and, rather than zigzag up, climbs it with a set of dizzying stairs.

In a society without carts or draft animals, no clear, consistent reason for roads so wide jumps out at present-day observers. Some roads are oriented toward points on the horizon where the sun rises or sets at the solstices. The placement of others may also have symbolic justifications. The routes may have been related to trade, since excavations in Chaco Canyon have turned up artifacts from central Mexico. Also, to build the Great Houses some 200,000 timbers must have been carried from faraway forested mountains. Perhaps these wide roads are like the broad roadways that ring modern cities in attempts to handle urban traffic.

A word is necessary here about the mound builders of the Mississippi Valley. While they seem to have relied on river transport and simple trails to travel, they also were building levees and pyramid-like mounds, at a time when the Egyptians were beginning to construct their own pyramids.

Long recognized as the products of a sophisticated society, these relics of settlements that were home to up to 30,000 people were thought by early Europeans to be far too "civilized" to be built by Native Americans, eliciting speculation that adventurers from more "advanced" places had built them. Archeological research, however, shows clearly that they were homegrown products of people who were organized and savvy.

Other public works projects in the New World were even more elaborate, and some, like the Inca road network that ran nearly the length of South America, astounded Europeans. Beginning in northern Ecuador, it surpassed even the Roman network, linking settlements nearly the entire length of western South America, and extending well into Chile. The Great Inka Road (Qhapaq Ñan, named a UNESCO World Heritage Site in 2014) carried goods, soldiers, treasure, and travelers over 40,000 kilometres (25,000 miles.) Along the dry coastal plain, the straight track was edged by stone markers, with way stations a day's travel apart where supplies and lodging could be had. In the higher country, the route switched back and forth up to the heights and leaped across chasms on suspension bridges made from ropes as thick as a man's torso. The Spaniards were particularly impressed by the bridges, because there was nothing like them in Europe.

Pedro Cieza de Léon, one of the first Europeans to see what the civilizations of the Andes had created, wrote in *Chronicles of Peru 1543*:

> In human memory I believe that there is no account of a road as great as this, running through deep valleys, high mountains, banks of snow, torrents of water, living rock and wild rivers....Oh! Can anything similar be claimed for Alexander or any of the powerful kings who ruled the world, that they were able to build such a road and provide the supplies found on it?[42]

NOVEMBER IN CUSCO, PERU, THE FORMER INCA CAPITAL, CAN BE glorious. The rainy season is just beginning, which means that a storm may blow in during the afternoon, leaving air so clear that the mountains surrounding the high valley glow with clarity. It is high—3,400 metres

(11,000 feet)—which means that even though it is only thirteen degrees south of the equator (on a par with sweltering Luanda, Angola in Africa), it never is very hot. Today, it is served by an international airport and modern highways, linking it with other centres in Peru. But when the Incas reigned, it was the centre of their empire, the point where all roads were ultimately headed.

Some of the vestiges of the Inca roads remain, either in the orientation of present-day streets or as stone passages along hillsides or through towns and cities. One of the most charming of these is in the centre of Cusco, running from the great palace of Qorikancha, on top of which the Iglesia Santo Domingo now stands. The way between two rows of buildings is no wider than the extended arms of two grown men. It runs straight as a die up toward the square whose name once meant "plaza of tranquility," but now is the Plaza de Armas.

The west coast of South America is an area of great seismic instability, and the Incas built with this in mind. Along this short street, you can see how stone blocks on the lower courses of the old buildings fit together flawlessly. They narrow upward to produce an inclination of ten to fifteen degrees, so that the weight falls solidly on the block beneath. The convex upper surface of one fits perfectly into the concave bottom of the block on top of it. Set together without mortar, the Inca constructions have frequently fared much better than more recent buildings during earthquakes.

The Qorikancha is a case in point. Built on the edge of a hill, the palace overlooks a grassy square that covers a buried and channeled stream that forms the depression through which a major street, the Avenida do Sol, now runs. The building was the secure treasure house of the last Incas, filled with gold: Qorikancha, indeed, means "room or space containing gold." But after the Spaniards captured the city, the structure was turned over to the Dominican Fathers to be used as a Roman Catholic Church. Part of the original building was torn down to remove reminders of the pagan past, and the stone blocks were used to build the church. Inside it's clear where the stone blocks were recycled, because they were cemented together with mortar. During a severe earthquake in 1950, the rebuilt structure was badly damaged, but the Inca foundations, which had not been touched, held.

Nearly five hundred years after the Spanish took over, many parts of the Inca road are still used on a daily basis by people in the country. The stretch that leads to Machu Picchu, the storied spiritual capital of the empire about 75 kilometres (46 miles) from Cusco, also sees thousands of tourists hike up to the sacred city. Clever engineering channels water around the trail, frequently leading to hydraulic systems that feed water into settlements. In places, the roadway is 10 to 15 metres (about 33 to 50 feet) wide, possibly built to accommodate the transport of large stone blocks used to construct buildings. In other places, the road is much narrower, sometimes only wide enough for two lines of llamas to pass each other on a steep hillside: since there were no draft animals in the New World until Europeans brought horses and donkeys, no wider routes were ordinarily needed.

Construction dates for much of the Great Inka Road have not been determined, but it's likely that the first segments date back more than a couple of thousand years. Like the Romans, the Incas, who were just the last of a series of South American powers, built on past constructions and were still integrating newly conquered regions into their empire when the Spanish arrived.

Oh yes, when the Spanish arrived, first on ships and then on horseback, change came too, as fast as a galloping horse or a fully rigged sailing ship running with the wind.

Chapter Eight

THE REVENGE
OF THE ROAD

MEANWHILE, BACK IN EUROPE, ROADS WERE TERRIBLE. Twenty-four years after the Inka Road wowed the first Spanish who travelled it, another Spanish expeditionary force set out from Italy to fight in Flanders. Here's what one soldier reported:

> Four and a half long leagues of very bad road, because there are two and a half leagues ascent to the top of the mountain—a narrow and very stony road—and after reaching the top we marched another league along a ridge of the mountain.... After crossing the top of the mountain there is a very bad descent, which lasts another league, the same kind of road as the ascent, and it leads down to... a miserable hamlet with a hundred small houses. While we crossed the mountain it snowed and the weather was awful.[1]

The Spanish Road, as it became known, was celebrated because, despite its shortcoming, at the time it was the best way that troops could move overland across Europe. Couriers travelling light took two weeks to travel the 800 kilometres (nearly 500 miles) between the headquarters in Spain of Philip II, the Habsburg king who ruled much of Europe for a few decades in the sixteenth century, and his vassals in the Netherlands. Compare that with how fast Herodotus reports Darius's couriers rode. Some two thousand years before, they could travel three times faster: they took only two weeks to cover the more than 2,900 kilometres (about 1,800 miles) from Susa (in what is now Iran) to Sardis on the edge of the Mediterranean coastal plateau.

In addition, getting a fighting force from southern Europe to the Netherlands was considerably more complicated than sending a message. That is why Philip spent so much money building the Spanish Road, and there's more than a little irony in the fact that it was financed with booty taken from the Americas. When the Spanish "treasure fleet" arrived in Seville in the fall of 1566, it brought with it four million ducats (the equivalent of U.S. $4 billion today), of which the crown could claim a fifth as its just due.[2] That sounds like an incredible sum, but Philip was a big spender. Faced with revolt in the Low Countries—the issues were religious as well as political, since part of the conflict was instigated by Protestants who did not want to be ruled by the Spanish Catholics—he put aside one million ducats for the campaign to quash the rebellion. In addition to upgrading bridges and existing roads that the expeditionary forces would travel, Philip had to provision the 10,000 troops, 6,000 servants and camp followers (frequently family), and 3,000 horses that made the trek. It took the force more than a month to cross the Alps from Milan, and another six weeks to travel to Brussels. Please note that this rate of travel covering the 900 kilometres (700 miles) was considered very good.

Today you could make the trip by train, crossing the Alps via one of the longest tunnels in the world, in fifteen hours and nine minutes.[3] Or you could drive it, according to Google at least, in nine hours and four minutes.[4] Those times indicate that something fundamental has changed in the way we get around over the 450 years since Philip commanded the construction of his road. As we shall see, those changes began in the part of Europe that Philip was trying to subjugate: the Netherlands and England.

The English-speaking world knows Philip best as the fellow who married Elizabeth I's older sister Mary I, and then sent the Spanish Armada against the country after her death. A devout Catholic, he considered

Good Queen Bess, a Protestant and therefore an imposter. He also undoubtedly wanted some of the wealth that England was claiming from its explorations. Despite the largesse his ships brought back from the New World, Philip was chronically short of cash: at one point, his foreign debts equalled 60 per cent of Spain's gross domestic product, and he defaulted on repaying them four separate times.

England, on the other hand, had already started down a path that would bring wealth Philip could never have imagined. The population was growing in England, and in some other places in Europe. Between 1500 and 1700, the population of western Europe increased by about 30 per cent.[5] The increase in what is now the United Kingdom was particularly striking: the population appears to have more than doubled in the period, from about four million to around eight and a half million. As a result there were ample numbers of people to work in industry and colonize new territory. As well, because of the new industry and more people to warm and house, a shortage of wood developed that led, in turn, to the need to look to another source of fuel: coal.

Wood and charcoal (the product of wood burned in the absence of air, and which burns hotter than an ordinary wood fire) had been long used for cooking, heating, and metallurgy. Coal had too: there's evidence that early Britons used it on funeral pyres, as well as for fires to dry grain. But coal was relatively little used compared to wood, until the wood supply disappeared in a literal cloud of smoke as thermal power was used to power burgeoning industry. (The fact that wood was needed to build ships and housing for the rising population was also a factor.)

At the time Philip II tried to put down the rebellion in the Dutch provinces, people there were using two other forms of energy: wind power (those beautiful Dutch windmills!) and peat. The latter material is made of partly decomposed vegetable matter found in acid bogs which can be cut, dried, and eventually burned. Bury it deep within the earth and wait a couple million years, and you'll have coal or perhaps petroleum. But peat—which might be considered a kind of under-done fossil fuel—is much easier to collect than those other hydrocarbons that fuel our lives today, since it lies on the surface of the land.[6] Furthermore, when it burns peat doesn't impart impurities to the substance that it is heating, unlike coal whose sulfur content initially made it unsuitable for many industrial uses. For these reasons, the Dutch prized peat, mined it assiduously for a couple of hundred years, and transported it around the low-lying country on barges travelling through lakes and on specially built canals.

There's peat in England, too—remember that the oldest traces of a road, the Sweet Track, was discovered by a peat cutter—but its peat bogs were not nearly as accessible as those in the Netherlands. Coal presented some of the same transportation problems as peat, but it packed more energy per pound, tipping the balance in its favour.

There are records of coal being shipped to London as early as the thirteenth century from Newcastle in the east of England, down the River Tyne, and then by sea to the Thames, and up that river to London. Newcastle Lane and Seacoal Lane, off Fleet Street in modern London, bear witness to the docks on the River Fleet (now buried) where the coal was off-loaded.

By the beginning of the 1600s—about the time when Good Queen Bess was nearing the end of her reign—coal accounted for three-quarters of the fuel consumption in London. By the end of the century, ways had been found to overcome the problems inherent in its impurities, and to increase the temperature at which coal-fired furnaces burned. With the invention of the steam engine, the demand for coal skyrocketed, and the search was on to make its mining easier and more profitable, and to move it more efficiently.

Canals, like those used in the Netherlands to transport peat, were one solution to the transportation problem. European travelers such as Marco Polo had reported on the Grand Canal in China—still the longest canal in the world—and the Jesuit missionary Matteo Ricci, who arrived in China in 1582, twenty years after the construction of the Spanish Road, travelled on the Grand Canal to Beijing.

While these stories may have been an inspiration, canals in Europe date back to before Marco Polo. The introduction of the pound lock—two locks separated by a stretch of canal where water level can be regulated easily—spurred their growth. The first one built primarily for trade was in France, when the Seine and the Loire rivers were joined in the early seventeenth century. Shortly thereafter, construction began on the

Canal du Midi which joins, in effect, the Mediterranean and the Atlantic. Completed in 1694 and 360 kilometres (223 miles) long, it includes a network of navigable waterways with 328 locks, aqueducts, bridges, tunnels, and other features. Many say it paved the way for the Industrial Revolution in France.[7]

Certainly, canals played an important role in England for a time also. The first major project, built by James Brindley for the aptly named third Duke of Bridgewater, was a huge commercial success. The duke had coal mines in North West England and wanted to find a way to decrease transport costs to the factories being built in what would become the heartland of British industry. In January 1761, the first load of coal to fuel steam-powered engines was shipped from the duke's mines to Manchester along the new canal, for half the cost of what transportation was previously. Inspired by that experience, more canals were built on English river systems, notably the Leeds and Liverpool canal, and the Thames and Severn canal in 1774 and 1789.

But that success marked the beginning of the end of the usefulness of canals because the invention of the steam engine opened the door to a new means of transport. The railroad, so much faster than even the post horses of Genghis Khan, was just around the corner.

Pulling loads on rails goes back as far as 600 BC, with the Diolkos (meaning "haul-over") at Corinth.[8] Greek theatres had tracks on which scenery could be moved, not surprising in a society which invented the idea of *deus ex machina*, the god coming down in a machine to solve problems or punish the wicked. Like the use of various technological innovations to make bling—smelted metals in particular—this almost frivolous use was followed by a far more practical one. On the Greek isle of Corinth, ships had to round a headland noted for its stormy weather. Well before the Common Era, thought had been given to avoid this dangerous passage by digging a canal across the isthmus, which is only about 6 kilometres (3.7 miles) wide. Then some bright person realized that a simpler way of getting payload from one side of the isthmus to the other would be to pull it on rails. Greek historians record at least eight occasions when warships were carried over the isthmus on sledges or wagons moving on rails. About a kilometre of the track has been excavated, although the possibility of finding more ruins isn't great, because of the damage done during the excavation of the current canal in 1893.

Rails also may have been used as tracks for hauling minerals out of mines in Portugal at Três Minas, and by German miners in the sixteenth century who pushed and pulled the *hunds* or cars themselves. But it wasn't until 1604 that the first well-documented railroad was built to move coal from the Strelley pits in Nottingham to the River Trent in the English Midlands.[9] Of course, the railroad only used animal power to haul the cars. The game changed, however, when the steam engine began to be used to power a train of cars.

Jump forward to a summer morning in 1803. It was four o'clock and a revolution was about to begin in the quiet dawn. The big red-haired man who had designed a new contraption paced up and down in the yard of a carriage builder on Leather Lane, not far from Gray's Inns Gardens in central London. Richard Trevithick, Captain Dick, was a Cornishman who had been developing steam engines for pumps in mines, and had bigger ideas about what could be done with the noisy, smoke-belching machines. A few months previously, he and his colleagues had built an engine that could move from place to place along conventional roadways—not on rails—which they briefly, but successfully, tried out. The machine travelled on its own power up a hill, to the great delight of crew and friends—indeed, to their too great delight perhaps. Since they were near a pub, they repaired to it for the "proper drinks" and roast goose, a person there remembered later.[10] They neglected to extinguish the fire under the boiler, however, and when the water had completely evaporated—apparently about the time that they'd finished their refreshments—the machine exploded.

This time there would be no such kerfuffle. Captain Dick and a helper stoked the firebox, and the son of his partner, John Vivian, climbed aboard the big-wheeled contraption, ready to roll through the quiet predawn streets. According to Vivian, the engine could hold eight to ten passengers and the waiting adventurers also got on. Off they went, along Tottenham Court Road as far as the Lord's Cricket Ground near what is now Regent's Park, hitting speeds of up to nine miles an hour. They turned back through Paddington and Islington (then on the edges of London) for a trip of about seven miles. Near the end of the trip, Vivian remembered Captain Dick coming next to him, asking how things were going. "I think we had better go on to Cornwall," he replied, and the intrepid inventor put his foot on the throttle to give the engine full power. They tore along, not stopping until they hit a garden wall and took down "seven or eight yards" of fence.

The run, they concluded, was nevertheless a success. The next year Trevithick built the Penydarren or "Pen-y-Darren" locomotive to haul iron from Merthyr Tydfil to Abercynon, Wales. Considered the first real steam railroad train, it was designed to carry 10 tons of iron, and once hauled a load of 25 tons, although it was too heavy for the cast plate rails, which broke under the weight. Nevertheless, the advantage of using metal rails was apparent because the smooth surface cut down resistance. As one observer wrote in the late nineteenth century about a demonstration of the superiority of rails:

> A good horse on an ordinary turnpike road can draw two thousand pounds, or one ton. … [B]ut when twelve wagons were loaded with stones, till each wagon weighed three tons, and the wagons were

Richard Trevithick built the Penydarren or "Pen-y-Darren" locomotive to haul iron in Wales in 1804. Considered the first real steam railroad train, it was designed to carry 10 tons of iron.
Photo: Hugh Llewelyn / Creative Commons Attribution-Sharealike 2.0 License

fastened together, the horse...drew the wagons with ease [along the rails,] six miles in two hours, having stopped four times, in order to show he had the power of starting, as well as drawing his great load.[11]

Working out a way to make rails that could carry heavier loads did not take long. Add a steam engine that could go faster than a horse, and the modern age had begun. As Thomas Jefferson wrote in 1802, "The introduction of so powerful an agent as steam [to a carriage on wheels] will make a great change in the situation of man."[12]

UNTIL THIS POINT, HUMANS HAD NEVER MOVED FASTER THAN one of Genghis Khan's battle ponies (perhaps 25 kilometres an hour or a bit more than 15 miles an hour for short stretches) or a sleek, fully-rigged ship sailing before the wind (the record dates from the mid-nineteenth century of 22 knots an hour or about 40 kilometres an hour.)[13] But with the steam locomotive travelling on rails, the pace accelerated. The average speed of a railroad coach in mid-nineteenth century Britain was 30 to 50 kilometres (about 20 to 30 miles) an hour, three times that of a stagecoach, and perhaps ten times faster than a person on foot.[14]

The British were the first off the block when it came to trains, but the rest of the world roared ahead soon after. By the late 1830s, trains were chugging in France, Belgium, Poland, Russia, the United States, and Canada, and even on the island of Cuba. Fuel for their engines was frequently considerably cheaper than food for the horses and men that they replaced as motive forces.

In Europe, the rail lines were engineered to be as straight and level as possible. This was partly due to the conviction that trains running on curved lines would be unstable, but also because labour was cheap and land to build the roads was expensive. Bringing trains into the centres of existing urban areas required reshaping cities. Tracks cut through existing housing usually in poorer sections where real estate prices were lower. In some places like Paris, where the rail lines ended at one of a half-dozen train stations sited around the city, getting goods from one railroad line to another was an enormous, time-wasting headache. For this reason, the centres of many cities were rejigged, with Paris the most shining example.[15] The case was different in many of the places where railroads opened up country to settlement, as the next great wave of human expansion rolled forward.

But first, a word about the effects of the Industrial Revolution on ordinary folks. There is no doubt that working and living conditions in the cities where the new factories were located were frequently horrible. Living next to a railroad line meant being constantly subjected to smoke from the engines, while the crowded housing almost always had primitive sewage systems—or none at all. The result was higher death rates in European cities than in the countryside and villages for most of the nineteenth century. Nevertheless, the population in countries undergoing development grew as it had never before, setting the stage for massive population movement, particularly to the New World where, as we've seen, diseases had decimated all the previously thriving civilizations.

"Over London–by Rail" gives a taste of what life was like in railroad-age London and other nineteenth-century cities.

Engraving by Gustave Doré, 1872 / Public Domain

Why was this? Part of it seems to be the way that new foods and new ways of transporting food evened out the supply, meaning that bad growing years in one region could be compensated by food imports. The impact shows up first in a drop in infant mortality. For example, between 1726 and 1751 in the British Isles the death rate in the first year of life was 195 per 1,000, but by 1821–26, it had dropped to 144 per 1,000.[16] What Jared Diamond would call a natural experiment in the effect of increased food occurred in Ireland two decades later. The potato, a native of the Andes, was introduced there in the seventeenth century, first as a novelty for the upper classes. As these largely British landowners forced peasants from their fields in order to produce meat and other crops for export in the beginning of the nineteenth century, the potato became the staple food for the poorest since a very small plot could produce enough to feed a family. It was a monotonous diet—a man could eat sixty potatoes a day, a woman, forty, and a child, twenty-five, with milk as a supplement—but it allowed for a reasonable level of health. At the time of the potato's introduction, the Irish population stood at about three million, but by 1841, it was between 8.3 and 8.5 million. Then came the accidental introduction of a fungus that devastated the potato crop in 1841–2, leading to the death of about one million people and the emigration of another 1.5 million in the year that followed.[17]

Demographic forces were at play elsewhere in the early nineteenth century, although not as dramatically as in Ireland. As a result, a large number of people were ready to try their luck in the supposedly unclaimed and empty lands across the water. Between 1800 and 1940, fifty million people left Europe for good, most to the western hemisphere although some also went to Australia and New Zealand.

Those who chose to go to the New World joined millions of Africans who were forced to go there, in striking contrast to the way Africans settled the rest of the world by walking out of the mother continent so long ago. Between the early 1500s when the Portuguese carried the first African slaves to South America and the end of the nineteenth century when slavery was finally abolished everywhere in the Americas, some twelve million African slaves were transported to the western hemisphere. At times, there were more Africans than Europeans arriving: one source says that between 1700 and the American Revolution in 1776, approximately 250,000 African slaves, 210,000 European immigrants, and 50,000 convicts landed in what is now the United States.[18]

"Landed" is the important word. They were the lucky ones to make it to terra firma after crossing on ships that were often so bad that 20 per cent of the passengers might die (the death rate was often even higher on slave ships.) No telling how many were lost as uncounted ships went down in ocean storms, too.

Once on land, some migrants tarried near the shore. Others, in North America particularly, went upstream on the great rivers that lead into the New World. Frequently at the beginning of this great migration there were few if any roads for them to follow, although the wilderness was not completely uncharted for them.

You'll remember that this was not the case when the first migrants left Africa for greener pastures, moving toward savannahs full of game, and rivers and seashores abounding in fish and water creatures. They had absolutely no idea where they were going, yet nevertheless they were fruitful and multiplied in their new homeland. It was a pattern that repeated itself each time humans met an unsettled frontier.

The same kind of slow but steady population expansion probably would have happened after European and African migrants arrived in the apparently under-populated country of the New World. But the newcomers this time came with a number of things that made the land more productive than it had been: crops like wheat, rice, sugar cane, olives, bananas, and coffee; new animals like cattle, pigs, chickens, sheep, horses, oxen, donkeys, and goats; as well as wheeled vehicles and plows, which replaced digging sticks. The exchange went the other way too. In addition to the potato, American crops like corn, manioc, chilies, and cocoa became important additions to the diet of the rest of the world. The result was better nutrition in general. Throughout the world population increased at a rate that would have been unimaginable in the 1800s. "The power of population is indefinitely greater than the power in the earth to produce subsistence for man," wrote Thomas Robert Malthus in 1798.[19] But he had not seen how much more acreage would become available for food production, or the way the nutritional value of the food that each acre produced would increase with new crops and new methods.

By the early nineteenth century, a wave of people began rolling toward "undeveloped territory" wherever it was. The movement was mostly from the centres of western Europe where population growth was greatest. Moving into the "vacant" land was extremely laborious when wagon roads and primitive trails were the only way to strike out from the seacoast and the rivers. One settler in upstate New York recalled her trip in the pre-railroad era when she travelled more than 600 kilometres (upward of 375 miles) in an ox cart:

> Our way lay chiefly through the forest, and we made but slow prog-ress. Oh! what a bitter cold night it was when we reached the swampy woods where the city of Rochester now stands. The oxen were cov-ered with icicles, and their breath sent up clouds of steam. 'Nathan,' says I to my man, 'you must stop and kindle a fire; I am dead.'[20]

However, once railroads were built to slice across prairies and through forests, the journey became somewhat easier. Even those critical of the Industrial Revolution were impressed by the power of the locomotive. Henry David Thoreau, who retreated to Walden Pond in the woods near Boston, wrote: "When I hear the iron horse make the hills echo with his snort like thunder, shaking the earth with his feet, and breathing fire and smoke from his nostrils...it seems as if the earth had got a race now worthy to inhabit it."[21]

The list of ambitious railroad projects is long. The Trans-Siberian from Moscow to Vladivostok was completed in 1904. India saw its first railroads as early as 1850, and by the turn of the century a complex system of trunk lines and local connector lines served the subcontinent. In both cases, strategic political concerns were part of the rationale for building the lines. Railroads could move troops and supplies far more efficiently than they could be transported overland: in Russia's case, it wanted to guarantee hegemony across northern Asia as far as Vladivostok, while India fortified its northern frontier. China was considerably slower off the mark. When the Qing rulers were approached about constructing railroads in the mid-nineteenth century, they are said to have replied that steam engines were "clever but useless" and that railroads would "deprive us of our defensive barriers, harm our fields and interfere with our *feng shui*."[22] But by 1911 the Chinese rail system had 9,000 kilometres (more than 5,500 miles) of track, with Beijing, the capital, at its centre, just as Paris was the centre of the French rail system.

The railroad also advanced into Africa, the home of our ancestors. Winston Churchill wrote about the building of the line from the eastern coast, south of the Horn of Africa: "Mombasa is the starting-point of one of the most wonderful railways in the world... [A] sure, swift road along which the white man and all that he brings with him, for good or ill, may penetrate into the heart of Africa as easily and safely as he may travel from London to Vienna."[23]

At the peak of railroad construction, there were 22 million kilometres (14 million miles) of track criss-crossing every continent in the world except Antarctica.[24]

In North America, the trains began to run in the 1830s, and by the time of the U.S. Civil War plans were underfoot to build transcontinental lines. The first, authorized in 1862, was built from both ends of the rail line—from the edge of San Francisco Bay and from Council Bluff, Iowa, where earlier rail lines ended. The two lines met in May 1869, not far from Ogden, Utah. In the next twenty years, five more lines were strung across the continent, three in the United States and two in Canada. A web of smaller lines stretched deep in the empty spaces, yet less than one hundred years later the heyday of passenger rail in North America had past, as once again road-building underwent a major change.

By the time my mother, my sister, and I were travelling, Walla Walla, Washington, the town where we were headed, was served only by a small freight line, even though when rail service began in 1875 the first train was packed with passengers—some riding on flatbed cars—celebrating what many hoped would be the beginning of greater prosperity.[25]

The town's name means "running waters" in Nez Perce, a local Amerindian language. A visit even in high summer when it hasn't rained in awhile shows how apt the name is. Tree-shaded streams originating in the Blue Mountains to the east tumble through the town, eventually joining with two larger streams that flow westward toward the Columbia River. The contrast between the Walla Walla Valley and the surrounding dry country is striking even today when irrigation elsewhere has enabled crops like the fabulous Walla Walla sweet onions, orchards full of peach and apple trees, and excellent vineyards.

The valley was a stopping place for sojourners travelling west on the Oregon Trail, beginning in the early 1830s. Starting near the confluence of the Missouri and the Mississippi rivers, the trail was first organized as a track for horse and foot traffic, beginning about 1811. Native Americans knew the way before that, of course: they'd guided the expedition ordered by U.S. President Thomas Jefferson to reconnoitre the Northwest Territory purchased by the U.S. from France in 1803. (One of the guides was a native woman, Sacajawea, whose husband was a Métis born in Québec: her baby son—on her back—shows up on a U.S. quarter, the only Canadian to do so!)

The Oregon Trail's basic trajectory led from the watershed of the Missouri, through the Rockies, and then down the watersheds of rivers running west toward the Pacific. By 1836, the trail had been widened into one that wagons could use. Even though it was probably no better than the Spanish Road in the sixteenth century, the first wagon train of migrants left for the West that spring, to be followed during the next three decades by some 400,000 settlers.

They moved into land that may have seemed empty, but had been the homeland of Native Americans for thousands of years. For example, near the western end of the trail, excavations at The Dalles—not far from where my mother, my sister, and I would change buses on our trip that summer—show that Amerindians fished salmon from the Columbia 9,000 years ago, if not before. In 1804, the Lewis and Clark expedition noted about twenty Amerindian lodges here, with salmon on racks being prepared for storage.[26] The language spoken by the tribes in the area is related to that spoken by those in the Klamath River watershed where, you'll remember, the very oldest indications of human presence in North America have been found. Like the Klamath, the Columbia could be used as a highway from the coast, and the abundant fish could sustain a thriving, growing population.

Migrants on the Oregon Trail had no idea of the locals' history. Their government said the land belonged to the United States and that settlement from the East was highly desired, so they started out with horses, mules, cattle, and supplies. The journey would take four months, and few wagon trains arrived in the valleys of the Oregon territory without significant loss of stock or humans.

Before the Trail was built, the sojourners from the East were exclusively male. The "white" men living at Fort Vancouver farther down the Columbia near its mouth, as well as others scattered over the land, frequently took wives among the native women, so from the beginning a mixed-race population was present. Their connection to the East was through the fur trade portage of the Hudson's Bay Company, which extended all the way across the continent to Montreal. But bring your women in and the stage is set for permanent, game-changing settlement. Narcissa Whitman, the wife of a Presbyterian minister who set up a mission near Walla Walla, is considered the first "white" woman to cross on the Trail, arriving in the fall of 1836. Significantly, she was pregnant at the time.

Some 400,000 sojourners followed the Oregon Trail westward in the middle of the nineteenth century, wearing down stone and leaving wheel ruts that can still be seen today.

Photo: Wusel007 / Creative Commons Attribution-Sharealike 3.0 Unported License

The Whitmans' mission began in 1837. There they not only ministered to the native population, trying to convert them to their brand of Christianity, but also helped out the growing stream of migrants. One of the early ones wrote in his journal in 1842 that Dr. Whitman has "a verry comfortable house and is farming to considerable extent. He has a Thrashing machine and grinding mill all under one roof driven by water power. Many Indians around him. [W]as never more pleased to see him or white people in my life, we were received with the utmost kindness."[27] The young migrant goes on to add that it was here that he learned of the death of a young man who had started out with him from Independence, Missouri, four months before.

Death was a constant companion on the Trail, and death would soon descend upon the Whitmans. In 1847, they were killed by a group of Native Americans of the Cayuse tribe who were outraged that the doctor's medicine seemed to work on the white settlers during an epidemic, but did nothing to save the native population. They thought that he was poisoning their people, so they attacked in retribution. However, the Cayuse probably succumbed to a disease for which they had no immunity. The survivors among the tribe also had their days numbered: there have been no Cayuse for more than a century.

How large the Native American population was back then is impossible to determine now, but in the 1830s the Nez Perce tribe—the largest in the area—was estimated to number about 6,000, whereas there were only a handful of whites. By the summer that my mother, my sister, and I visited the area, the proportions had completely reversed: only slightly more than 1 per cent of the entire population of the state of Washington was listed as Native Americans, be they descendants of the Nez Perce or other tribes. The rest were almost entirely the descendants of Europeans.[28] This demographic flip-flop happened because of a double whammy: death by disease, and the amazing reproductive success of the newcomers.

My father's family illustrates this latter point. His grandparents travelled the Oregon Trail sometime before 1858. That year James E. Cusker (he was twenty-four and born in Washington, DC) and Alta Clementine Hayworth (she, sixteen and born in Missouri) were married in the

Willamette Valley of Oregon. They farmed various parcels around Walla Walla, and raised eleven of their twelve children to adulthood. Their fruitfulness was not unusual. Studies have shown that a woman can give birth to a dozen or so children if she doesn't use contraception.[29] Just as humans ever since the first Great Expansion have thrived when entering new, empty (or nearly empty) territory, these settlers did very well for themselves. My husband's father's family had a similar experience. Moving into new country in Kansas about the same time, they had nine children of whom eight lived until their eighties: only one died as a toddler due to "the summer complaint" that was probably an infant diarrhea.

James and Clementine likely first saw the Columbia after their separate treks across the continent just above Biggs Junction, which was the crossroads where my mother, my sister, and I were supposed to change buses from a north-to-south line to an east-to-west one. A short section of the Oregon Trail is visible still on a bench above the junction, and several settlers wrote in their journals about the delight they felt when they forded the John Day River, crested a hill, and looked down on the great river.[30] Today, the little town is located where two major highways intersect: Interstate 97 and U.S. 84; the former crosses the Columbia on the Sam Hill Memorial Bridge, opened a few years after we passed through. A half-dozen motels, restaurants, and gas bars make up the town; but when we were there, it was not much more than a wide spot in the road, with one store, an eatery, and a couple of gas pumps. Behind ran the Union Pacific mainline, but no passenger trains stopped there.

We were travelling by bus, not train, of course. Partly, that may have been because trains were more expensive than buses to take, and at that point money was tight in our family. More importantly, though, trains only travelled where their tracks took them. To travel from Southern California to the corner where Washington, Oregon, and Idaho meet, we'd have to take a train swinging east to Utah, change rail lines there and head west, and we'd still have to make part of the journey by ordinary road. On paper, it looked like taking the bus would be simpler and more direct, even though we had to change buses at Biggs Junction.

But the bus driver had been direct when he looked at our tickets: "Are you for real, lady? Nobody gets off there."

Just us: a woman and two dirty, tired, squabbling children who, it turned out, had missed their connection. Because of road construction—and that summer it seemed that roads were under construction everywhere in the West—we were late getting to the crossroads and the bus going east had already left. Our driver was hesitant about letting us off in the gathering darkness. The next bus wouldn't come until morning, so we would have to spend the night sitting up on the hard benches of the truck stop that served also as a bus station. As we waited, we heard freight trains on the tracks thundering past just south of us, their horns blaring, as if taunting us because where they were going and where we wanted to go were irreconcilable.

Compared to the travails of those who travelled the Oregon Trail, our situation a hundred or so years later was a piece of cake. But I remember the tension as my mother tried to figure out what to do, the cigarettes she chain-smoked, her attempt to cash a traveller's cheque, the long-distance, collect phone call she placed after much discussion with the people who ran the place. No, she told my grandfather, we wouldn't be in Pendleton to meet him. We wouldn't be leaving until morning, we wouldn't arrive in Pendleton until nearly midday, she said, and then she settled us down on the benches to sleep.

But sometime in the middle of the night, my grandfather arrived, having driven the 140 miles from Walla Walla to pick us up. I remember tears and hugs, and curling up in the back seat of his big Lincoln. The road was smooth, the continent had been tamed, and although we didn't have a name for it, the "Grandparent Effect" still operated.

Nor did we realize as we sped through the warm night, with the smells of growing things blowing through the open windows, that the highway was about to become King.

Chapter Nine

SPEEDING

OR JACK KEROUAC, THE RAILROAD CARRIED WITH IT AN allure of adventure. He wrote in *On the Road*: "I heard the Denver and Rio Grande locomotive howling off to the mountains. I wanted to pursue my star further." And he explained his writing techniques in railroad terms: he "intended to clack along all the way like a steam engine pulling a one-hundred-car freight with a talky caboose at the end.... [S]wift writing is confessional and pure and all excited with the life of it."[1] But significantly, he didn't do much of his wandering by train. Although he worked as a brakeman at one point, most of the adventures recounted in *On the Road* were on the bus or in a private vehicle. The latter might be a farm truck or a beat-up '37 Ford Sedan or (once or twice) a brand new luxury car. It didn't really matter, as long as a there was paved road, gasoline, and the desire to get someplace.

When he was rambling and we were travelling, the United States was embarking on a great wave of highway construction. The impetus came from two things. The first was the increasing popularity of the automobile among ordinary folk, as well as the use of trucks to transport goods. The second was inspired by strategic concerns, and therefore was not unlike the railroad building by Russia and India in the late nineteenth century, which was designed to consolidate those countries' defenses.

Even though the idea of a vehicle that could travel on its own along ordinary roads dates back to Richard Trevithick's sojourn on the streets of London with his steam contraption in 1803, it wasn't until more than a hundred years later that the age of the automobile began. (The word "automobile" is a French invention, derived from Greek *auto* or self and Latin *mobilis*, moveable.)[2] Inventors experimented for decades with steam and electricity, but the gasoline-powered internal combustion engine proved to be the safest and easiest to operate.

By the turn of the nineteenth century, several European countries had fledgling automobile manufacturers, but in 1908 Henry Ford set the pattern for putting people all over the world in the driver's seat with his Model T, a mass-produced, dependable, and affordable machine. Ford cut down cost by rationalizing the steps needed to produce the car. For example, the Model T famously was available only in black for most of its production run, not because Ford particularly liked the colour, but

Henry Ford was the first to mass-produce a car that ordinary folk could afford. His Model T ushered in the age of the automobile.

Photo: Harry Shipler, 1910 / Public Domain

because at first no other colour of paint dried quickly enough for the assembly line.[3] Ford's methods cut the number of man hours needed to produce a car from twelve and a half to one and a half hours with a concomitant decrease in cost: he boasted that his cars could be easily bought by any worker in his factories, since the Model T cost about three months' wages.

To some extent, the car won over the rural population before it did urbanites. This is partly because, in cities, streetcars and urban railroads (including subways) already carried many passengers. Also city distances were frequently short enough so that people could walk to work and play. In the country, however, things were different. The tough early cars were game for travel on unpaved, ungraded roads, and farmers found them great for hauling goods to and from town.

My grandfather who met my mother, my sister, and me owned one of them from about 1916 to 1919. There's a photo of him sitting proudly in the Overland Touring Car that he somehow acquired when he, my grandmother, my mother, and aunt were living in eastern Montana. Unlike the part of my father's family that had travelled the Oregon Trail, my mother's family had fetched up in the western United States during World War I, after several years living on the Canadian prairie while my grandfather worked on the Canadian Pacific Railway. After crossing the U.S.–Canada border so he could work on the Great Northern Railroad, they attempted to homestead on land the Great Northern had opened up to settlers. Bad move, it seems, for a man who'd never had much experience with agriculture. But with the Overland, he found a way to supplement the family's coffers: he met other settlers at the train in Glasgow, Montana, and took them out to their claims.

In later years he always had a nice car, and when we took our trip he'd settled down to buying a new Lincoln Continental every year or so. The car we had back in San Diego wasn't as big or as expensive—a 1949 Mercury, that sat at home most of the time since my mother didn't drive and my father at that point took the bus to work.

Yes, buses in Southern California. There were buses, and people took them until governments at all levels began to push the automobile as the answer to every problem in urban life. A few years after our trip, it became hard to get downtown by public transportation from our house, and my father began driving to work. He'd leave early to avoid the rush hour since the new divided highways were already becoming snarled with cars, in a classic "if you build it, they will come" scenario.

We were all caught up in the automobile age. You could get your driver's license at sixteen—even younger in California for one brief period if you took a driver's education course, which I did, passing my driver's test when I was fifteen and a half. Even my mother finally succumbed, learning to drive (although never very well) at age forty-five. Driving and cars had become a necessity in most of North America and large parts of the rest of the world.

Problems with car dependence, however, were recognized as early as the 1920s. Le Corbusier, the influential Swiss architect and urban planner, was fulminating about traffic in the fall of 1928: "In the early evening twilight on the Champs-Élysées it was as though the world had suddenly gone mad. After the emptiness of the summer the traffic was more furious than ever. ... To leave your house meant that once you had crossed your threshold you were a possible sacrifice to death in the shape of innumerable motors."[4] His proposed solution was to rebuild cities so that vehicles would be completely separate from pedestrian traffic, with people living in high-rise housing set in parks.

His ideas about housing were taken up all over the world, although in many places the government agencies who built the high-rises didn't really understand their architectural origin. In the war-ravaged cities of Europe and the Soviet Union, his apartment blocks became the norm for social housing after World War II. In North America, his ideas lay behind dozens of urban renewal projects designed ostensibly to replace slum housing. But, except where the high-rises were designed for the wealthy or where careful social engineering prevailed (as in Singapore), they proved not to be very good places to live. Thirty years later, many of the developments had deteriorated terribly, and some, notably ones in St. Louis and Chicago, were razed.

Le Corbusier's ideas about roads for vehicles have not worn well either. He scorned the pattern of roads in most European cities, calling them the "pack-donkey's way" because the animal "meanders along. ... [H]e zigzags in order to avoid the larger stones, or to ease the climb or to gain a little shade; he takes the line of least resistance."

Look back at the history of roads, and you can see that's exactly the way most of the tracks humans have followed began. Le Corbusier saw no good in it, calling it contrary to human nature: "Man walks in a straight line because he has a goal and knows where he is going; he has made up his mind to reach some particular place and he goes straight to it." Cities laid out by the Romans and new ones founded in North America were better designed, he said, because they used geometric principles to lay out street grids. But even they could not meet the challenge of the automobile, because their streets were too narrow and mixed pedestrian with vehicular traffic. What was needed, Le Corbusier said, was to build high-speed, limited-access highways cutting through the hearts of rebuilt cities.

These highways looked lovely on the drawing board and in aerial photographs. There was something magical in their appeal, too, as Sigfried Giedion rhapsodized in 1953 in his book on city planning *Space, Time*

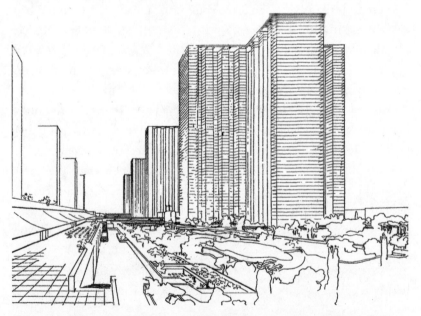

The Swiss architect Le Corbusier proposed rebuilding cities to separate vehicle traffic from pedestrians completely, with people living in high-rise housing set in parks. His ideas were copied around the world, sometimes with disastrous results.

From Le Corbusier, The City of To-Morrow

and Architecture: "Riding up and down the long sweeping grades produces an exhilarating dual feeling, one of being connected with the soil and yet of hovering just above it."[5]

In short, highways promised something akin to that transcendent experience that Jack Kerouac was looking for on the road. His description of his arrival in Los Angeles with his girlfriend Bea hints at that: "I looked greedily out of the window: stucco houses and palms and drive-ins, the whole mad thing, the ragged promised land, the fantastic end of America."[6]

That was a time when the United States and Canada were starting a frenzy of highway building. In the U.S., the Interstate highway system was under construction: authorized in 1952, it was designed to incorporate existing good roads across the country, upgrade others, and build new ones.[7] Under President Dwight Eisenhower—who, as a young soldier in 1919, had taken sixty-two days to cross the country in a military convoy—the program was given long-term funding that saw more than 78,000 kilometres (48,600 miles) of good highway, with 14,700 interchanges and 55,500 bridges in place by the turn of the twenty-first century. In Canada, the Trans-Canada Highway—not built to the same standard as the U.S. Interstate system—began in 1949.

The routes reflected strategic considerations. Eisenhower and many of his planners had seen first-hand the importance of a good highway system when they confronted the roads built by the Fascist governments in Germany and Italy before World War II.[8] One of the Interstates' main criteria was linking major population centres to allow for rapid movement from one coast to another, one border to the other. In some cases, doing this meant going where no vehicle had gone before, constructing tunnels and long grades in mountains, slicing straight across seemingly empty country in other places.

The background to these highways was the existing grid of roads, many of which reflected the way much of North America was surveyed in the nineteenth century in preparation for divvying up the land to settlers. Ironically, the basis for the geometry of surveying goes back to something as non-Euclidean as that donkey Le Corbusier so disliked: the amount of land a man was supposed to be able to work in a day, or four square perches.

Each perch was 16.5 feet long (a bit more than 5 metres), and to measure an area surveyors used a chain that was four perches long (22 yards or approximately 20 metres).[9] Each chain was divided into one hundred links, neatly combining the decimal system with less standard units. An acre was ten chains by ten chains, 640 acres was one square mile or a section.

At first, homesteads in the U.S. were a quarter section, but as the frontier was advanced into drier country the basic grant went up to a section. (Even that wasn't enough for my grandparents' to make a go of it at the end of World War I in eastern Montana.) The survey lines served as the basis for a network of roads, running straight east-west, and north-south at intervals outlining land earmarked for townships. (In Canada, similar principles were used.) Only a few of these roads were eventually developed, but some of those became upgraded into the Interstate system.

In other places, the Interstate highways followed tracks that had been in use for centuries. For example, the route we took on our bus trip north from Los Angeles was not too far from the Siskiyou Trail, first used by Native Americans to travel up and down California's inland valleys. In the 1830s, cattle drives followed the trail from the part of California still held at that time by Mexico, north into the Oregon territory. In the twentieth century, paved roads followed the old routes rather closely.

When it came time to consider how to integrate the new and growing highway system into cities, many saw it as an opportunity to change the geography of urban areas as dramatically as Haussmann had in Paris in the mid-1800s.

In general, highway standards call for speeds of at least 80 kilometres (50 miles) per hour, with limited access through dedicated entrance and exit lanes. Wherever possible, traffic should be able to roll continuously through or around urban areas. The ideal situation was to be able to travel from the centre of one city to another without having to stop at a traffic light or even to slow down.

Robert Moses, the czar of planning in New York City for twenty-five years, was famous for his schemes to cut highways through the Big Apple. Comparing himself to Haussmann, he frowned on narrow streets in the centre of the city, and razed hundreds of buildings in order to build throughways. It took the legendary urbanist Jane Jacobs and her friends—"a bunch of mothers," Moses scoffed—to stop him from razing the heart of Greenwich Village. Their successful action in the late 1960s was the beginning salvo in the war against making the automobile king of transportation.[10]

Le Corbusier, who died in 1964, would have scoffed at the revolt against construction of urban highways. At one point, he advocated pulling down all of the buildings in the centre of Paris in order to replace centuries of architecture with his high-rises, parks, and connecting highways. The French only partially gave in to the charms of geometric design and swooping autoroutes. The historic central arrondissements were saved, and while some highways were built slicing into it, many are now closed to vehicular traffic on Sundays. As in many other European cities, automobile and truck traffic is discouraged in Paris today, while high-rise buildings exist practically without exception only on the outskirts. But in other places, other countries, the temptation of Le Corbusier's seductive ideas and drawings was too hard to resist, with consequences that will not be easily rectified.

The most striking example of the strong points and the terrible weaknesses of this approach to urban development is the Brazilian capital Brasília, which was being built just as Kerouac's *On the Road* was published. The plans for the new city were revolutionary, although the idea of building a capital from scratch was not. Other countries had done it: Washington, DC is only one example, one that had some influence on what happened in Brazil. In that country, the desire to build a new capital had been around since shortly after Brazil was settled in the sixteenth century. Rio de Janeiro, the beautifully situated city on the Atlantic coast, had functioned as the capital, but from the beginning there were security fears about its location, since an invader might attack from the sea. Moving the capital inland was little more than a dream, however, until the mid-1950s when presidential candidate Juscelino Kubitschek promised that, if elected, he would build a new capital city by the end of his five-year term. Shortly after he won, an international competition was held to choose a plan for the new city.

To some extent the die was cast in advance, since modernist architect Oscar Niemeyer, who designed the United Nations headquarters in

New York, had already been chosen to design the major buildings. The competition's winner, Lúcio Costa, nevertheless was something of a surprise, since his plan, unlike the voluminous, detailed ones submitted by other contestants, was presented on four large cards without a technical plan or drawing attached. He took the relatively flatland of Brazil's central plain and proposed a spread-out city that would be monumental. Frequently, its layout is compared to a bird with outstretched wings or an airplane, seen from above. The central axis would feature broad, automobile-friendly thoroughfares along which the buildings of government would be set, housing executive, legislative, and judicial arms of the government, as well as all the ministries. Extending out from either side would be curving boulevards of housing, the north and south wings (the *Asa Sul* and *Asa Norte*). Organized in super blocks called Superquadras, the basic style was a six- or seven-storey apartment building with elevators, along with three-storey walk-up buildings and a few ranks of row housing. It looked very much like something that Le Corbusier might sketch out.

Despite the vagueness of the plan—or maybe because of it—five years later the new city was open for business. Within ten years the city had reached its maximum planned population of 250,000 surrounded by a wide greenbelt. Fifty years after that, the city was choked with cars, and more than two million people lived beyond the greenbelt in more or less planned communities. The biggest employer in the area was the government, and people had to get to offices either in private cars, on buses, or on a Metrô system that goes only a short distance into the country.

When I visited Brasília in the South American spring of 2013, the place seemed strangely familiar to me. Not only were the gardens full of plants I remember from my childhood in San Diego—poinsettias, plumbago, hibiscus, and bougainvillea—but, standing on a corner, I was confronted with the problems I remembered from back then: how to cross the street. In a flash, I was back on the waterfront drive that separated San Diego's city centre buildings from the pleasure-craft pier. In both cases, pedestrians had been left out of the equation.

The Monumental Axis that forms the backbone of Brasília descends a long slope toward a lake. When I flew into the city in the late afternoon the day before, its vaunted avian shape was sort of visible. By the time I was on the ground, night had fallen so my entrance to the city was along a high-speed, well-lit roadway with only a few cars on it. My guide, architecture professor Silvia Ficher, offered a running commentary on the weak points of the city's design, as she drove me down the boulevards toward the lakefront for a look at the first building finished in the hectic construction period: the Presidential Palace.[11] From a distance, it looked like the beautiful dream of a modernist architect. When we turned back up the boulevards toward the hotel district where I was staying, the Monumental Axis looked as impressive as any grand concourse I'd ever seen. What was missing were signs of people, except in a former slum quarter which some of the workers, who built the city, had built for their own use.

Costa's plan had anticipated that most of the construction workers— lured from high unemployment regions elsewhere in Brazil—would go back home when the city was completed. Therefore, housing for them had been sketchily planned, and many of the workers built their own shanty towns with no sewage, no water, and no transportation. Most of these were razed in the years following the opening of the city in 1960,

Brazil's capital Brasília was inspired by Le Corbusier's ideas about cities. Today it features some great architecture, like the cathedral designed by Oscar Niemeyer, but it's no place to be a pedestrian.

Author Photo, 2013

but a few on the outskirts were "regularized" into independent municipalities: there are sixteen surrounding the city centre now. Others closer
in were completely razed, with only one, Vila Planalto, remaining. In the
intervening years, this one has become a "heritage" site, a monument
to the tens of thousands of people who worked day and night to build
Brasília. Located not far from the Plaza of the Three Powers—Praça dos
Três Poderes, the seat of government—it had just been named an historical sector when I was there, and that warm evening, people sat out
in cantinas, drinking and eating, with music floating into the night air.
Its many restaurants are favourite lunch spots for the civil servants who
work not far away in the graceful buildings that line the Monumental
Axis. Because of the way different land uses are segregated in the city,
there are few restaurants to serve the workers, besides cafeterias in the
buildings themselves.

Unlike most cities, Brasília did not grow outward from a central core.
Construction went on in all parts of the basic plan, the *Plano Piloto*, from
the beginning. Distances between government buildings were designed
to be large so that the structures would stand out against the emptiness
of the public spaces. The result was a city where distances are usually too
far to walk.

This became abundantly clear to me in the morning when I went out
to reconnoitre. My hotel was in a cluster about even with the top of the
slope of the grand axis, which lies between two one-way boulevards, each
with four lanes of traffic running roughly north and south. My thought
was to walk over, watch people coming to work, get the lay of the land.
At the brink of the hill stands a television tower that is one of the tallest
structures in Brazil. Opened shortly after the official establishment of
the city, at 224 metres (735 feet, or about half the height of Toronto's CN
Tower) the tower is the third tallest structure in Brazil. The tower still has
pride of place in the city, even though it is no longer as essential for communication since a shorter structure for broadcasting digital television
signals was opened in 2012 to the north of the city.

Looking toward the original tower from the Praça dos Três Poderes—
where the judicial, executive, and legislative branches of government
have their headquarters in a complex of architectural elegance—is like

looking from the Capitol steps in Washington, DC toward the Lincoln Memorial, or from the Trocadéro or the École Militaire in Paris toward the Eiffel Tower. The big difference is that of scale. The Washington esplanade is three kilometres, or almost two miles long, a distance that lends itself nicely to a pleasant stroll. In Paris, the distance is even shorter: from the eastern end of the grassy concourse to its western extension on the other side of the Seine is about a kilometre and a half, and the Eiffel Tower itself lies in the middle. Their equivalent in Brasília is nearly three times as long as the Washington esplanade and nine times as long as the one in Paris. To make the walk in Brasília on a hot day is a chore.

I did, but I seemed to be one of few pedestrians making the trek. Buses run up and down the boulevards. So do taxis and private automobiles. But sidewalks along the boulevards are not wide enough to handle crowds, while the grassy linear park in the middle obviously isn't designed for foot traffic. In places, people trying to get from offices on one side to those on the other side, nearly a kilometre away, have worn footpaths in the grass down to the red soil that underlies the capital. But it's clear that if you had an appointment on one side and worked on the other, you'd be best off taking a cab because otherwise you might get killed trying to cut across the boulevards. There are only nine stoplights, or one for every kilometre. At the noon hour, brave but foolhardy souls opt not to go to a corner with a light, but run across the lanes of traffic. Perhaps it's not surprising that Brasília and it suburbs, the Distrito Federal, have a rate of traffic accident mortality—19 per 100,000 people—that is much higher than the European average of 10 per 100,000. [12]

If you live in one of the Superquadras, the neighbourhood-sized apartment block complexes that were designed to be the cornerstone of Brasília's residential housing, you probably wouldn't find the absence of concern for pedestrians along the Monumental Axis a problem. That's because each complex houses about 8,000 to 10,000 people and is served by a small shopping centre, along with elementary schools and churches accessible on foot through tropical gardens. In theory, you wouldn't have to go outside your little neighbourhood for services. In practice, each Superquadra is rather well served by public transport too, and contains parking for a portion of the units. The problem—beside the fact that instead of one car per unit, each unit now may have two or three vehi-cles—is that less than a tenth of the Distrito Federal's population lives in them. The result is long, long queues of cars and buses transporting people who live on the periphery into the central city.

But it isn't just the desire to see the urbanist vision of Le Corbusier, Costa, and Niemeyer realized that led to Brasília's car-centred develop-ment. The same president who was behind the city's construction also greatly encouraged the country's automobile industry. As one architec-ture professor at the Universidade de Brasília lamented to me, reflecting on Brasília and most other Brazilian cities, "As long as the automobile industry has so much clout in financial policy, cities will continue to be congested."[13]

The building of Brasília also had long-term effects on the nation's road system elsewhere. One of the arguments for locating the new cap-ital on Brazil's central plain is that it is near the geographic centre of the country. Of course, those who used that argument were fully aware that roads linking that centre to the rest of Brazil were rudimentary at best, and would require much construction. Therefore, one of Kubitschek's projects was the completion of a roadway, the Belém-Brasília Highway, from the northeast of the country to the new capital. Initially unpaved, it was the route taken by thousands of workers leaving the poor regions of the state of Pará, lured by the offer of jobs in building the new capi-tal. Like several other roads constructed to unite the country and open isolated parts, such as the interstate highway BR-364 in the vast Amazon region, it has had massive effects on the environment. Areas previously unreachable became available for agriculture or for the forest industry. The effects of such road building will be visited in the next chapter.

But in the meantime, as I looked at the brilliant blue sky on that hot spring day, I decided to take refuge inside one of the Superquadras. There the air was cooler under the shade of trees planted fifty years previously when the complex was first built. A group of toddlers were playing in a small playground, while not far away an elderly woman sat watching. She was accompanied by a much younger woman, possibly a paid compan-ion. The people who moved in here when the complex was built had a chance to buy the apartments in the 1990s, and many did. Now, these original residents have aged, just as the buildings of the new capital have. Concrete, please note, doesn't weather as well as stone. Even the outside of buildings like Niemeyer's stunning cathedral needed to be painted or at least scrubbed down that spring day. Patches of greenish mould blemished it in shady places, like moss on the north side of trees in another climate, another hemisphere.

For some, Brasília is a cautionary tale about what happens when you buy into the car-based urban paradigm that reigned in the second half of the twentieth century. The country invested incredible sums in building the new city, and as the nation's capital and showcase it can still count on resources that automobile-friendly cities elsewhere in the world can't. At a time when road infrastructure in North America is aging rapidly without adequate plans for repair—"Some U.S. state leaders have tried to make a virtue out of cutting highway funding," one observer noted in 2010—highways in the *Plano Piloto* at least look in wonderful shape.[14] Air quality is generally good, perhaps because the city is located in a region that is not very densely populated. The Distrito Federal has about 492 inhabitants per square kilometre, but it is surrounded by the state of Goiás, with a density of 19 per square kilometre. Note, however, that Brasília has not done a review of its contribution to greenhouse gas emissions, unlike many other Latin American cities, so the full effect of its car-dependency is unknown.[15]

What can be done about this? As was already noted, some densely populated European cities—seduced in the twentieth century into expanding highway systems by Le Corbusier's ideas and the auto mystique—have turned their backs on automobile transport, particularly since the turn of the twenty-first century. London taxes automobiles coming into the centre of the city, while Copenhagen and Amsterdam give priority to bicycle transit. Elsewhere, some Asian cities have invested heavily in public transportation: the Shanghai metro system is now the longest in the world, for example.[16] Some U.S.$70 billion in new transit projects involving more than 470 miles of transit lines were under construction in 2016, according to the industry newsletter *The Transport Public*.[17] Talking about "increased density" around "transport nodes" is current. So is the realization that where planners and developers did not buy into the automobile or freeway paradigm, it will be easier to redress the problems of greenhouse gases and concomitant climate change.

Brazil, a little ironically, provides a very good example of what might be done to set things straight. The city of Curitiba, in the south of the country, shows that working with what you have can lead to brilliant solutions to problems.

It was cooler when I visited there just before my sojourn in Brasília: in Brazil, going south is like going north in North America. With a city population of about 1.9 million (and 3.2 million in the metropolitan region), Curitiba is not substantially different in size from Brasília and its suburbs, but in many respects it could not be more different. First of all, it is a relatively old city.[18] Settlement began in 1693, and the city itself was inaugurated in 1746. Because it was not on the coast where most action during the colonial period was concentrated, Curitiba's growth lagged behind that of seaside cities; but by 1843 it had 17,000 inhabitants, about the same as São Paulo, currently one of the largest cities in the world and which also lies inland.

Ten years later, Curitiba's first city plan was drawn up, basically recording what development had already occurred. Nevertheless, it is credited with being a deciding factor when Curitiba was named the capital of the new state of Paraná, which was carved out of the larger São Paulo state in 1853. By 1940, the population had grown to 120,000, organized in part on a standard grid pattern surrounding a central square.

Traffic was a mess then and, inspired by Le Corbusier's ideas of separating different sorts of traffic and land usages, a complete reorganization of the city was proposed by French architect Alfred Agache in 1943, in the middle of World War II. The designs his team came up with show circular boulevards dividing the city into sectors for business, education, government, and the like. The central square would shelter massive underground parking garages that could also be used as air-raid shelters in case of attack: neighbouring Argentina had recently signed on with the Axis powers, while Brazil was leaning toward the Allies. But wartime is no time to start reconstructing a city, and after the war, political and economic factors collaborated to push the plan to the side. Revamping Curitiba along Le Corbusian lines would just cost too much, everyone agreed.

Something had to be done to channel the growth of the city, however. Just as Brasília was opening to great fanfare, leaders in Curitiba decided to turn in a direction that was at complete odds with the automobile-based plan for the capital. Their aim was to provide attractive public transportation and to revitalize the city's centre, instead of tearing it down to build highways. The basic idea was to establish a developmental axis running roughly north and south, with zoning and property tax incentives designed to encourage density along transit corridors served by an integrated, rapid bus system. In order to counter persistent flooding problems, large, low-lying areas of the city were set aside as parks which could be used to stock overflow water in times of flooding. Cars were banished from a stretch of the city centre, too. Merchants initially were appalled by the idea, but after its opening—city crews worked day and night to install flower pots and children's art in a few days—the attraction was so successful merchants asked that a larger stretch be car-free.

"We were building a sustainable city long before the term became popular," says Carlos Alberto Guillén of the Secretaria de Meio Ambiente (the Environment Secretariat), who has worked for the city since he was a teenager.[19] Its success has been immense: the Siemens/ Economist report *Latin America Green Index* puts Curitiba in a class by

Curitiba, in contrast to car-centred Brasília, has a rapid bus system that is world-renowned. Passengers pay their fare and enter from elegant bus shelters.
Author Photo

itself.[20] Visitors come from all over the world to see what and how this has been accomplished.

The transportation system lies at the heart of Curitiba's success. Moving 2.5 million passengers a day, the integrated system includes articulated express buses that can carry up to 270 passengers. They connect with buses that serve more local areas, and feeder buses that connect outlying suburbs. The aim is to have public transit no farther than 300 metres (about 980 feet or less than three football-field lengths) from every resident's door. The express buses have dedicated lanes and frequently whiz past private cars that are stuck in traffic. I found out just how efficient they are the hard way: I tried to take a taxi at rush hour to the other side of town, and arrived much later than I liked. But on the way back, an express bus that stopped right across the street from my meeting sped me to my hotel in ten minutes, three stops away.

The Environment Secretariat headquarters, where I met Guillén on my first morning in Curitiba, can be seen as emblematic of the city. Set on a busy, four-lane street divided by a median strip (yes, the city does have them), it is perched on the edge of a portion of a temperate rainforest: the Atlantic Forest, the *Mata Atlântica*. As an immensely rich ecosystem that once covered much of southeast Brazil, this forest remnant surrounding Curitiba receives 1,000 millimetres (nearly 40 inches) of rain a year.

The secretariat's rustic-looking buildings are built out of local timber, much of it salvaged from downed trees. They also include a wealth of recycled treasures: an old ox-cart wheel that provides stretchers for a staircase, panelling and wood stoves saved when old buildings were torn down, and huge logs that once carried electric wires and would have been trashed by the electric company had not the secretariat come to the rescue.

Outside, at the top of a slope that leads down to a park along the River Barguí, it was drizzling. So thick was the foliage on the trees, however, that when Guillén took me for a short walk on the nature trail, we didn't get wet.

"You can't go anywhere in Curitiba, can't take a tourist picture, without seeing a reminder of the city's attitude toward sustainability and the environment," he said, as we picked our way along a boardwalk slippery in places from dripping trees. I heard bird calls, and when I commented he said that 350 species of birds have been identified in the ecosystem, including twenty-two that are found nowhere else. In the distance, an araucaria, the emblematic tree of southern Brazil, stood high above the forest's understorey. The conifer is almost limbless for five-sixths of its height, and then bursts out into an umbrella of branches. Its straight trunks were prized for building, and it was logged so rapaciously that it has become endangered.

The air smelled good, a mix of damp earth and something floral, with an undertone of wet cedar bark that reminded me of walking through another temperate rainforest in British Columbia. That area, you'll remember, was home to some of the first adventurers to the western hemisphere from Asia when the Ice Ages were ending, and until recently First Nations peoples lived abundantly on the bounty from the sea and the shore. Archeological remains suggest the same happened here, but as Europeans advanced, the native population suffered as it did else-where in the New World. By the time Curitiba's Environment Secretariat wanted to build a structure with a thatched roof in the indigenous style to show how suited it was for the climate, nobody around Curitiba knew how to do it, although the technique had been used as late as one hundred years ago. Guillén explained that Amerindians from farther away were engaged to do the job and teach the skills necessary to keep the building maintained.

The structures are fascinating and charming but are just a small bit of what makes Curitiba special. The real story is the city's commitment to guiding its development, to changing its form. Inspired by the success of the first axis of transportation and development, it is now in the process of setting up another, parallel axis along a formerly high-speed, congested roadway that runs east. City officials say they expect that the zoning and tax credit incentives now in place will lead to growth similar to what occurred earlier on the first axis over a twenty-year period. This will not solve all the problems—with increasing prosperity, many middle-class people are buying cars that they may not use to go to work during the week, but for which they want parking spaces that older residential buildings don't have. Coupled with the arrival of large shopping centres located at the end of transit corridors that provide plentiful parking, fewer people are choosing to live in the centre and to shop there, city planners say.[21]

Keeping a handle on growth in the twenty-nine municipalities outside Curitiba proper is also a challenge. A big incentive for suburbs to cooperate with Curitiba's urban plan is that they then can be involved in certain federal programs such as social housing. (Sewers, water, and electricity are responsibilities of the state of Paraná.) And the transportation system, which is controlled by the city government, sets the norms for levels of service provided by the private companies that do the heavy lifting, and plays a big role in guiding growth.

Plans call for more environmentally-friendly vehicles throughout the system, and consideration is being given to increased use of bikes for transport. The city currently has 120 kilometres of bike trails, mostly laid out in the 1970s to connect parks when the idea was to provide a network for leisure cycling. The trails to be added will serve a clientele biking to work or shopping, and the city is discussing with Lyon, France, how to set up a bike-share program like the one begun there ten years ago.

One thing Curitiba won't be tempted to do is push its transportation system to another level by investing in light rail or subway construction. "There was talk about a metro back when we started setting up the integrated bus system," Daniele Moraes said. Like the Agache plan, however, the idea was too expensive: "We're not likely to go that way, given the success of what we've done for far less."

Wise decision, I thought a few days later when I rode the Metrô in Brasília, which only serves one sector of the conurbation beyond the limits of the *Plano Piloto*. The Metrô cars were crowded at rush hour, but so were the highways we saw from the train. The folks in Curitiba were putting their money in the right services, I thought later when I heard that the new light rail link in Brasília, which was supposed to be finished for the 2014 FIFA World Cup of soccer games, was not completed in time and, worse, would serve the airport and little else. Better to put all the money and effort into improving surface transit, making it easier to get around on foot. Significantly, Curitiba also hosted some World Cup games, but just added more buses and taxis to the transit mix to accommodate visitors.

There are some who say that the Curitiba solution won't work elsewhere, that in many chaotic cities in the developing world, lack of government clout and resources means that any increase in the standard of living will translate into more vehicles clogging routes, with the accompanying increase in greenhouse gas emissions and frayed urban life. But even there, help may be on the way. Nairobi, for example, where the public transit system collapsed in the 1990s, is now served by a network of independent buses and taxis that operates relatively efficiently, and in the near future those lucky enough to have a smart phone (and they are legion) can use an app to plot the best way to get around by using the *matatus* (privately owned minibuses).[22]

Sadly, I couldn't stay long in either Curitiba or Brasília: not enough time.

Time, time, time: that mutable constant which underlies everything we do. In Curitiba, they say it will take a couple of decades to develop the city's new population corridor. Brasília's Monumental Axis is now fifty-seven years old. The Interstate highway system in the U.S. is sixty-seven. The first Model T was produced not quite 110 years ago. Richard Trevithick drove his steam vehicle through the streets of London 105 years before that. The years go rocketing past, as that other cult writer Joseph Heller said in *Catch 22*.

Over time, the spread of humans around the globe, our quarrels, and our search for resources have had profound effects on the landscape. Hunting and gathering, growing food, cutting timber, wearing tracks as we go from place to place: all have altered things, as we've seen. But these changes have sped up in the last two centuries like a runaway car with the accelerator depressed and the brakes out of order. The big question is one Kerouac asked in *On the Road*: "Whither goest thou, America, in thy shiny car in the night?"[23] Only it applies not only to America, but to us all.

Chapter Ten

ON THE ROAD, II

T IME. YES, IT IS TIME TO REACH BACK MILLIONS OF YEARS, as well as hop forward several decades from the bus trip my mother, my sister, and I took that summer.

Let's go backward first. Across the Columbia River from Biggs Junction, where we paused involuntarily on our journey, there is striking evidence of the forces inside the earth and an intimation of humans' place in the grand picture.[1] Along this stretch, the great river has cut through layers and layers of black basalt that look like a dark palisade set off by the parched vegetation on top and the river channel below. While I don't remember noticing it—even though there was a full moon, fatigue and concern seem to have wiped out any memory—I've since seen the residue of lava which began pouring out of the earth from fissures to the east perhaps sixteen million years ago.[2] This action occurred between two periods of volcanic activity. The first created the ancestral Cascade Mountains. The second produced the eruption of Mount Mazama in southern Oregon, witnessed by some of the first human residents of North America, and also the Mount St. Helens explosion in 1980 that anyone today can revisit on YouTube videos.[3] Not far away is an emblem of the twentieth century: the Hanford Nuclear Reservation where thousands of liters of nuclear waste are stored. Few people want to entertain the prospect of what would happen if the earth began to move again, as it obviously has done in the past.[4]

Now go forward to another bus trip, one I took sixty years after that first one with my family. The second trip was motivated by two desires: to see more evidence of the forces of the earth and to learn how a new road was changing the landscape and the world. My trajectory took me from Cusco, Peru, where the remains of Inca roads are ever-present, over the Andes, and into the Amazon basin past switchback trails laid out a millennium or more ago by Amerindians. Doing so, I travelled a new route that the Peruvian and Brazilian governments hope will radically increase exchanges of people and goods. It took me a day and a half, including a night spent at a comfortable lodge near the banks of the Madre de Dios River.

Conditions before the new highway (called the Estrada do Pacífico in Brazil and the Carretera Interoceánica in Peru) was completed were orders of magnitude worse. Passengers travelled that first stretch on improvised means, such as platforms on top of tanker trucks taking fuel to the gateway to the Amazon basin at Puerto Maldonado. In the early twenty-first century, the journey took *National Geographic* writer Ted Conover seventy-two hours. There was talk then of building a new route, but he reported that few expected it would ever be built, so travellers had become accustomed to unreliable and frequently perilous transportation.[5]

But ten years later the new route was finally completed. In principle, you can take it from the Atlantic Coast near São Paulo, Brazil—the port of Santos is only 50 kilometres away—to the Pacific Ocean in Peru, a minimum five-day journey of 5,000 kilometres (about 3,100 miles) by bus. In Brazil, the route as far as the border on the western edge of the Amazon basin has been in place since at least 2002. But in Peru, the stretch of road over the Andes from Cusco to the Brazilian border has only been operational really since 2012.[6]

Commercial considerations lie behind the route's construction. Getting Brazilian products like soybeans and machinery to Pacific ports was that country's motivation, while Peru hoped to get better access to its more prosperous neighbour. So far, the calculation seems to be paying off in terms of trade, for Brazil at least. Between 2009 and 2014, Peruvian imports from Brazil increased by 266 per cent, while its exports to Brazil increased by 44.2 per cent. But the road construction has had effects that are much harder to measure.[7]

I. Forest Brown, a researcher at the Woods Hole Research Center who is working out of Rio Branco, Brazil (where I ended my bus trip), says that building roads has effects far wider than the few metres on each side of the road that a traveller sees from a bus or car.[8] The zone affected extends for kilometres on each side, which means that each road cut through a previously inaccessible region leaves behind a wide swath, since the main road often is the starting point for other roads cutting into forests. Each of them carries with it a zone of disturbance, if not destruction, along its length. Aerial photos show smaller roads shooting off from larger routes, each lined by a zone of deforestation so that the whole looks, ironically, like a child's drawing of a tall tree with regularly spaced branches. Each bare zone is much less humid than the forest, and since vegetation in tropical forests hasn't evolved to deal with that, the zones are particularly vulnerable to the effects of drought, whether as the result of local deforestation or planet-wide climate change.[9]

Needless to say, a trip on top of a tanker truck was not how I wanted to investigate what the new Estrada-Carretera highway had wrought. Thank goodness, it's possible now to take a luxury double-decker bus, complete with pretty stewardesses and box lunches, from Cusco to Puerto Maldonado any day of the week, and another bus, somewhat more modest but still comfortable, onward to Rio Branco twice a week.

One of the advantages of being of grandmotherly age is that it gives me license to talk to anyone without fear of being taken for a flirt or a busybody. I like to travel by myself, too, because that way I don't have to think about the wishes or whims of a companion. So, on the bus from Cusco I found myself sitting in the best seat on the bus's second level, directly over the driver.[10] The day was clear and the atmosphere on the bus festive. Across the aisle sat a couple who spoke Quechua to each other, he with weathered face and hands, aged perhaps fifty; she considerably younger, with a long black braid bouncing down her back, and wearing a flouncing, multi-layered skirt of the sort that Andean women have been wearing since the arrival of the Spanish. They held hands for much of the trip, munching throughout on a sack of coca leaves.

Next to me was nineteen-year-old Diego, leaving Cusco after a visit with his sisters, and headed for a boom town on the other side of the Andes. Yes, he spoke Quechua, too. One of the official languages in Peru today, Quechua had been used by the Incas as a unifying force in their empire, which included several conquered ethnic groups who spoke other languages. It is widely used still throughout the Andes. My seatmate had gone to school in Spanish, however, he said. How much education he had, I couldn't figure out: my Portuguese is much better than my Spanish so our conversation went by fits and starts as I churned up my memory to find the right words. He wanted to know what I was doing on the bus, however: obviously, he was as curious about me as I was about him. I could almost hear him think, "Lady, are you for real?" like the bus driver who questioned my mother about getting off at Biggs Junction.

Leaving Cusco, the ancient Inca capital, the bus headed down a wide valley. The highway is divided, like an expressway in richer parts of the world, but here squatters had taken up residence in the median, and traffic was light. Nor was the turnoff to the Estrada-Carretera what you'd expect as a link to such an iconic highway. We passed through a built-up area on an ordinary urban street until we'd climbed out of the valley and could look westward toward a range of green, somewhat rounded mountains. Traffic continued to be light: we passed a Coca-Cola truck going up and, heading downward, several trucks carrying milled lumber, as well as others transporting road construction equipment.

Obviously, you don't build a highway through the most rugged part of a mountain range. This road climbs steadily but the high, rugged snow-capped peaks rise in the distance. Small settlements dot the route: I saw herds of llamas grazing on nearby slopes, and in the middle of the afternoon, kids on their way home from school. Just before the second highest pass—4,125 metres (13,533 feet)—a flock of boys aged nine or ten whizzed along the road on bicycles. Near the highest pass—4,725 metres (15,502 feet), considerably higher than Mount Whitney, the highest peak in the lower forty-eight states—a small group of llamas made their way along the road underneath the single-strand electric wire that more or less followed the road, connecting isolated buildings to the world of electricity.

The relatively gradual rise through the rounded mountains of this region is not unique in the Andes. Charles Darwin—who, like Kerouac, went travelling as a young man and then wrote a famous book about it— encountered this when he took a break in his voyage around the world to travel the roads of western South America by mule. Passing over the cordillera from Chile into what is now Argentina, he commented on what he saw near the top:

> We reached a singular basin-like plain, called the Valle del Yeso. It was covered by a little dry pasture, and we had the pleasant sight of a herd of cattle amidst the surrounding rocky deserts. ... We set out early in the morning, and continued to follow the course of

The highest pass on the transcontinental highway, called Estrada do Pacífico in Brazil and Carretera Interoceánica in Peru, is 4,725 metres (15,502 feet), but the peaks of the Andes Cordillera are still higher.

Author Photo

the river, which had become very small, till we arrived at the foot of the ridge that separates the waters flowing into the Pacific and Atlantic Oceans. The road, which as yet had been good with a steady but very gradual ascent, now changed into a steep zigzag track up the great range.

But the view was glorious at the top and worth the struggle:

The atmosphere resplendently clear; the sky an intense blue; the profound valleys; the wild broken forms: the heaps of ruins, piled up during the lapse of ages; the bright-coloured rocks, contrasted with the quiet mountains of snow, all these together produced a scene no one could have imagined. Neither plant nor bird, excepting a few condors wheeling around the higher pinnacles, distracted my attention from the inanimate mass. I felt glad that I was alone: it was like watching a thunderstorm, or hearing in full orchestra a chorus of the *Messiah*.[11]

Yes, indeed, I thought when I read this description: Darwin nailed it. But I wasn't alone when the bus reached the top of the continental divide, and my travel companions did not seem to be as enthralled by the scenery as I was. The stewardess had put a movie on by then, and although it was hard to see in the bright afternoon light, the televisions mounted in the ceiling got more attention than what was happening outside. And, curiously, the bus company conspired to keep us from paying much attention, once we started down the eastern slope.

Darwin noted that the Andes rise more abruptly from the plains of Argentina to the east than from the foothills of Chile to the west. The same profile is found in California, where the Sierra Nevada Mountains slope relatively gradually from the state's central valleys—the ones we travelled that summer—and then plunge abruptly from the crest line so that the eastern side of Mount Whitney is like a sheer wall. The precipitous profile is caused by the way the forces of the earth have forced up the blocks of volcanic rocks that form the foundations of the mountains. The descent is equally abrupt where the Estrada-Carretera crosses the Andes, even though the summit is not as craggy as the one Darwin described, nor as barren as the passes over which California's Amerindians transported obsidian from one side of the Sierra Nevada to the other.

I didn't see tilted sedimentary rocks like those that amazed me when we travelled north in California, but Darwin, crossing the ridge of the Andes somewhat farther south than my bus ride, saw some particularly remarkable ones. The Portillo line of peaks, the highest in that part of the cordillera, includes:

> beds of a conglomerate several thousand feet in thickness, which have been upheaved by the red granite, and dip at an angle of 45°. ... I was astonished to find that this conglomerate was partly composed of pebbles, derived from the rocks, with their fossil shells, of [another] range; and partly of red potash-granite, like that of the Portillo. In most parts, perhaps in all parts, of the Cordillera ... each line has been formed by repeated upheavals and injections; and that the several parallel lines are of different ages. Only thus can we gain time at all sufficient to explain [what] these great ... mountains have suffered.[12]

Time—another, completely different kind of time from what we live in now.

Darwin's side trip into the Andes took him and his party a month. Today, bus riders can leave Cusco near noon and travel through the mountains during daylight, or leave in the evening and miss the scenery. If you're travelling frequently, the latter might be your choice, but for me, there was no question which I'd rather do. When I saw what the descent into the Amazon basin was like, I decided that travel by day was wise from a safety point of view, too. The road is good, new and well-maintained, but driving the hairpin curves at night must challenge the best driver. The bus company seems to think it's wise to keep the passengers' minds off the danger, because as soon as we'd started down, the stewardess flipped off the movies and began passing out Bingo cards.

"No, gracias," I said, when she handed one to me. The young man next to me took a card, but drifted deeper into the music he was listening to through his earbuds. The Quechua couple played: it appeared to be the first time the man had seen the game, and the stewardess had to explain the rules.

As I said, the countryside we passed through had been mostly green. The four days of rain that had preceded my journey may have accounted for the freshness of the colour, but on the east side the abundance of rain also caused several mini-floods where more runoff bounded down the slopes than stream beds could channel. Twice we passed signs pointing out a *camino viejo*, "old road," that was even more serpentine. Then, near the town of Marcapata (from the Quechua words *pata* meaning "above" or "terraces," and *marca* meaning "homeland,") signs announcing archeological sites began showing up. Stair-like footpaths made of stone crossed terraces still being worked by women in the Andes' signature circle skirts, with long black braids, and wielding mattocks. Trails like these have run for centuries from the Amazon basin to the other side of the Andes' crest. One, the Caminho do Peabiru, was used by the Portuguese explorer Aleixo Garcia to reach the Inca Empire in 1524–25, making him and his companions the first Europeans to see the splendor of the Incas: Francisco Pizarro, the conqueror of Peru, didn't arrive until three years later, coming from the north.

As we descended farther, the green became more vibrant until the slopes glowed in the afternoon light. A river rushed not far away, headed in the same direction we were.

I couldn't take my eyes off the highway. Sitting as I was, directly above the driver, I watched his strategy for ruling the road. Ordinarily, traffic coming uphill has the right-of-way, but the bus driver apparently believed that "might makes right," that is, any smaller vehicle should get out of the way of the big bus. At moments, he ran us halfway down the oncoming lane, as if playing chicken with other drivers. They'd move over until they were hugging the road's shoulder on their side, skimming either a cliff rising abruptly or a drop-off that opened to the valley floor. Then the bus would roar past, the ruling road warrior.

Not that there was much traffic for a road that was supposed to open up trade from one ocean to another. When we stopped for supper in a village at the bottom of the valley which cut like a knife through the mountains, I counted only three cars going in the opposite direction.

Dogs lazed in the middle of the road in the sun, getting up and moseying out of the way only when they heard approaching vehicles.

Until this point, the negative effects of the new highway seemed minimal. Yes, it probably was easier for outside influences to impinge on traditional ways of life, but the altitude, and lack of trees and valuable minerals to extract—so far at least—have meant that there hasn't been a "resources rush." Aerial photographs and satellite maps to date show little deforestation of the steep valleys on the east side. Indeed, the Marcapata Valley has become celebrated for its birdlife, and the success of eco-tourism may help protect it.

Farther down the highway, the story was very different. In the mountains, the water in streams and rivers was clear, but as we approached the eastern flatlands, water courses became choked with red silt. Gold-mining operations and logging, both legal and contraband, had ripped open the forest so that erosion sullied great stretches of formerly lush Amazonia. To some extent, the Estrada-Carretera is not responsible for this despoiling of the land, because it began long before the transoceanic route was opened. Getting over the Andes, remember, had been difficult

Bus stop on the Estrada-Carretera, 2013: The highway drops down into the Amazon basin on the east side, where luxury buses stop in a sleepy village. Opponents argue that new roads open up the territory with disastrous consequences for the environment and people. *Author Photo*

but not impossible. And in flatter territory, the rivers' potential use as highways for transport gained importance. Timber could be sent down streams to the Madre de Dios River, from which valuable mahogany logs could find their way to market.

But with the new road, all this has intensified. As evening fell, the highway ran straight as a die through landscapes I could only guess at. Stops at settlements became more frequent. At one settlement about two hours from my destination, Puerto Maldonado, the Quechua-speaking couple gathered their things and climbed off. From the luggage compartment under the bus, they recuperated a huge mound of vegetation—coca leaves, perhaps—bound up in what looked like a blanket or a shawl.

At the largest settlement before we reached our stopping point, my seat companion got off, carrying only his jacket, two loaves of bread he'd bought at an earlier stop, and a small pack. I watched him walk briskly, confidently down the road, past bars where men and a few women sat outside drinking in the hot evening. Smoke from the grills of a dozen tiny restaurants clouded the air. A skinny girl no more than thirteen or fourteen stood next to the road, wearing shorts, a halter top, and high heels, stopping men as they passed. I thought of Nighttown where another young man, Stephen Dedalus, went adventuring, seventy-five years after Darwin and fifty years before Jack Kerouac:

> Skeleton tracks, red and green will-o'-the-wisps and danger signals. Rows of flimsy houses with gaping doors.... Snakes of river fog creep slowly. From drains, clefts, cesspools, middens arise on all sides stagnant fumes. A glow leaps in the south beyond the seaward reaches of the river. ... The call: Wait, my love, and I'll be with you.[13]

The settlement seemed to have no name, although hundreds of people were out that evening, eating, drinking, looking for pleasure or trouble. Like many other settlements that lined this stretch of the Estrada-Carretera, it was a *pueblo de plástico*, made up of flimsy plastic structures. Not a good place for old lady gringos like me, so I wasn't tempted to get out for a short look around. Even Monte Reel, a *New York*

Times reporter at least thirty years younger than I, was chased out when he tried to investigate a pueblo as he travelled the Estrada-Carretera shortly before I did.[14]

Critics of the transcontinental highway project had argued that it would bring more drugs, prostitution, and environmental destruction to the people who lived along it, and it looks like they were right. Although I couldn't see them in the darkness, the roads shooting off into the countryside along this stretch of highway lead to illicit gold mining in streams and logging on dry land. The wasted landscape is plainly visible from Google satellite maps, and I thought of that time long ago when gold and decorative woods were among the few things prized enough to be transported long distances on early roads.

This destruction comes as no surprise to anyone who has looked at the impact of earlier projects in Brazil. Remember that when Brasília was built, highways also had to be built both to connect the new capital to the rest of the country and to bring in people and supplies to build it. The 2,000 kilometre (1,243 mile) highway from Belém to Brasília turned into "a spider web of secondary roads and a 400-kilometre-wide swath of forest destruction across the eastern Brazilian Amazon," says forestry expert William Laurance.[15] About 95 per cent of all deforestation occurs within 50 kilometres (about 30 miles) of roads, he adds. And, says physicist Enea Salati of the Brazilian Sustainable Development Foundation, only half in jest: "The best thing you could do for the Amazon is to bomb all the roads."

That's not going to happen, of course. But the lack of maintenance on the Brazilian side of the Estrada-Carretera highway appears to be contributing to the slower-than-hoped-for increase in goods transported on the road, which may translate into a temporary slowing of the new highway's effects.

I took the bus headed to Brazil from Puerto Maldonado about noon the day after my bus trip from Cusco. Before I left, I had a chance to wander around a bit, and was favourably impressed by what I saw. The town was buzzing with activity, much of it aimed at serving tourists who want to see the wonders of the Amazon basin. Transportation is mainly by motorbikes, which burn much less fuel than cars and buses: gasoline and diesel fuel must still be trucked in across the Andes, although gas prices seemed to be about the same there as in Cusco. Taxis are three-wheeled motorbikes with a passenger compartment attached, similar to those I've seen elsewhere, particularly in India. Official motorcycle cabbies wearing helmets and numbered yellow vests pick up one passenger at a time. There are lovely plantings of tropical flowers in public spaces, walls where short bits of poetry are painted, and a promenade along the river near a handsome suspension bridge which was the last link in the Interoceanic Highway to be completed.

On the other side of the river, however, the view deteriorated. Obviously, the original forest had been cut years before, and while the road was relatively new, sheets of mud from runoff covered it in many places. Things got worse as we approached and then crossed the border into Brazil. In the 1970s and 1980s, the Brazilian government encouraged settlement and road building in the western borderlands, partly to provide a buffer with Peru, which was then being besieged by the Shining Path guerillas, and partly to put dibs on the mineral and timber wealth in the region. About the same time, a major paved interstate highway, BR-364, was built from the centre of Brazil northwestward to another point on the border between Peru and Brazil, in the state of Acre. It opened the door to much deforestation and exploitation of the Amazon region, although protests by locals in the state of Acre appear to have limited the despoiling to some extent.

Rio Branco, Acre's capital, was where my bus was headed. The journey was about as long as the one between Cusco and Puerto Maldonado, and if you timed your buses right you could make the entire journey from the Inca capital to Rio Branco in a little under twenty-four hours. That's just what a quartet of women in their late thirties or early forties had done. The day before—a Monday—had been a holiday in Brazil, and they'd combined a couple of vacation days from their government office jobs with the long weekend so they could visit Machu Picchu, the sacred city of the Incas not far from Cusco. Three of them were clearly tired after much sightseeing and travel stuffed into a few days, but the fourth was running on overdrive. As she climbed aboard, she checked out the other passengers and homed in on a trio of young men who had settled down in the first two rows on the right side.

Now, the year after *On the Road* was published, Ritchie Valens, a Mexican-American kid the same age as Kerouac's girlfriend Bea, recorded a Mexican folk song that became an enormous hit all over North America. His version of "La Bamba" swept the charts in 1958, at a point in my life when I listened to hit tunes on the radio as much as I could. The song was far more part of my youth than Kerouac ever was, and at one time I could sing all the words. So, when the lady on her way back from an excellent Peruvian adventure began singing the chorus, I immediately snapped to attention. It took a few moments for me to figure out why she was singing: her explanation, in rapid-fire Portuguese, leapt past me before I could catch it. But then I saw she was serenading a handsome, mahogany-skinned guy with a huge Rastafarian hairdo and wearing sweats in South African colours. He was called, it seems, Bomba (not "Bamba" as both the Brazilian lady and I first thought), and was a *capoeira* ace from Ecuador on his way to do a show in Rio Branco. The two other guys, skinny little Falcão (or Falcon) and his stockier friend who seemed too shy to give his name, were also *capoeristas*. They were somewhat embarrassed by Bomba, but he was older and apparently a far better master than they of the Brazilian martial art, so they let him charm the ladies. Including me.

Bomba said he was originally from Senegal, and in part to test him I started speaking French. No problem: he was fluent with an accent that suggested very good schools in France. His English also was terrific, and so, it seems, was his Spanish: obviously he was not a poor boy, just as Kerouac, who at one point studied on a scholarship at Columbia University, was not a guy unacquainted with highbrow culture. Bomba was travelling on an Ecuadorian passport, which he got, he said, because he was such a good athlete and Ecuador wanted him to compete for that country.

At first, there was much chit-chat on the bus, with people going up and down the aisle gossiping. I tried to listen in, but really I wanted to look out the window. It was raining and the low places along the sides of the road were all filled with red, silty water. A few cows stood on a hillock surveying what was left of the forest, mute evidence to the fact that 62 per cent of all deforested land in Brazil is used for cattle pasture.[16] At a couple of places, road crews were rebuilding approaches to bridges that apparently had been washed out during floods. The speed limit was 50 kilometres (about 30 miles) an hour, but even though there were no police patrols, the driver kept within the speed limit. Travelling faster and hitting one of the big holes in the pavement could mean a broken suspension.

The young male steward handed out a small box with snacks, and played two movies that were hard to see in the afternoon light. The three *capoeiristas* watched or listened to headphones. But I kept watching the landscape out the window.

From just looking at this sadly used land, there was no way of knowing what kind of trees had once grown on it. The state of Acre is famous—or infamous—for its rubber production from *Hevea brasiliensis*, the rubber tree native to Brazil. During the rubber boom at the beginning of the twentieth century, latex (the raw material for making the many rubber products we use now) was collected from the trees. Workers (*seringueiros*) cut grooves in the trees so the sticky sap ran out into containers, in a process similar to the way maple sap is collected in Canada, the country where I live now. The difference was that, in the lust for getting the most from every rubber tree, the grooves encircled the trees so that after one tapping they died.

During this period, the only way to get the latex out of the Amazon forest was by water, so it was sent by boat down the Madre de Dios River to the mighty Amazon, and thence to the wider world. But rubber tree seeds from the Amazon region had been spirited out of Brazil in the late nineteenth century to Britain, where seedlings were started at the Royal Botanic Gardens at Kew. In a successful attempt to break Brazil's monopoly on rubber production, the British encouraged cultivation of rubber trees throughout the tropical regions of the British Empire.[17] By 1920, so much rubber was coming from these upstart plantations that the bottom fell out of the rubber market. The effects were devastating on the people who had done the rubber tapping in Amazonia.

During World War II, the demand for latex from Brazil picked up somewhat. More was needed for the war effort, at a time when the Asian plantations were under Japanese control. This led to another push into Amazonia. The environmental consequences were less severe than those of the first boom, since the tapping technique had changed to one rather like that used on maple trees, which can produce sap year after year. But new territory was open to production, and the conditions the rubber tappers worked and lived in were extremely harsh. The building of BR-364 accelerated the movement of rubber companies into previously untouched lands, at a time when competition was growing from natural rubber harvested elsewhere and from recently-developed synthetic rubber. The result was deteriorating conditions, and the birth of a home-grown protest movement.

Stop here for a moment to consider a bit of irony: new roads mean greater demand for tires. If it weren't for the need for millions of tires to roll on the world's highways, the demand for rubber would be far less. So, viewed from the perspective of a rubber worker the spiral of demand and destruction grew worse and worse.

The history of rubber production is filled with horrors, including the tactics of King Leopold II of Belgium, who ruled the Congo at the turn of the twentieth century as his own private empire. Perhaps half the population perished, as he forced workers to gather latex from vines not nearly as productive as Brazilian rubber trees. They worked under threat of having hands and feet cut off: this was the real backdrop for Joseph Conrad's *Heart of Darkness*, which we talked about earlier when we discussed the importance of rivers.[18]

In Brazil, the mortality rate was less than in the Congo, but in the 1970s and early 1980s the game changed again, as land owners began throwing rubber tappers out of the Amazon forest in order to exploit it more intensely. Small farmers and ranchers were also encroaching on the forest, wanting to turn it over to crops like soybeans or to raising cattle. Tellingly, one of the main exports the Estrada-Carretera is expected to carry is soybeans to Pacific ports for shipment to Asia.

The effect of cutting down trees has worked its way through the environment. Their foliage previously slowed down rain—even dense downpours—so that the precipitation could be more readily absorbed by the soil. The brown, silty water of the Rio Acre running through Rio Branco (which was named after a nineteenth century Brazilian politician and statesman, and not as a comment on the quality of the water) shows just what can happen. So, too, were the floods that stopped traffic completely for days, a few months after I travelled the road from Peru. Heavy rains were more than the ecosystem could handle.

The protest movement against this became one of the rare success stories in the history of the twentieth century's environmental conflicts. Chico Mendes, a man from a small settlement in the state of Acre who began his career as a child rubber tapper, organized the tappers and their families. They successfully advocated creating "extractive reserves." In these more or less protected forest areas, locals could live off the proceeds from collecting wild Brazil nuts and the tropical fruit *açaí* that has become something of a health food craze.[19] Also, latex collected in the reserves is used by a condom factory, whose production is bought by the Brazilian government for distribution in public health programs.[20]

Becoming increasingly savvy when it came to local and international politics and marketing, Mendes's friends won power in the Acre elections in 1999. Since then, they have been able to slow the destruction of the forest somewhat. (It helped that Brazil was about to undergo a major political change when Lula (Luiz Inácio Lula da Silva,) the Partido dos Trabalhadores (Workers' Party) candidate, became president of Brazil in 2003.)

But twenty-five years before my sojourn in the state of Acre, Mendes was murdered on the order of two owners of rubber tree stands. He has become a symbol of forces that hope to turn the tide on destruction.[21] "At first I thought I was fighting to save the rubber trees; then I thought I was fighting to save the Amazon

"At first I thought I was fighting to save the rubber trees; then I thought I was fighting to save the Amazon rainforest. Now I realize I am fighting for humanity," said Chico Mendes, legendary environmental activist who was murdered in 1988.

Photo: Miranda Smith / Creative Commons Attribution-Sharealike 3.0 Unported License

rainforest. Now I realize I am fighting for humanity," Mendes is frequently quoted as saying.[22]

That's not overstating the case: grassroots protest movements can change the world, Naomi Klein insists in *This Changes Everything*, her well-documented but very long book about climate change and the bankruptcy of capitalism. While Klein never mentions Mendes in her book, throughout it she argues that real change has to come from the bottom, not the top. Decent wages and working conditions are needed to give people the time to fight the good fight, she adds. That's exactly the model that Mendes developed in the backwoods of Amazonia four decades ago.

I didn't ask anyone on the bus from Puerto Maldonado to Rio Branco what they thought of Mendes or the effects of the Estrada-Carretera. The travelling ladies obviously were pleased that it opened up adventures to them, and so perhaps were the others, but as the trip went on, they became less talkative. Two of the *capoeiristas*, Falcão and his sidekick, tried to pick up a radio signal as we bumped along some of the badly worn roads just inside Brazil. They weren't successful, and the absence of cellphone chatter among the other passengers indicated that this area was beyond good transmission, too.

Sometime after sunset, we stopped at Brasiléia, a town not far from the border with Peru, and not far from Bolivia either. Everyone piled into a *lanchonete* for supper, a pay-per-kilo cafeteria with a wide range of relatively inexpensive dishes. The food in these places is generally good, and the temptation is great to eat too much, particularly when you've been cooped up most of the day. But I noticed that two of the *capoeiristas* didn't buy anything but soft drinks, although Bomba held court with the ladies, putting away a massive plate of barbecue with several sides. Perhaps this was the difference between a *capoeira* ace who was making reasonable money from the martial art that mixes force with music, and the young guys just starting out on the circuit? Maybe, but I also was reminded of another meaning of *capoeira*.

Many of the moves and traditions of *capoeira* are vestiges of the culture that slaves from the West Coast of Africa brought with them when they were forcibly transported to Brazil. Their masters were wary of the practice, and more than once, the martial art was outlawed. But the slaves persisted, slipping clandestinely from place to place through paths earlier cut or burned through the forest by Amerindians. The second-growth grass and bushes that grew up along these passages were called *capoeira*, from the Tupi words *ka'a* or "underbrush" and *uera* or "formerly used land."[23] The scraggly vegetation of the countryside we were passing through certainly fell into that category. The short stature of the two young *capoeiristas* made them living representations of the struggle necessary to survive, even thrive, in a world that has been changed drastically by the passage of humans.

The destruction of forests opened up by roads is not unique to Amazonia. What I saw on this stretch of the Estrada-Carretera didn't look much different from the logged-over sections of Ontario or Quebec in summer: scruffy grass and other low plants, plus a few, widely spaced trees. Long before, the Mata Atlântica, the temperate rain forest to the east in which Curitiba is situated, practically disappeared. Elsewhere in the world, forests are being cut down wantonly. A recent African study based on satellite images shows more than 50,000 kilometres (about 30,000 miles) of logging roads in the Congo basin which have been pushed into the forest since the 1970s.[24] In Russia, cutting of the boreal forest continues.[25]

Deforestation damages more than the forest itself. The year after I took my bus trip, São Paulo, Brazil's biggest city, suffered the worst water crisis in its history.[26] It was directly related to the cutting down of the Atlantic rainforest, the Mata Atlântica, that once surrounded the city. The cycle of absorption of water by the forest, its slow release back into the atmosphere and its return as rain had been severely disrupted.

The prospect of more crises like this can summon up nightmarish visions, like those found in Cormac McCarthy's tenth novel, *The Road*. The novel tells the story of a father and young son roaming America after some sort of apocalypse. Nothing grows, the air is full of toxic chemicals. The pair keeps going south, travelling on decaying roads, escaping from one horror only to come up against another.

As mournful as Kerouac's *On the Road* is exuberant, *The Road* reflects a great change in the general outlook which developed in the fifty years between the two books. Say what you will about *On the Road*—and after reading it a couple of times, I've come to think it's both sexist and self-indulgent—the narrator assumes that things will get better, not worse. Having lived through a childhood clouded by the Great Depression and an early youth overshadowed by World War II, Kerouac and his friends wanted to burst the bounds, to crash through to joy. McCarthy, on the other hand, writes a story devoid of hope, where all the terrible things that humans have wrought have now settled down over humanity like a killing fog.

There have been times working on this book (reading, travelling, and talking to people about what roads have meant and done to us) when I've been extremely discouraged about where the roads we've built have taken us. The election of Donald Trump as president of the United States and the impeachment of progressive Brazilian president Dilma Rousseff two months earlier do not augur well. Our dependence on fossil fuels, our disregard for the landscape, our seeming inability to stop long enough in our headlong rush in order to make the adjustments necessary to rescue the climate: all these have made me pessimistic. There is, however, a seed of hope not found in McCarthy's book that was apparent outside the window of the bus I rode in South America: what Dylan Thomas called the "force that through the green fuse drives the flower."[27]

Life. Leaves. The *capoeira*, in its many forms.

The naturally occurring landscapes that are most like what McCarthy describes are those that follow a volcanic eruption. Consider the biggest one that living North Americans know about first-hand: the explosion of Mount St. Helens in 1980. Photographs taken shortly after the ash settled and the rumbles quieted show complete desolation. All living matter has been removed down to the underlying rock: the trees kilometres away from the crater are nothing but blasted snags, the animals have disappeared, there appears to be nothing growing. But fast forward a couple of years, and the landscape changes. Fireweed blooms in mid-summer; willows have begun to grow around pools of rainwater; animals, big and small, return to try their luck in a new environment.

Early Amerindians returned to the valleys and hills near Mount Mazama in Oregon: the artifacts they left behind are eloquent witnesses. Not even the incredible Mount Toba explosion in our distant past stopped our ancestors from being fruitful and multiplying. Humans came very close to being wiped out on the shores of the Red Sea, and it's clear that only a relatively small number successfully made the crossing from Asia to North America. A few survived, and travelled on. Not without wreaking havoc, not without terrible losses, not without changing the landscape along the roads they travelled. But there is consolation, even at this point when we seem to be so close to collective destruction of the world as we know it: some things still might be done to avert the worst.

For example, take the matter of what we've done to forests. First, experts say, we should stop deforestation. To do that, governments all over the world will have to control road building into forested areas. William Laurance says that, among the "many human drivers of environmental change, [it] is one of the most readily amenable to policy modification. In practical terms, it is far easier to cancel or relocate a road project than it is to, say, reduce human overpopulation or halt harmful climate change."[28]

Then we should replant forests, both urban and rural. But the new forests should not be simple one-species, tree-planting projects of the sort that have become the rite of passage for Canadian young people in the last thirty years. Nor should forests be changed into tree farms: in 2015, Indonesia was aflame with fires that were set to clear forests, so the land could be replanted in oil palms.[29] These fires, on some days, produced as much greenhouse gas as the entire United States.

The effects of reforestation could be extremely positive in sequestering greenhouse gases and possibly reversing climate change. Researchers at the Max Planck Institute for Meteorology have found that a considerable amount of carbon dioxide, the greenhouse gas believed to be most responsible for climate change, was removed from the atmosphere when forests came back following the decimation of the Amerindian population and after the end of the Mongol Empire, with its demand for pasture lands.[30] Principal researcher Julia Pongratz says that, because about a quarter of the earth's land surface is used by people in some way, "we are now in a position to make land-use decisions that will diminish our impact on climate and the carbon cycle. We cannot ignore the knowledge we have gained."[31]

Reforestation will not be easy, in part because imported pests and climate change that has already occurred have cut down options when it comes to choosing what species to use to rebuild forests. A case in point are the ash trees on my street that were chopped down in the summer of 2015 in an attempt to stop the ravages of the emerald ash borer, an insect from Asia that was first detected in North America in 2002. Ironically, many of the ash trees had been planted forty years ago to replace those killed by Dutch elm disease, another imported malady. Because millions of trees will have to be planted just to make up for the ones lost, increasing urban forests is going to be very difficult.

Then, there is the problem of replacing forests lost to fire. The summer of 2015 also saw enormous fires across the North American West, after four years of drought that was aggravated, if not caused, by the forces unleashed through runaway greenhouse gas emissions. Those forests may never regrow as they once were because the pine cones and seeds, which ordinarily would give birth to new trees, were burned in the exceptionally hot fires.[32]

Yet, forests can and do return, although the species in second growth are frequently not the most desired. Evidence of this is the tree-lined rivers that the second wave of Europeans saw in the seventeenth century when they arrived after the native population had been decimated by disease brought by the first European explorers. So is the curious discovery of a mysterious people who once lived in the Amazon basin. In a region west of Rio Branco where much of the forest cover has been removed, a series of low, earthen work structures have been recently discerned, bearing witness to an unknown Amerindian culture that had disappeared from view when the forest grew back.[33]

However, reforestation on a global scale alone would not be enough to stop climate change completely. Major changes to the way we live in cities, in both the developed and developing world, would be necessary too. Dependence on the private automobile and on coal-fired electricity plants are just two of the major challenges. How to meet them is far from clear. More cities like Curitiba would certainly help, but even the advent of the so-called paperless age has not cut the demand for forest products. Industry projections expect that demand will increase at a rate of 2.4 per cent a year until at least 2020—not for printing papers, but for packing.[34]

So, it's more likely than not that global warming will continue. The ice caps will continue to melt—the ice on Comox Glacier in British Columbia, mentioned before, will be gone in twenty-five years, scientists predict. Mount Shasta, that beautiful mountain at the end of the Great Valley of California that I saw so long ago, was nearly bare of snow in 2015, after years of drought. In the future, rising sea levels will submerge the lowlands of Southern California, and the cliffs I scrambled on when I was a child, where my mother showed me those layers of sedimentary rock, will be washed away.[35] Much of the Amazon basin will be flooded, too. Sea waters will enter the St. Lawrence valley so that Mount Royal, on whose slopes I live now, becomes an island once again in a great salt sea. Ironically, it is possible that much of the web of roads built in the last fifty years will be as transitory as a message written on wet sand at low tide, becoming routes that only exploring divers of the future will see.

Who will be around to witness this is anyone's guess.

AFTER DARK, THE BUS ATTENDANT PUT ON *THE WOLVERINE*, AN action film that the *capoeiristas* had been asking for ever since he mentioned it at our supper stop. It had been recently released, so it was not one they'd be likely to see otherwise on their limited budgets. The fact that they'd heard about it says a lot about the way the world is interconnected today, in a way that transcends the physical roads we travel.

The beginning of the film spooked me. In a prequel which appears not to have been part of the North American version, a little boy's fingers sprout sword-like claws during a family drama someplace in North America. He grows up to take part in a series of conflicts from the mid-nineteenth century to the present. Since the film was dubbed in Spanish, it took me a quarter of an hour to realize that we were deep within the world of Wolverine, an immortal superhero. Also known as Logan, he considers the fact that he can suffer but cannot die a curse, and has retreated into snow-clad mountains in the Yukon. But he is called into service by a Japanese industrialist whom he once saved. Acrobatic chases and spectacular special effects follow.

The thrills were good for keeping my mind off the erratic oncoming traffic, but the interesting question that the film poses about where humans fit into eternity only occurred to me later. The Wolverine should have died a hundred years ago, but he fights on, hesitant to love because if he had a wife, children, and friends, they would all die but he won't. By the end of the film, he's ready to continue combating evil, and in so doing he seems to find a measure of grace that will allow him to go on, if not grow older. The Wolverine will live to see the seas rise, the temperature soar, civilization as we know it struggle and possibly fall. That is indeed a curse, particularly if there is nothing even a superhero can do about it.

What did the two *capoeiristas* think? A half-hour into the film, they'd already fallen asleep. Bomba was snoring gently too.

What's next on the road through time is hard to discern. Even harder to see is what must be done to avoid the effects of mankind's road building.
Author Photo

So it was I who sat up in the night watching the far-fetched tale, won-dering what Chico Mendes, that all-too-mortal hero, would think. Perhaps that it was a shame people can only find peace in a fantasy world? Or that rest is not for the wicked, and that there is much for all of us to do?

The people who can't sleep—the old people who wake up early and the careless young who stay up late—are the most expendable to the village. When danger threatens, they were—and maybe are— an early warning system for the group. I guess that's what I was doing on that bus trip, keeping a grandmotherly vigil in the night as we sped along that road, and now, later, bearing witness to what was and what might be.

NOTES

Chapter One. On the Road, 1

1 No one alive but me remembers this trip, so I've had no way to cross-check exactly what happened. The trajectory, road conditions, and possible means of transport have been verified, and all the accompanying information was carefully researched.

2 Currently, there are four methods for dating based on changes in atoms. Radiocarbon dating uses the rate of decay of carbon-14, an unstable isotope of carbon, into carbon-12, the stable one. It is accurate up to about 50,000 years ago. Potassium-argon measures the rate of decay of potassium-40 into argon-40 in rocks that have passed through a volcanic explosion, and has been used to date rocks up to four billion years old. A more recent method tracks the change from argon-40 to argon-39 in matter as small as a grain of sand, and can provide far more precise dating in recent rock. The decay of different isotopes of uranium is particularly useful in dating stalagmites in caves and coral in ancient seas: it's good for dates of up to 490,000 years ago. Objects like grains of sand and tooth enamel can be dated through changes in their crystal structure caused by the ambient radiation in the medium in which they are buried. Depending on the method, dates as old as two million years can be determined.

3 Diana Marcum, "Bea Kozera dies at 92; 'On the Road' character was based on her," *Los Angeles Times*, August 24, 2013, http://www.latimes.com/local/obituaries/la-me-beatrice-kozera-20130825-story.html.

4   Gerald Nicosia, author of *Memory Babe: A Critical Biography of Jack Kerouac*, was quoted by Diana Marcum in her article for the *Los Angeles Times* above.

5   Jack Kerouac, *On the Road: The Original Scroll*, ed. Howard Cunnell (New York: Penguin Books, 2007), 183.

Chapter Two. Bottleneck on the Road from Eden

1   Jennifer L. Thompson and Andrew J. Nelson, "Middle Childhood and Modern Human Origins," *Human Nature* 22 (2011): 249–80, doi: 10.1007/s12110-011-9119-3. Note, too, that I was just this age when I took the bus trip that opened my eyes to the world. Huck Finn was twelve when his adventures began, you may also recall.

2   Turtles and other slow-moving prey show up with great frequency in the sites where anatomically modern humans lived. It is only later that birds, which were harder to catch because they move more quickly, could be caught. See Mary C. Stiner, Natalie D. Munro, and Todd A. Surovell, "The Tortoise and the Hare: Small-Game Use, the Broad-Spectrum Revolution, and Paleolithic Demography," *Current Anthropology* 41, no. 1 (February 2000): 39–73.

3   Imagining what life was like so long ago has a respectable tradition. The acclaimed paleontologist Richard Leakey in his book *Origins Reconsidered: In Search of What Makes Us Human*—written with Roger Lewin (New York: Anchor Books, 1993)—begins with a gripping description of how a boy, about the age of our friends but a *Homo erectus* rather than *Homo sapiens*, found his death while hunting with his group on the shores of a lake in East Africa. Leakey's scientific credentials are impeccable, whereas I'm only a quintessential intelligent layperson; but when I came across his description, well after I'd written the first draft of this account, I felt justified.

4   Jared Diamond and James A. Robinson, eds., *Natural Experiments of History* (Cambridge, MA: Harvard University Press, 2010), 22. In surveying, taking sightlines from at least three points whose coordinates are known allows precise fixing of a point in the landscape.

5   Michael Hopkin, "Ethiopia is top choice for cradle of *Homo sapiens*: Radioactive dating finds that fossil skulls are 195,000 years old," *Nature*, February 16, 2005, doi: 10.1038/news050214-10.

6   See my book *Green City: People, Nature and Urban Places* (Montreal: Véhicule Press, 2006) for a discussion of what our predilection for savannah landscape has produced.

7   J. H. Heerwagen and G. H. Orians, "Humans, Habitats and Aesthetics," in *The Biophilia Hypothesis*, eds. S. R. Kellert and E. O. Wilson, 138–172 (Washington, DC: Island Press, 1995).

8   Kenneth Miller, "Archaeologists Find Earliest Evidence of Humans Cooking
    With Fire," *Discover Magazine,* May 9, 2013, http://discovermagazine.
    com/2013/may/ 09-archaeologists-find-earliest-evidence- of-humans-
    cooking-with-fire.

9   Geoff Bailey, "The Red Sea, Coastal Landscapes, and Hominin Dispersals," in
    *The Evolution of Human Populations in Arabia: Paleoenvironments, Prehistory
    and Genetics,* eds. Michael D. Petraglia and Jeffrey I. Rose, 15–37 (Dordrecht,
    Netherlands: Springer, 2009).

10 Wu Liu et al., "The earliest unequivocally modern humans in southern
    China," *Nature,* October 14, 2015, doi: 10.1038/nature15696.

11 Carl Zimmer, "A Single Migration from Africa Populated the World,
    Studies Find," *New York Times,* September 21, 2016, http://www.nytimes.
    com/2016/09/22/science/ancient-dna-human-history.html?r=0.

12 Nicholas Wade, "Why Humans and Their Fur Parted Ways," *New York Times,*
    August 19, 2003, http://www.nytimes.com/2003/08/19/science/why-
    humans-and-their-fur-parted-ways.html?pagewanted=all&src=pm.

13 Kathleen McAuliffe, "Human evolution kicks into high gear," NBC
    News, February 10, 2009, http://www.nbcnews.com/id/29123062/ns/
    technology_and_science-science/t/human-evolution-kicks-high-gear/#.
    UDJFH4WKBNQ.

14 Heng Li and Richard Durbin, "Inference of human population history from
    individual whole-genome sequences," *Nature* 475 (July 28, 2011): 493–6,
    doi: 10.1038/nature10231.

15 Lyn Wadley et al., "Middle Stone Age Bedding Construction and Settlement
    Patterns at Sibudu, South Africa," *Science* 334, no. 6061 (December 9, 2011):
    1388-91, doi: 10.1126/science.1213317.

16 Danielle Torrent, "UF study of lice DNA shows humans first wore clothes
    170,000 years ago," *News: University of Florida,* January 6, 2011, http://news.
    ufl.edu/archive/2011/01/uf-study-of-lice-dna-shows-humans-first-wore-
    clothes-170000-years-ago.php.

17 Timothy Taylor, *The Artificial Ape: How Technology Changed the Course of
    Human Evolution* (London: Palgrave Macmillan Trade, 2010).

18 Brendan Borrell, "From The Trenches: Bon Voyage, Caveman," *Archaeology:
    A Publication of the Archaeological Institute of America* 63, no. 3 (May/June
    2010), http://archive.archaeology.org/1005/trenches/voyage.html.

19 Author's interview with Michael Bisson, June 26, 2013.

20 For a detailed description of what the landscape looked like, see Michael
    D. Petraglia and Jeffrey I. Rose, eds., *The Evolution of Human Populations in
    Arabia: Paleoenvironments, Prehistory and Genetics* (Dordrecht, Netherlands:
    Springer, 2009).

21 Archeological evidence on display at the Australian Museum helps to date the earliest occupation of Australia. "The Malakunanja II rock shelter in Arnhem Land has been dated to around 55,000 years old and is currently gaining support as Australia's oldest site" (Fran Dorey, "The spread of people to Australia," *Australia Museum*, October 30, 2015, http://australianmuseum. net.au/The-spread-of-people-to-Australia/#sthash.7Rxcs8sQ.dpuf.)

22 James Devitt, "Finding Showing Human Ancestor Older than Previously Thought Offers New Insights into Evolution," *New York University*, http:// www.nyu.edu/about/news-publications/news/2011/06/29/finding-showing-human-ancestor-older-than-previously-thought-offers-new-insights-into-evolution.html.

23 Nicholas Wade, "Phonetic Clues Hint Language Is Africa-Born," *New York Times*, April 14, 2011, http://www.nytimes.com/2011/04/15/science/15language.html.

24 This video of the Red Sea was taken from space by the crew of Expedition 29, on board the International Space Station. The flight goes from north to south. The clouds at the end obscure the opening of the sea at Bab al-Mandab, called the Gate of Grief because of its tricky, strong currents. *Day Pass down the Red Sea*, September 17, 2011, http://vimeo.com/31962605.

Chapter Three. Into the Woods

1 David F. Lancy and M. Annette Grove, "'Getting Noticed': Middle Childhood in Cross-Cultural Perspective," *Human Nature* 22, no. 3 (September 2011): 281–302.

2 The Samburu tribe in modern Kenya use red ochre to make elaborate designs for many ritual purposes. See Marcy Mendelson, "Warrior Graduation Ceremony Reveals Kenya at a Crossroads," *National Geographic*, September 22, 2013, http://news.nationalgeographic.com/news/2013/09/130921-samburu-moran-warrior-graduation-ceremony-kenya-culture/.

3 Francesco d'Errico et al., "Additional evidence on the use of personal ornaments in the Middle Paleolithic of North Africa," *Proceedings of the National Academy of Sciences of the United States of America (PNAS)* 106, no. 38 (August 28, 2009): 16051–56, doi:10.1073/pnas.0903532106.

4 Brenna M. Henn, L. L. Cavalli-Sforza, and Marcus W. Feldman, "The great human expansion," *PNAS* 109, no. 44 (October 2013): 17758–64, doi:10.1073/pnas.1212380109.

5 Steve Webb, Matthew L. Cupper, and Richard Robins, "Pleistocene human footprints from the Willandra Lakes, southeastern Australia," *Journal of Human Evolution* 50, no. 4 (2005): 405–13, http://epublications.bond.edu.au/hss_pubs/40/.

6   The description of the land on the east side of the Red Sea on the
    Arabian Peninsula, including the kind of plants and animals early modern
    humans might have found, is drawn from several articles by Geoff Bailey,
    particularly "The Red Sea, Coastal Landscapes, and Hominin Dispersals,"
    15–37.

7   Henn, "The great human expansion," 17758–64. Note that these are only
    estimates, and that in areas rich in game or fish resources, the territory per
    person could be somewhat smaller.

8   Omkar Deshpande et al., "A serial founder effect model for human settlement
    out of Africa," *Proceedings of the Royal Society B: Biological Sciences* 276, no.
    1655 (September 2008): 291–300, doi: 10.1098/rspb.2008.0750.

9   Kit Opie and Camilla Power, "Grandmothering and Female Coalitions:
    A Basis for Matrilineal Priority?" in *Early Human Kinship: From Sex to
    Social Reproduction*, eds. Nicholas J. Allen, Hilary Callan, Robin Dunbar,
    and Wendy James, 168–86 (Malden, MA: Blackwell, 2008), http://www.
    academia.edu/177474/Grandmothering_and_Female_Coalitions_A_
    Basis_for_Matrilineal_Priority.

10 Nicholas Blurton Jones, "Bushman Birth Spacing: A Test for Optimal
    Interbirth Intervals," *Ethology and Sociobiology* 7, no.2 (1986): 91–105, doi:
    10.1016/0162-3095(86)90002-6.

11 The experience of older female killer whales appears to be essential for
    the group's survival. Nicholas Weiler, "Menopausal killer whales are
    family leaders," *Science*, March 5, 2015, http://news.sciencemag.org/
    biology/2015/03/menopausal-killer-whales-are-family-leaders, doi:
    10.1126/science.aab0277.

12 Elizabeth Kolbert, "Ice Memory: Does a glacier hold the secret of how
    civilization began—and how it may end?" *New Yorker*, January 7, 2002,
    http://www.newyorker.com/magazine/2002/01/07/ice-memory.

13 Michael Balter, *The Goddess and the Bull: Çatalhöyük: An Archaeological
    Journey to the Dawn of Civilization* (New York: Free Press, 2007).

14 Numbers 20:11.

15 Willy Tegel et al., "Early Neolithic Water Wells Reveal the World's Oldest
    Wood Architecture," PLOS (December 19, 2012), doi: 10.1371/journal.
    pone.0051374.

16 Diamond, *Gun, Germs, and Steel*, 98–113.

17 Diamond, *Guns, Germs, and Steel*, 120.

18 Catherine Breton et al., "The origins of the domestication of the olive tree," C.
    R. *Biologies* 332 (2009): 1059–64.

19 Li Liu et al., "The earliest rice domestication in China," *Antiquity* 81, no. 313
    (September 2007): 316–31, http://antiquity.ac.uk/projgall/liu1/.

20 Lawrence R. Heaney, "A Synopsis of Climatic and Vegetational Change in Southeast Asia," *Climatic Change* 19, no. 1 (January 1991): 53–61, doi: 10.1007/BF00142213.

21 For a graphic picture comparing forests today and in the past, see the simulations by NASA's Earth Observatory: http://earthobservatory.nasa.gov/ Features/BorealMigration/boreal_migration2.php.

22 Germain Bayon et al., "Intensifying Weathering and Land Use in Iron Age Central Africa," *Science* 335, no. 6073 (March 2012): 1219–22, doi: 10.1126/ science.1215400.

23 *The Epic of Gilgamesh*, trans. N. K. Sanders (Assyrian International News Agency), Tablet 4, 8, http://www.aina.org/books/eog/eog.pdf.

24 Robert Pogue Harrison's book *Forests: The Shadow of Civilization* (Chicago: The University of Chicago Press, 1992) is an interesting analysis drawing on literary texts of the Western world to explain what he believes is our civilization's very ambivalent attitude toward forests. His analysis of Gilgamesh's psychological state as the Sumerian king goes to conquer the forest is thought-provoking, to say the least. But he takes little notice of the fact that civilization developed on savannahs and grasslands.

25 E. E. Kuzmina, *The Prehistory of the Silk Road*, ed. Victor H. Mair (Philadelphia: University of Pennsylvania Press, 2008).

26 Mark Elvin, *The Retreat of the Elephants: An Environmental History of China* (New Haven and London: Yale University Press, 2004), 40.

27 An interesting discussion of fire-making and other Stone Age skills can be found on an eclectic website called Stone Age Skills, which was created by a modern woodsman, Walter Muma: http://stoneageskills.com/articles/ percussionfierstarting.html.

28 *Discover Firemaking: An Introductory Guide*, compiled by Ollie Douglas (Oxford, UK: Pitts River Museum of Anthropology and Archeology, 2010), https://www.prm.ox.ac.uk/sites/default/files/imported/basic/pdf/Fire_ Making_fs.pdf. The guide was published in conjunction with the exhibition "Methods of Firemaking" shown at the Pitts River Museum.

29 Lloyd C. Hulbert, "Causes of Fire Effects in Tallgrass Prairie," *Ecology* 69, no. 1 (February 1988): 46–58, doi: 10.2307/1943159.

30 Charles C. Mann, *1491: New Revelations of the Americas Before Columbus* (New York: Vintage Books, 2005), 281–82.

31 Several references can be found in the *Diaries* of George Nelson, found in the Baldwin Collection of the Toronto Public Library at http://www. torontopubliclibrary.ca/books-video-music/specialized-collections/ historical-baldwin-manuscripts.

32   Madhav Gadgil and Ramachandra Guha, *This Fissured Land: An Ecological History of India* (Berkeley and Los Angeles: University of California Press, 1992).

33   Mait Metspalu et al., "Shared and Unique Components of Human Population Structure and Genome-Wide Signals of Positive Selection in South Asia," *The American Journal of Human Genetics* 89, no. 6 (December 9, 2011): 731–44, doi: 10.1016/j.ajhg.2011.11.010.

34   Peter Blood, ed., "Agriculture," *Pakistan: A Country Study,* http://countrystudies.us/pakistan/49.htm.

35   One of its main cities, Harappa, was effectively forgotten until the early twentieth century when railroad engineers of the British Raj found its ruins as they looked for rocks and rip-rap to use as railway ballast.

36   Kuzmina, *The Prehistory of the Silk Road*, 25–32.

37   Lisa Respers France, "The words and comedy of Sid Caesar," CNN, http://www.cnn.com/2014/02/12/showbiz/celebrity-news-gossip/sid-caesar-comedy/.

38   Elvin, *The Retreat of the Elephants*, 45.

Chapter Four. The Things They Carried

1   O. Soffer, J. M. Adovasio, and D. C. Hyland, "The 'Venus' Figurines: Textiles, Basketry, Gender, and Status in the Upper Paleolithic," *Current Anthropology* 41, no. 4 (August–October 2000): 511–37.

2   The University Record, "Surgeons use Stone Age technology for delicate surgery," University of Michigan, September 10, 1997, http://ur.umich.edu/9798/Sep10_97/surgery.htm.

3   Yaroslav V. Kuzmin, "Long-Distance Obsidian Transport in Prehistoric Northeast Asia," *Bulletin of the Indo-Pacific Prehistory Association* 32 (2012): 1–5, doi: http://dx.doi.org/10.7152/bippa.v32i0.9997, http://journals.lib.washington.edu/index.php/BIPPA/article/view/9997.

4   Yaroslav V. Kuzmin et al., "Obsidian use at the Ushki Lake complex, Kamchatka Peninsula (Northeastern Siberia): implications for terminal Pleistocene and early Holocene human migrations in Beringia," *Journal of Archaeological Science* 35, no. 8 (August 2008): 2179–87, doi:10.1016/j.jas.2008.02.001.

5   Andrew Sherratt, "The Obsidian Trade in the Near East, 14,000 to 6500 BC," *ArchAtlas*, Version 4.1 (2005), http://www.archatlas.org/ObsidianRoutes/obsidian.php (accessed September 1, 2016).

6   Other routes were along the Euphrates, which suggests that obsidian was moved by water; but more about water routes in chapter 6, "Across the Water."

7   Silkroad Foundation, "History of Silk," http://www.silk-road.com/artl/silkhistory.shtml.

8   In Book VI of the epic *Gilgamesh*, the goddess Ishtar tempts Gilgamesh with a chariot of lapis lazuli and gold.

9   Ebih-Il, the Superintendent of Mari, statuette now in the Louvre, Paris. See: http://www.louvre.fr/en/oeuvre-notices/ebih-il-superintendent-mari.

10 Jessica Cox, "Trade and Power: The Role of Naqada as a Trading Centre in Predynastic Egypt," *Monash University Publications*, 2012, https://www.academia.edu/2980599/Trade_and_Power_The_Role_of_Naqada_as_a_Trading_Centre_in_Predynastic_Egypt.

11 Aljazeera documentary, https://www.youtube.com/watch?v=pwyc5uRxvYE.

12 Kelsey Michal Ajango, "New Thoughts on the Trade of Lapis Lazuli in the Ancient Near East: c. 3000–2000 B.C." (BA thesis, University of Wisconsin, 2010), http://digital.library.wisc.edu/1793/64508.

13 J. M. de Navarro, "Prehistoric Routes between Northern Europe and Italy Defined by the Amber Trade," *The Geographical Journal* 66, no. 6 (December 1925): 481–503, doi: 10.2307/1783003. See also Anna J. Mukherjee et al., "The Qatna lion: scientific confirmation of Baltic amber in late Bronze Age Syria," *Antiquity* 82 (2008): 49–59.

14 See blog by Edward Pegler, "A primer on old-world metals before the Copper age (revised)," Armchair Prehistory, August 30, 2015, http://armchairprehistory.com/2015/08/30/a-primer-on-old-world-metals-before-the-copper-age/.

15 E. Huysecom et al., "The emergence of pottery in Africa during the 10th millennium calBC: new evidence from Ounjougou (Mali)," *Antiquity* 83, no. 322 (2009): 905–17, https://doc.rero.ch/record/19037/files/mag_epa_2.pdf.

16 Benjamin W. Roberts et al., "Development of metallurgy in Eurasia," *Antiquity* 83, no.322 (December 2009): 1012–22, doi: http://dx.doi.org/10.1017/S0003598X00099312.

17 David W. Anthony, *The Horse, the Wheel and Language: How Bronze-Age Riders from the Eurasian Steppes Shaped the Modern World* (Princeton: Princeton University Press, 2007), 200.

18 Ibid., 221–224.

19 Malcolm Gladwell, *Outliers: The Story of Success* (New York: Little, Brown and Company, 2008), 175.

20 Ibid.

Chapter Five. Warriors' Roads

1   See "Charge of the Light Brigade" by Alfred, Lord Tennyson, which was first published December 9, 1854, accessed on the Poetry Foundation website at: https://www.poetryfoundation.org/poems-and-poets/poems/detail/45319.

2   Jesse Greenspan, "The Charge of the Light Brigade, 160 Years Ago," *History in the Headlines,* October 24, 2014, http://www.history.com/news/the-charge-of-the-light-brigade-160-years-ago.

3   For an explanation of this ancient forestry method, see: http://www.coppice.co.uk/.

4   Dendrochronologists have produced a series of tree ring chronology for the British Isles that extend from 4989 to 381 BCE. See J. Hillam et al., "Dendrochronology of the English Neolithic," Antiquity 64, no. 243, (June 1990): 210–20, doi: http://dx.doi.org/10.1017/S0003598X00077826.

5   Some timbers recovered at Plumstead date between 3910 and 3970 BCE, using radioactive carbon dating. See Diccon Hart et al., "Archaeological Investigations at Belmarsh West, London Borough of Greenwich Post-Excavation Assessment and Project Design for Publication," ASE Project Report: 2009056, Project No. 3541, March 2009.

6   John Noble Wilford, "World's Oldest Paved Road Found in Egypt," *New York Times,* May 8, 1994, http://www.nytimes.com/1994/05/08/world/world-s-oldest-paved-road-found-in-egypt.html.

7   April Holloway, "The 9,500-year-old honeycomb city of Çatalhöyük," *Ancient Origins,* September 19, 2013, http://www.ancient-origins.net/ancient-places-asia/9500-year-old-honeycomb-city-atalh-y-k-00840#!boPUoE. Some researchers suggest that the roofs of houses were in effect plazas and functioned as streets, too. That would solve the problem of mud and flooded routes during periods of rain.

8   Carrie Gracie, "Qin Shi Huang: The ruthless emperor who burned books," BBC News, October 15, 2012, http://www.bbc.com/news/magazine-19922863.

9   Darius I was of the Achaemenid dynasty. Persia knew other dynasties, but to avoid complicating things too much, the generic term "Persian" will be used here to describe the dynasty.

10 In 1992, the Metropolitan Museum of Art in New York hosted an exhibit "The Royal City of Susa: Ancient Near Eastern Treasures in the Louvre." Its catalogue not only contains photos of some of the gems of the exhibit, but also includes essays on both the art found in the city and on its history: *Royal City of Susa: Ancient Near Eastern Treasures in the Louvre,* eds. Prudence O. Harper, Joan Aruz, and Françoise Tallon (New York: Metropolitan Museum of Art, re-issued 2013).

11   Bryan Walsh, "The 10 Most Air-Polluted Cities in the World,"
     Time, September 27, 2011, http://science.time.com/2011/09/27/
     the-10-most-air-polluted-cities-in-the-world/.

12   The Greek historian Herodotus devotes most of his book *The Histories* to Darius
     and his unsuccessful attempt to subdue Greek city states. (See particularly
     Chapters VI–VII. Herodotus, *The Histories*, trans. Aubrey de Sélincourt
     (London: Penguin Classics, 1972.) Darius himself left several monuments,
     written in as many as three languages, attesting to his accomplishments. He also
     is mentioned in the Bible as ordering the rebuilding of the Jewish temple in
     Jerusalem. Archaeological research corroborates most of his claims.

13   Iran Chamber Society, "Words of Darius the Great in Biston's Inscription,"
     History of Iran, http://www.iranchamber.com/history/darius/darius_
     inscription_biston.php#sthash.S16cbzjP.dpuf.

14   De Morgan, while he appreciated what he was uncovering, also proceeded
     in a way that makes modern archaeologists cringe. Instead of carefully
     keeping track of the layers, the dirt was hauled away "as in a public works
     project," with relatively few records kept. See article on "Jacques de Morgan"
     at the *Encyclopedia Iranica*, piloted by Columbia University: http://www.
     iranicaonline.org/articles/de-morgan.

15   A short video, *Iranian city of Shush*, made for Iranian television by
     Press TV allows a close look at these. See: http://www.youtube.com/
     watch?v=IdBMau99lXU.

16   Herodotus, *The Histories*, Book 5, Sections 52 and 53, 330–331.

17   Ibid.

18   "Mongol couriers were expected to ride the full distances themselves,
     carrying the letters on their persons for total security. Consequently they
     forced their bodies to the absolute physical limits of endurance riding day and
     night, rarely stopping for food or rest, their bodies strapped up tightly with
     leather belts to keep them upright in the saddle." Tim Severin, *In Search of
     Genghis Khan* (Sydney, Auckland, Johannesburg: Hutchison, 1991), 137.

19   Another feat was the construction of a canal connecting the Nile with the
     Red Sea. Its existence was corroborated in the nineteenth century, when three
     separate markers were found celebrating this accomplishment.

20   Rodney S. Young, "Gordion on the Royal Road," *Proceedings of the American
     Philosophical Society* 107, no. 4 (August 15, 1963): 348–64.

21   See David French, "Pre- and Early-Roman Roads of Asia Minor. The Persian
     Royal Road," *Iran* 36 (1998): 15–43, doi: 10.2307/4299973.

22   P. Pétrequin et al., "Jade. Grandes haches alpines du Néolithique européen.
     Ve et IVe Millénaires av. J-C," Presses Universitaires de Franche-Comté,
     Besançon.

23 For grand pictures of old Chinese roads, see China Scenic, "Ancient Paths of Taihang Mountains," http://www.chinascenic.com/magazine/ancient-paths-of-taihang-mountains-209.html.

24 Charles Sanft, *Communication and Cooperation in Early Imperial China: Publicizing the Qin Dynasty* (Albany, NY: SUNY Press, 2014).

25 Logan Thompson, "Roman Roads," *History Today* 47, no. 2 (1997), http://www.historytoday.com/logan-thompson/roman-roads.

26 See documentary: The History Channel, *Roman Roads: Paths to Empire* (1997), https://www.youtube.com/watch?v=GdmoYkgv1WI.

27 For grand pictures of Roman aqueducts that still exist, see Steve Levenstein, "Bridges That Babble On: 15 Amazing Roman Aqueducts," *Web Urbanist*, http://weburbanist.com/2010/09/26/bridges-that-babble-on-15-amazing-roman-aqueducts/.

28 For pictures of Roman baths, see Historvius, "Roman Baths–List of Surviving Roman Baths," http://www.historvius.com/roman-baths/fr267.

29 Virgilio Hipollito Correia, *Conímbriga: Brief Guide of the Ruins and Museum*, a publication of the Conímbriga Monographic Museum, Conímbriga, Portugal. This short publication bears no date, and appears to be available only at the museum, where I bought it in 2013.

30 The distance from Izmir to Shush is about 2,031 kilometres (1,262 miles) by air and 2,515 kilometres (1,563 miles) by land; while Rome to Coimbra is 1,758 kilometres (1,092 miles) by air and 2,356 kilometres (1,464 miles) by land.

31 To be sure, Portuguese retains echoes of languages spoken before and after Roman rule by the "barbarians," the Visigoths of various stripes. For example, the words for "glove" in many Latinate languages are related: in Spanish, it's *guante*; in French, *gant*; and Italian, *guanto*. But the Portuguese word is *luva* and, like the English word, comes from the proto-Gothic word for hand or palm of the hand, *galofo*.

Chapter Six. Across the Water

1 The Plakias Stone Age Project, http://plakiasstoneageproject.com/project-overview/. The only early modern human remains found on Crete have been dated to around 50,000 BCE, which would suggest that they are ancestors of people who left Africa after the first great wave of modern human expansion. See also: Thomas F. Strasser et al., "Stone Age Seafaring in the Mediterranean: Evidence from the Plakias Region for Lower Palaeolithic and Mesolithic Habitation of Crete," *Hesperia: The Journal of the American School of Classical Studies at Athens* 79, no. 2 (April-June 2010): 145–90, http://www.jstor.org/stable/40835484.

2   American Association for the Advancement of Science, "The First Seafarers," by Science News Staff, March 11, 1998, http://www.sciencemag.org/ news/1998/03/first-seafarers.

3   *The Sea Is My Brother* was written in 1942, but not published until 2011 by Da Capo Press as *The Sea Is My Brother: The Lost Novel.*

4   For a lovely view of the Mondego, see the prize-winning film *Mondego* by Daniel Pinheiro, (WILDSTEP Productions, 2011), http://vimeo. com/31170389.

5   Louvre Museum, "Frieze of the Transportation of Timber," http://www. louvre.fr/en/oeuvre-notices/frieze-transportation-timber.

6   From *The Odyssey* by Homer, translated by Samuel Butler, Book XII "The Sirens, Scylla and Charybdis, the Cattle of the Sun," https://www.gutenberg. org/files/1727/1727-h/1727-h.htm, accessed September 19, 2016.

7   Rene Wanders, "The Pesse Boat," *Boot van Pesse,* http://www.bootvanpesse.com.

8   See the Groupement de recherches archéologiques subacquatiques website at http://archsubgras.free.fr/pnavancien.html. And that of the museum where this boat is now displayed: http://www.musee-prehistoire-idf.fr/ pirogue-mesolithique-pin.

9   P. Breunig, "The 8000-year-old dugout canoe from Dufuna (NE Nigeria)," in *Aspects of African Archaeology,* eds. G. Pwiti and R. Soper, 461–68 (Harare: University of Zimbabwe Publications, 1994). See also: Femi Macaulay, "The discovery of an 8,000-year-old dugout canoe in northern Nigeria is shedding new light on Africa's distant past," http://www.egyptsearch.com/forums/ ultimatebb.cgi?ubb=get_topic;f=8;t=003581.

10   People's Daily Online, "China's Boat-building Dates Back 7,500 Years: Archaeologists," *Beijing Time,* November 21, 2002, http://en.people. cn/200211/21/eng20021121_107216.shtml.

11   Smithsonian Institution, "Gobustan Petroglyphs," http://gobustan.si.edu/ subject_matter.

12   Joseph Conrad, *Heart of Darkness* (New York: Dover Editions, 1991), 35.

13   Mark Twain, *The Adventures of Huckleberry Finn* (Berkeley, Los Angeles, London: University of California Press, 1985), 89.

14   Herodotus, *The Histories,* Book Four, 53.

15   The first section, the Hong Gou, is mentioned in diplomatic dispatches in 330 BCE, but scholars now think it dates from the sixth century BCE. The second section, the Hang Gou, is dated more clearly since it was part of the attempt of a king of a southern province to consolidate his taking of territory to the north of his domain, with construction beginning in 486 BCE.

16   Editorial, "The Heritage of the Grand Canal," *China Heritage Quarterly,* no. 9, March 2007.

17   Oxford Reference, "an army marches on its stomach," http://www.
     oxfordreference.com/view/10.1093/oi/authority.20110803095425331.

18   David Kessler and Peter Temin, "The organization of the grain trade in the
     early Roman Empire," *The Economic History Review* 60, no. 2 (2007): 313–32,
     doi: 10.1111/j.1468-0289.2006.00360.x.

19   Eric H. Cline, *1177 BC: The Year Civilization Collapsed* (Princeton: Princeton
     University Press, 2014). The title is a considerable overstatement—certainly
     civilization in China and South America continued, completely untouched by
     the Sea Peoples drama, but it has some truth from a western Eurasian standpoint.

20   Ibid., 9.

21   Brandon L. Drake, "The influence of climatic change on the Late Bronze Age
     Collapse and the Greek Dark Ages," *Journal of Archaeological Science* 39, no. 6
     (May 2012): 1862–70, doi: 10.1016/j.jas.2012.01.029.

22   Jack Kerouac, *Desolation Angels* (New York: Open Road Media, 2016), 77.
     The novel was first published in 1965 by Coward-McCann, and the *Ben-Hur*
     movie epic came out in 1959.

23   Simon James, "The Roman galley slave: *Ben-Hur* and the birth of a factoid,"
     Public Archaeology 2, no. 1 (2001): 35–49, doi.org/10.1179/pua.2001.2.1.35.

24   David Christian, "Silk Roads or Steppe Roads? The Silk
     Roads in World History," *Journal of World History* 11, no. 1
     (2000): 1–26, http://www.medievalists.net/2011/12/18/
     silk-roads-or-steppe-roads-the-silk-roads-in-world-history/.

25   James Legge, trans. and ed., *A Record of Buddhistic Kingdoms Being an Account
     by the Chinese Monk Fa-Hien of His Travels in India and Ceylon (AD 399-414)
     in Search of the Buddhist Books of Discipline* (Oxford: Clarendon Press, 1886),
     9–36, quoted in Daniel C. Waugh, "The Journey of Faxian to India," https://
     depts.washington.edu/silkroad/texts/faxian.html.

26   Christian, "Silk Roads or Steppe Roads?" 1–26.

27   Tatiana Zerjal et al., "The Genetic Legacy of the Mongols," *The American
     Journal of Human Genetics* 72, no. 3 (March 2003): 717–21, doi: http://
     dx.doi.org/10.1086/367774

28   Jack Weatherford, *Genghis Khan and the Making of the Modern World* (New
     York: Crown Publishers, 2004).

29   Franck Billé, "Batu Khan c. 1205–1255—Conqueror of much of Eurasia;
     Great Khan of the Golden Horde," in *Berkshire Dictionary of Chinese Biography,
     Volume 2* (Great Barrington, MA: Berkshire Publishing Group, 2014), 748–60.

30   The original Middle English reads: "This noble kyng was cleped Cambyuskan,
     / Which in his tyme was of so greet renoun / That ther was nowhere in no
     regioun / So excellent a lord in alle thyng." *The Works of Geoffrey Chaucer*, ed.
     F. N. Robinson (Boston: Houghton Mifflin Company, 1957), 128.

31   AVERT, "History of HIV and AIDS Overview," http://www.avert.org/history-hiv-aids-africa.htm.

32   Weatherford, *Genghis Khan*, 247.

33   The extremely important role the Portuguese played in the European voyages of exploration is too often forgotten, which is why I wrote *Making Waves: The Continuing Portuguese Adventure* (Montreal: Véhicule Press, 2010).

Chapter Seven. Mystery Roads

1   Mann, *1491*, 120–24.

2   Russell Thornton, "Population History of Native North Americans," in *A Population History of North America*, eds. Michael R. Haines and Richard H. Steckel, 9–50 (Cambridge, UK: Cambridge University Press, 2000).

3   Some individuals have a genetic heritage indicating occasional mixing with people from elsewhere in the world. But when that might have occurred is hard to say, although attempts are being made to do just that. Recent announcements of contact between Easter Islanders and South American natives are an example. In both recent studies, the mixing came in the last thousand years, and perhaps even more recently. See: Will Dunham, "Easter Island's ancient inhabitants weren't so lonely after all," *Reuters*, October 23, 2014, http://www.reuters.com/article/2014/10/23/us-science-easterisland-idUSKCN0IC28C20141023.

4   Not far away, the U.S. Air Force has maintained a major base, Cannon AFB, since World War II. This military use of the area is in contrast with the objects that have been found from the Clovis culture, which are more prosaic tools of hunting, not of warfare. As in Eurasia, the transformation of tools must have taken awhile before the territorial imperative brought forth the need for tools of warfare with neighbours. When there are no neighbours, there's no need to fight them.

5   John H. Blitz, "Adoption of the Bow in Prehistoric North America," *North American Archaeologist* 9, no. 2 (1988): 123–45.

6   For a fascinating account of the Clovis discoveries, see Mann, *1491*, 164–78.

7   Thomas Kuhn, *The Structure of Scientific Revolutions* (Chicago: University of Chicago Press, 1962).

8   For more on Luther Cressman, see the television documentary program *Luther Cressman, Quest for First People*, by Kami Horton, on Oregon Public Broadcasting, April 30, 2014: http://www.opb.org/television/programs/oregonexperience/segment/luther-cressman-quest-for-first-people/.

9   Thomas J. Connolly, "Fort Rock Cave," *The Oregon Encyclopedia, a project of the Oregon Historical Society,* www.oregonencyclopedia.org/articles/fort_rock_cave/pdf/.

10   Joseph M. Licciardi, "Chronology of latest Pleistocene lake-level fluctuations in the pluvial Lake Chewaucan basin, Oregon, USA," *Journal of Quaternary Science* 16, no. 6 (2001): 545–53, doi: 10.1002/jqs.619.

11   C. Melvin Aikens, "Great Basin," chap. 2 in *Archeology of Oregon,* 1993, published by the U.S. Bureau of Land Management, Washington and Oregon Section and accessed at: http://www.blm.gov/or/resources/heritage/files/AOO-chapter2.pdf. This is from a series of publications put on the Internet by the U.S. Bureau of Land Management section for Washington and Oregon.

12   Lionel E. Jackson Jr. and Michael C. Wilson, "The Ice-Free Corridor Revisited," *Geotimes,* February 2004. http://www.geotimes.org/feb04/feature_Revisited.html#links.

13   Kelly E. Graf, Caroline V. Ketron, and Michael R. Waters, eds., *Paleoamerican Odyssey* (College Station, TX: Texas A&M University Press, 2014), http://www.tamupress.com/product/Paleoamerican-Odyssey,7924.aspx. Thirty-one studies were presented at the 2013 conference by the same name, which was hosted in Santa Fe, New Mexico, by the Center for the Study of the First Americans.

14   Vladimir V. Pitulkoa et al., "The oldest art of the Eurasian Arctic: personal ornaments and symbolic objects from Yana RHS, Arctic Siberia," *Antiquity* 86, no. 333 (January 2012): 642–59, doi: http://dx.doi.org/10.1017/S0003598X00047827.

15   Jacques Cinq-Mars and Richard E. Morlan, "Bluefish Caves and Old Crow Basin: A New Rapport," in *Ice Age Peoples of North America. Environments, Origins, and Adaptations of the First Americans,* eds. Robson Bonnichsen and Karen L. Turnmire, 200–12 (Corvallis: Oregon State University Press for the Center for the Study of the First Americans, 1999).

16   Erika Tamm et al. "Beringian Standstill and Spread of Native American Founders," *PLOS* (September 2007). doi:10.1371/journal.pone.0000829.

17   To read more see Bruce Bower, "Stone Age Siberians May Have Rarely Hunted Mammoths," *The Archaeology News Network,* June 12, 2013, http://archaeologynewsnetwork.blogspot.ca/2013/06/stone-age-siberians-may-have-rarely.html#.VE7GX4WKBNQ.

18   Bruce Bradley and Dennis Stanford, "The North Atlantic ice-edge corridor: A possible Palaeolithic route to the New World," *World Archaeology Special Issue "Debates in World Archaeology"* 36, no. 4 (2004): 459–78, doi.org/10.1080/0043824042000303656.

19   John Stang, "Skull found on shore of Columbia," *Tri-City Herald,* July 29, 1996.

20 Douglas W. Owsley and Richard L. Jantz, eds., *Kennewick Man: The Scientific Investigation of an Ancient American Skeleton* (College Station, TX: Texas A&M University Press, 2014).

21 Carl Zimmer, "New DNA Results Show Kennewick Man Was Native American," *New York Times,* June 18, 2015, http://www.nytimes.com/2015/06/19/science/new-dna-results-show-kennewick-man-was-native-american.html?_r=0.

22 Joel Achenbach, "Girl's 12,000-year-old skeleton may solve a mystery," *Washington Post,* May 15, 2014. http://www.washingtonpost.com/national/health-science/girls-12000-year-old-skeleton-may-solve-a-mystery/2014/05/15/e45a6330-da90-11e3-8009-71de85b9c527_story.html.

23 James C. Chatters et al., "Late Pleistocene Human Skeleton and mtDNA Link Paleoamericans and Modern Native Americans," *Science* 344, no. 6185 (May 16, 2014): 750–4, doi: 10.1126/science.1252619.

24 Jay T. Sturdevant, "Still an Open Book: Analysis of the Current Pre-Clovis vs. Clovis Debate from the Site of Meadowcroft Rockshelter, Pennsylvania and Monte Verde, Chile," *Nebraska Anthropologist* 15, Paper 125 (1999), http://digitalcommons.unl.edu/nebanthro/125.

25 Mark Hume, "Underwater discovery near Haida Gwaii could rewrite human history," *Globe and Mail,* September 23, 2014, http://www.theglobeandmail.com/news/british-columbia/bc-researchers-may-have-found-earliest-site-of-human-habitation-in-canada/article20737278/.

26 For a careful overview and consideration of the sites that don't fit the theories, see: Bonnie L. Pitblado, "A Tale of Two Migrations: Reconciling Recent Biological and Archaeological Evidence for the Pleistocene Peopling of the Americas," *Journal of Archaeological Research* 19, no. 4 (December 2011): 327–75.

27 Steven R. Holen, "Taphonomy of two last glacial maximum mammoth sites in the central Great Plains of North America: A preliminary report on La Sena and Lovewell," *Quaternary International* 142–143 (January 2006): 30–43, doi:10.1016/j.quaint.2005.03.003.

28 While Guidon's initial articles were published in English, much of the work has circulated in French or Portuguese, which seems to have put it outside the circle of North American academic knowledge. It's a lot easier to find Spanish-language research cited by North American scientists than ones written by European or Brazilian scientists.

29 Eric Boëda et al., "A new late Pleistocene archaeological sequence in South America: the Vale da Pedra Furada (Piau´i, Brazil)," *Antiquity* 88, no. 341 (September 2014): 927–41. Paper with supplementary material can be found

at: http://antiquity.ac.uk/projgall/boeda341/downloads/ant20130183_
supplement.pdf. It should be noted that some objects discovered in the same
area look as if they were shaped by humans and appear to date to 100,000 BCE.
This assertion has caused even more controversy. The only hominins who
could have made them would have been *Homo erectus*, and no remains have
been found anywhere else in the western hemisphere. But categorically saying
that this early prehuman could not have made it to South America might be
hasty, since evidence indicates that *Homo erectus* made it to the islands of
Flores in Indonesia and Crete in the Mediterranean at least that long ago.

30   And if this isn't a big enough question, there's another which we won't
go into here: What about assertions that there are artifacts even older, as
old as 300,000 years? They could only have been made by *Homo erectus*.
Investigator Mario Beltrão has argued for a couple decades in favour of their
authenticity, and is supported by French archeologist Henry de Lumley.
See: Juan Schobinger, "200.000 años del hombre en América: ¿qué pensar?"
Espacio, Tiempo y Forma, Serie I, Prehistoria y Arqueología 1 (1988): 375–95,
doi: http://dx.doi.org/10.5944/etfi.1.1988.4500. When confronted with
the puzzle of how early man could have got to South America, Beltrão's
champions point to the fact that it now seems clear *Homo erectus* made it
to Crete and to Flores in Indonesia, which would have required voyages in
boats. The big question is whether an island-hopping trip across the Atlantic
would have been possible.

31   Dunham, "Easter Island's ancient inhabitants," http://www.reuters.com/
article/2014/10/23/us-science-easterisland-idUSKCN0IC28C20141023.

32   Gideon Shelach, "On the Invention of Pottery," *Science* 336, no. 6089 (June
2012): 1644–45, doi: 10.1126/science.1224119.

33   A. C. Roosevelt et al., "Eighth Millennium Pottery from a Prehistoric Shell
Midden in the Brazilian Amazon," *Science* 254, no. 5038 (January 1992):
1621–24, doi: 10.1126/science.254.5038.1621.

34   John E. Clark and Dennis Gosser, "Reinventing Mesoamerica's First Pottery,"
in *The Emergence of Pottery: Technology and Innovation in Ancient Societies*,
eds. William Barnett and John W. Hoopes, 209–21 (Washington, DC:
Smithsonian Institution Press, 1995).

35   Huysecom, "The emergence of pottery," 905–17.

36   Álvaro Montenegro et al., "Modelling pre-historic transoceanic crossings
into the Americas," *Quaternary Science Reviews* 25, nos. 11–12 (June 2006):
1323–38, doi:10.1016/j.quascirev.2005.11.008.

37   Logan Kistler et al., "Transoceanic drift and the domestication of African bottle
gourds in the Americas," PNAS 111, no. 8 (January 10, 2014), doi: 10.1073/
pnas.1318678111, http://www.pnas.org/content/111/8/2937.short.

38   Adauto Araújo et al., "Parasites as Probes for Prehistoric Human Migrations?" *Papers in Natural Resources*, Paper 69, http://digitalcommons.unl.edu/ natrespapers/69.

39   William M. Denevan, "The Pristine Myth: The Landscape of the Americas in 1492," http://jan.ucc.nau.edu/~alcoze/for398/class/pristinemyth.html.

40   Second Letter of Hernando Cortés to Charles v, *Hernán Cortés, The Dispatches of Hernando Cortés, The Conqueror of Mexico, addressed to the Emperor Charles V, written during the conquest, and containing a narrative of its events* (New York: Wiley and Putnam, 1843), accessed at Early Americas Digital Archive, University of Maryland, http://mith.umd.edu/eada/html/ display.php?docs=cortez_letter2.xml.

41   See the website of the National Park Service, for more information on Chaco culture in the National Historical Park New Mexico: http://www.nps.gov/ chcu/historyculture/index.htm.

42   Quoted in John Hyslop, *The Inka Road System* (Orlando: Academic Press, 1984), 341.

Chapter Eight. The Revenge of the Road

1   Geoffrey Parker, "The Spanish Road to the Netherlands," MHQ: *The Quarterly Journal of Military History*, September 28, 2012, http://www.historynet.com/ the-spanish-road-to-the-netherlands.htm.

2   Figuring one ducat equals one peso (which in turn was worth twenty-five grams of gold), at 2013 prices that would equal about U.S.$1,000 per ducat.

3   Leaving Milan at about 5:30 p.m., changing trains at Brig on the other side of the Alps, again at Basel in Switzerland, and Cologne in Germany, you'd arrive at Brussels-Midi station at about 8:30 the next morning.

4   To see Google's calculation, go to https://maps.google.ca/maps?q=milan+ to+brussels+by+car&oe=utf-8&rls=org.mozilla:en-US:official&client= firefox-a&gfe_rd=cr&um=1&ie=UTF-8&sa=X&ei=EQj3VP7_ H4WWgwTDoYHQAw&ved=0CAcQ_AUoAQ&output=classic&dg=brw.

5   Angus Maddison, *Contours of the World Economy, 1-2030 AD: Essays in Macro-Economic History* (Oxford: Oxford University Press, 2007), app. B, 229–248.

6   Kris De Decker, "Medieval smokestacks: fossil fuels in pre-industrial times," *Low Tech Magazine*, September 2011, http://www.lowtechmagazine. com/2011/09/peat-and-coal-fossil-fuels-in-pre-industrial-times.html.

7   Citation for the Canal du Midi as a World Heritage site can be found at: United Nations Educational, Scientific and Cultural Organization, "Canal du Midi," *World Heritage List*, http://whc.unesco.org/en/list/770.

8   M. J. T. Lewis, "Railways in the Greek and Roman World," in *Early Railways. A Selection of Papers from the First International Early Railways Conference*, eds. Andy Guy and Jim Rees, 8-19, http://www.yieldopedia.com/paneladmin/reports/fb8f151d1ee5d60af0482d429fd27c10.pdf.

9   Waggonway Research Circle, *The Wollaton Wagonway of 1604: A Waggonway Research Circle guide* (Portland, Dorset: Island Publishing, 2005), www.island-publishing.co.uk/WRC_mirror/woll_wag_leaflet_a4.pdf.

10   H. W. Dickinson and Arthur Titley, *Richard Trevithick: The Engineer and the Man* (Cambridge: Cambridge University Press, 2010), 57.

11   Harry M. Flint, *The railroads of the United States: their history and statistics comprising the progress and present condition of the various lines with their earnings and expenses; to which are added a synopsis of the railroad laws of the United States and an article on the comparative merits of iron and steel rails* (Philadelphia: John. E. Potter and Company: 1868), 12-13, https://ia600404.us.archive.org/23/items/railroadsunitedooflingoog/railroadsunitedooflingoog.pdf.

12   Thomas Jefferson, *The Papers of Thomas Jefferson Digital Edition*, ed. James P. McClure and J. Jefferson Looney (Charlottesville: University of Virginia Press, Rotunda, 2008–2015), http://rotunda.upress.virginia.edu/founders/TSJN-01-38-02-0514. Original Source: Main Series, Volume 38 (1 July–12 November 1802).

13   John Vidal, "Modern cargo ships slow to the speed of the sailing clippers," *The Guardian*, July 25, 2010, http://www.theguardian.com/environment/2010/jul/25/slow-ships-cut-greenhouse-emissions.

14   Wolfgang Schivelbusch, *The Railway Journey: The Industrialization of Time and Space in the Nineteenth Century* (Berkeley and Los Angeles: University of California Press, 2014), 33.

15   For an extensive discussion of Napoléon III and Baron Georges-Eugène Haussmann's plan, see my book *The Walkable City: From Haussmann's Boulevards to Jane Jacobs' Streets and Beyond* (Montreal, QC: Véhicule Press, 2008), 41–50.

16   See Angus Maddison, "The Contours of World Development," in *The World Economy: Volume 1: A Millennial Perspective and Volume 2: Historical Statistics*, 29–50 (Paris: OECD Publishing, 2006), http://dx.doi.org/10.1787/9789264022621-3-en.This series of data covering more than a thousand years is an impressive source of information about the economic state of the world and its population.

17   Wesley Johnston, "Prelude to Famine 4: Demographics," http://www.wesleyjohnston.com/users/ireland/past/famine/demographics_pre.html.

18   EyeWitness to History, "Passage To America, 1750," http://www.eyewitnesstohistory.com/passage.htm.

19   Thomas Robert Malthus, *An Essay on the Principle of Population* (London: J. Johnson, 1798), Chapter I, Paragraph 17, accessed at http://www.econlib.org/library/Malthus/malPop.html.

20   Susannah Moodie, "Uncle Joe and His Family," chap. VII in *Roughing It in the Bush*, 2d ed. (London: Richard Bentley, 1852), http://digital.library.upenn.edu/women/moodie/roughing/roughing.html#I-03 September 19, 2016.

21   Henry David Thoreau, "Sounds," chap. 4, paragraph 8, in *Walden; or, Life in the Woods* (Boston: Ticknor and Fields, 1854), accessed at "The Thoreau Reader: Annotated works of Henry David Thoreau," ed. Richard Lenat, http://thoreau.eserver.org/walden04.html.

22   Wikipedia, "Qing Dynasty," *History of Rail Transport in China*, https://en.wikipedia.org/wiki/History_of_rail_transport_in_China.

23   Winston Churchill, *My African Journey* (Toronto: William Briggs, 1909), 4.

24   "Railroad," http://www.fem.unicamp.br/~em313/paginas/consulte/railroad.htm.

25   Walla Walla County, Official County Government Site, "History of Walla Walla," http://www.co.walla-walla.wa.us/history.shtml.

26   Virginia L. Butler and Jim E. O'Connor, "9,000 years of salmon fishing on the Columbia River, North America," *Quaternary Research* 62, no. 1 (July 2004): 1–8. doi:10.1016/j.yqres.2004.03.002.

27   Medorem Crawford, *Journal of Medorem Crawford: an account of his trip across the plains with the Oregon Pioneers of 1842*, ed. F. G. Young (Eugene, Oregon: Star Job Office, 1897), 20, http://www.sos.wa.gov/legacy/publications_detail.aspx?p=11.

28   National Geographic, "Lewis and Clark Interactive Journey Log," http://www.nationalgeographic.com/lewisandclark/record_tribes_013_12_17.html.

29   Joseph W. Eaton and Albert J. Mayer, *Man's Capacity to Reproduce: The Demography of a Unique Population* (Glencoe, IL.: The Free Press, 1954).

30   See photos taken by Lyn Topinka, and other photos in her collection, on her personal webpage: Columbia River Images, http://columbiariverimages.com/Regions/Places/biggs_oregon.html.

Chapter Nine. Speeding

1   Jack Kerouac interview by Ted Berrigan: "Jack Kerouac, The Art of Fiction No. 41," *The Paris Review*. No. 43 (Summer 1968), http://www.theparisreview.org/interviews/4260/the-art-of-fiction-no-41-jack-kerouac.

2   The French military engineer Nicolas-Joseph Cugnot built two steam-powered tricycles in the 1760s, but they could carry only one passenger

and had severe technical problems. See *Encyclopaedia Britannica Online*, s.v. "Nicolas Joseph Cugnot," http://www.britannica.com/EBchecked/topic/145966/Nicolas-Joseph-Cugnot (accessed September 19, 2016).

3   Fact sheet from the Smithsonian Institution: Prepared by the Division of the History of Technology,Transportation Collections, National Museum of American History, in cooperation with Public Inquiry Services, "Early Cars: Fact Sheet for Children," http://www.si.edu/Encyclopedia_SI/nmah/earlycars.htm.

4   Le Corbusier, *The City of To-morrow and Its Planning*, trans. Frederick Etchells (New York: Dover Publications Inc, 1987), xxiii.

5   Sigfried Giedion, *Space, Time and Architecture: The Growth of a New Tradition* (Cambridge MA: Harvard University Press, 1941), 729.

6   Kerouac, *On the Road: The Original Scroll*, 185.

7   For a short history of the Interstate system, with emphasis on California, please see California Department of Transportation, "California Celebrates 50 Years of the Interstate Highway System," http://www.dot.ca.gov/interstate/.

8   W. Dick and A. Lichtenberg, "The myth of Hitler's role in building the autobahn," *Deutsche Welle*, August 4, 2012, http://www.dw.de/the-myth-of-hitlers-role-in-building-the-autobahn/a-16144981.

9   Explanation taken from Andro Linklater, *Measuring America: How an Untamed Wilderness Shaped the United States and Fulfilled the Promise of Democracy* (New York: Walker and Company, 2002), 14–18.

10 For a more complete consideration of the relation between Haussmann, Moses and Jacobs, see my book *The Walkable City*.

11 Many thanks to Silvia Ficher and Pedro P. Palazzo of the Universidade de Brasília for their help, which included guided tours of the city and many references that I followed up.

12 Eduardo A. Vasconcellos and Michael Sivak, *Road Safety in Brazil: Challenges and Opportunities*, Report No. UMTRI-2009-29 (Ann Arbor, MI: The University of Michigan Transportation Research Institute, August 2009), https://deepblue.lib.umich.edu/bitstream/handle/2027.42/63586/102260.pdf. Note that other parts of Brazil have even higher mortality rates. The highest is in the state of Santa Catarina.

13 Personal communication.

14 Stephen Blank, "North American Infrastructure: A less than optimistic outlook. Will repairing old transportation systems be good enough to meet increasing demands?" OpenCanada, October 28, 2014, http://opencanada.org/features/north-american-infrastructure-and-competitiveness-a-less-than-optimistic-outlook/.

15   Calculated from Instituto Brasileiro de Geografia e Estatística (IBGE) figures
     for 2014. The IBGE is the Brazilian national agency collecting data on the
     country. To view the report, see ftp://ftp.ibge.gov.br/Estimativas_de_
     Populacao/Estimativas_2014/estimativa_dou_2014.pdf.

16   "Shanghai now the world's longest metro," *Railway Gazette*, May 4, 2010, http://
     www.railwaygazette.com/news/single-view/view/shanghai-now-the-worlds-
     longest-metro.html.

17   Yonah Freemark, "Openings and Construction Starts Planned for 2016,"
     http://www.thetransportpolitic.com/2016/01/06/openings-and-
     construction-starts-planned-for-2016/.

18   Many thanks to Daniele Moraes and Rennan Stelle of the Instituto de
     Pesquisa e Planejamento de Curitiba, the city's planning agency, and Silvia
     Mara dos Santos Ramos of URBS, Curitiba's transit agency, who spent several
     hours with me, outlining the city's history and its plans for the future.

19   Author's interview with Carlos Alberto Guillén, November 22, 2013.

20   *Latin American Green City Index: Assessing the environmental performance of
     Latin America's major cities* is a research project conducted by the Economist
     Intelligence Unit, sponsored by Siemens. For more information, see page 48,
     accessed at https://www.siemens.com/entry/cc/features/greencityindex.../
     report_latam_en.pdf.

21   Author's interviews with Daniele Moraes and Rennan Stelle, November 22,
     2013.

22   Transit App, "How We Mapped the Worlds' Weirdest Streets," https://
     medium.com/@transitapp/hello-nairobi-cc27bb5a73b7.

23   Kerouac, *On the Road*, 159.

Chapter Ten. On the Road, II

1   For a fascinating closer look, see David D. Alt and Donald W. Hyndman,
     Roadside Geology of Washington (Missoula, MN: Mountain Press Publishing
     Company, 1984).

2   Again and again the molten rock spread out over the land until it covered
     three-quarters of Washington, much of northern Oregon, and part of Idaho.
     Now called the Columbia Plateau, it stretches from nearly the Rockies to the
     Cascades, an area of 160,000 square kilometres (63,000 square miles.) In
     places, it is as thick as 1.8 kilometres (6,800 feet).

3   See for example Cowlitz County Tourism, *Mount St. Helens: 30 Years
     of Change* (Compel Media LLC, 2010), https://www.youtube.com/
     watch?v=Ifohb8_2WhE.

4   Anna King, "Lessons from Japan: Is Hanford Ready to Withstand a Big
     Earthquake?" *Seattle Magazine,* August 2011, http://www.seattlemag.com/
     article/lessons-japan-hanford-ready-withstand-big-earthquake.

5   Ted Conover, "Peru's Long Haul: Highway to Riches or Ruin?" *National Geo-
     graphic,* June 2003, http://ngm.nationalgeographic.com/ngm/0306/feature5/.

6   The presidents of the two countries actually cut the ribbon in 2011, but the
     bridge over the Madre de Dios had to be repaired over the following few months.

7   For export and import figures, see the report of the Brazilian government
     Ministério das Relações Exteriores Departamento de Promoção
     Comercial e Investimentos, *Peru Comércio Exterior,* February 2014,
     http://ois.sebrae.com.br/wp-content/uploads/2015/01/INDPeru.
     pdf. But the effect on Peru's balance of trade is not as positive: "¿Por
     qué la interoceánica no eleva aún el comercio con Brasil?" Economia,
     El Comercio, April 28, 2014, http://elcomercio.pe/economia/peru/
     que-interoceanica-no-eleva-aun-comercio-brasil-noticia-1725638.

8   See "Estrada Interoceânica: os impactos sociais sobre as cidades da região,"
     a special report produced by the Brazilian news agency, *Estadão,* October
     23, 2012, at http://economia.estadao.com.br/noticias/geral,estrada-
     interoceanica-os-impactos-sociais-sobre-as-cidades-da-regiao,131992e.

9   For an animation showing the number of forest fires in the Amazon basin
     between January 2013 and December 31 2014, see: InfoAmazonia, "Fire
     animation January 2012 to Dec. 2014," http://infoamazonia.org/projects/
     fire/. Source: Data © OpenStreetMap (and) contributors, CC-BY-SA
     InfoAmazonia, CartoDB.

10   A note about the trajectory I took on this journey: Montreal to Cusco by
     plane, Cusco to Puerto Maldonado by bus, overnight in Puerto Maldonado,
     bus to Rio Branco, Brazil. Plane to Curitiba, then plane to Brasília, and finally
     back to Montreal by plane.

11   Charles Darwin, *Journal of Researches into the Natural History and Geology
     of the countries visited during the voyage of HMS Beagle round the world,* 2d ed.
     (London: John Murray, 1845), 157. See also http://charles-darwin.classic-
     literature.co.uk/the-voyage-of-the-beagle/ebook-page-157.asp.

12   Ibid., 387.

13   The Nighttown section of *Ulysses.* See James Joyce, *Ulysses,* ed. Jeri Johnson
     (London: Oxford's World Classics, 2011), 412.

14   I'm indebted to Monte Reel for information about the settlements along this
     stretch of the Estrada-Carretera. His article for the *New York Times Magazine*
     "Traveling From Ocean to Ocean Across South America," February 19, 2014,
     confirmed my impressions of the Nighttown allure of the places. See http://
     www.nytimes.com/2014/02/23/magazine/south-america-road-trip.html.

15   William Laurance, "As Roads Spread in Rainforests, The Environmental Toll
     Grows," *Environment 360,* January 19, 2012, http://e360.yale.edu/feature/as_
     roads_spread_in_tropical_rain_forests_environmental_toll_grows/2485/.

16   Union of Concerned Scientists, "New Deforestation Data From Brazil Shows
     Continued Progress," *Common Dreams,* December 6, 2011, http://www.
     commondreams.org/newswire/2011/12/06/new-deforestation-data-brazil-
     shows-continued-progress.

17   See my book *Recreating Eden: A Natural History of Botanical Gardens*
     (Montreal: Véhicule Press, 2001) for the cloak-and-dagger tale of how British
     botanists stole the seeds.

18   See *The Guardian,* "The hidden holocaust," review of Adam Hochschilds's
     *King Leopold's Ghost: A Story of Greed, Terror, and Heroism in Colonial
     Africa* (London: Pan Macmillan, 1998), http://www.theguardian.com/
     theguardian/1999/may/13/features11.g22.

19   John Colapinto, "Strange Fruit: The rise and fall of açaí," *New Yorker,*
     May 30, 2011, http://www.newyorker.com/magazine/2011/05/30/
     strange-fruit-john-colapinto.

20   "The new rubber boomlet," The Brazilian Amazon, *The Economist,* December
     12, 2012, http://www.economist.com/news/americas/21567380-brazilian-
     state-acre-pioneering-approach-development-seeks-make-most.

21   Kate Evans, "Martyr of the Amazon: The legacy of Chico Mendes," December
     20, 2013 http://www.trust.org/item/20131220074605-dgjmi?view=print.

22   Among other places, the quote is found in the material accompanying
     an exhibition about Chico Mendes in Manchester, UK, in 2015: http://
     metaceptive.net/eco-brazil-chico-mendes-forests-and-water/.

23   Read more about the etymology of "capoeira" from Capoeira Connection,
     "What does the word capoeira mean?" http://capoeira-connection.com/
     capoeira/2011/10/what-does-the-word-capoeira-mean/#sthash.JdbPN3Jm.dp.

24   Nadine T. Laporte et al., "Expansion of Industrial Logging in Central Africa,"
     Science 316, no. 5830 (June 8, 2007): 1451, doi:10.1126/science.1141057.

25   Angelina Davydova, "Why Russia's Forests Must Be Protected," *World
     Economic Forum,* January 16, 2015, https://www.weforum.org/
     agenda/2015/01/why-russias-forests-must-be-protected/.

26   Simon Romero, "Taps Start to Run Dry in Brazil's Largest City," *New York
     Times,* February 16, 2015, http://www.nytimes.com/2015/02/17/world/
     americas/drought-pushes-sao-paulo-brazil-toward-water-crisis.html.

27   Dylan Thomas, "The Force that through the Green Fuse Drives the
     Flower," *The Poems of Dylan Thomas* (New York: New Directions, 1952).
     Accessed September 20, 2015 at https://www.poets.org/poetsorg/poem/
     force-through-green-fuse-drives-flower.

28   Laurance, "As Roads Spread in Rainforests," http://e360.yale.edu/
     feature/as_roads_spread_in_tropical_rain_forests_environmental_toll_
     grows/2485/.

29   George Monbiot, "Indonesia is burning. So why is the world looking away?"
     The Guardian, October 30, 2015. http://www.theguardian.com/
     commentisfree/2015/oct/30/indonesia-fires-disaster-21st-century-world-media.

30   Julia Pongratz et al., "Coupled climate–carbon simulations indicate
     minor global effects of wars and epidemics on atmospheric CO_2 between
     AD 800 and 1850," *The Holocene* 21, no. 5 (August 2011): 843-851, doi:
     10.1177/0959683610386981, http://hol.sagepub.com/content/21/5/843.

31   See the press release announcing the release of the study by Pongratz et al.:
     Carnegie Institution for Science, "War, Plague No Match for Deforestation
     in Driving CO_2 Buildup," January 20, 2011, https://carnegiescience.edu/
     news/war-plague-no-match-deforestation-driving-co2-buildup (accessed
     September 20, 2016).

32   John Schwartz, "As Fires Grow, a New Landscape Appears in the West," *New
     York Times,* September 21, 2015, http://www.nytimes.com/2015/09/22/
     science/as-fires-grow-a-new-landscape-appears-in-the-west.html.

33   Simon Romero, "Once Hidden by Forest, Carvings in Land Attest to
     Amazon's Lost World," *New York Times*, January 14, 2012, http://www.
     nytimes.com/2012/01/15/world/americas/land-carvings-attest-to-
     amazons-lost-world.html.

34   Newsprint demand is down but packaging demand will continue to grow, as
     countries like China increase consumer use. See: Jonathan Brandt, "Paper
     demand stacks up," HSBC *News and Insight*, August 11, 2014, http://www.
     hsbc.com/news-and-insight/insight-archive/2014/paper-demand-stacks-up.

35   Reuters has produced an excellent series called *The crisis of rising sea
     levels: Water's Edge* about the effects of rising sea levels around the
     world. See http://www.reuters.com/investigates/special-report/
     waters-edge-the-crisis-of-rising-sea-levels/.

BIBLIOGRAPHY

Achenbach, Joel. "Girl's 12,000-year-old skeleton may solve a mystery." *Washington Post,* May 15, 2014. http://www.washingtonpost.com/national/health-science/girls-12000-year-old-skeleton-may-solve-a-mystery/2014/05/15/e45a6330-da90-11e3-8009-71de85b9c527_story.html.

Ajango, Kelsey Michal. "New Thoughts on the Trade of Lapis Lazuli in the Ancient Near East: c. 3000–2000 BC" BA Thesis, University of Wisconsin, 2010. http://digital.library.wisc.edu/1793/64508.

Alt, David D., and Donald W. Hyndman. *Roadside Geology of Washington.* Missoula, MN: Mountain Press Publishing Company, 1984.

Anthony, David W. *The Horse, the Wheel and Language: How Bronze-Age Riders from the Eurasian Steppes Shaped the Modern World.* Princeton: Princeton University Press, 2007.

Araújo, Adauto, Karl J. Reinhard, Luiz F. Ferreira, and Scott Lyell Gardner. "Parasites as Probes for Prehistoric Human Migrations?" *Papers in Natural Resources.* Paper 69. http://digitalcommons.unl.edu/natrespapers/69.

Bailey, Geoff. "The Red Sea, Coastal Landscapes, and Hominin Dispersals" In *The Evolution of Human Populations in Arabia: Paleoenvironments, Prehistory and Genetics,* edited by Michael D. Petraglia and Jeffrey I. Rose, 15–37. Dordrecht, Netherlands: Springer, 2009.

Balter, Michael. *The Goddess and the Bull: Çatalhöyük: An Archaeological Journey to the Dawn of Civilization.* New York: Free Press, 2007.

Bayon, Germain, Bernard Dennielou, Joël Etoubleau, Emmanuel Ponzevera, Samuel Toucanne, and Sylvain Bermell. "Intensifying Weathering and Land Use in Iron Age Central Africa." *Science* 335, no. 6073 (March 2012): 1219–22, doi:10.1126/science.1215400.

Billé, Franck. "Batu Khan c. 1205–1255—Conqueror of much of Eurasia; Great Khan of the Golden Horde." *Berkshire Dictionary of Chinese Biography, Volume 2.* Great Barrington, MA: Berkshire Publishing Group, 2014. 748–60.

Blank, Stephen. "North American Infrastructure: A less than optimistic outlook. Will repairing old transportation systems be good enough to meet increasing demands?" OpenCanada, October 28, 2014. http://opencanada.org/features/north-american-infrastructure-and-competitiveness-a-less-than-optimistic-outlook/.

Blitz, John H. "Adoption of the Bow in Prehistoric North America." *North American Archaeologist* 9, no. 2 (1988): 123–45.

Blurton Jones, Nicholas. "Bushman Birth Spacing: A Test for Optimal Interbirth Intervals." *Ethology and Sociobiology* 7, no. 2 (1986): 91–105. doi: 10.1016/0162-3095(86)90002-6.

Boëda, Eric, Ignacio Clemente-Conte, Michel Fontugne, Christelle Lahaye, Mario Pino, Gisele Daltrini Felice, Niède Guidon, Sirlei Hoeltz, Antoine Lourdeau, Marina Pagli, Anne-Marie Pessis, Sibeli Viana, Amélie Da Costa, and Eric Douville. "A new late Pleistocene archaeological sequence in South America: the Vale da Pedra Furada (Piauí, Brazil)." *Antiquity* 88, no. 341 (September 2014): 927–41. http://antiquity.ac.uk/projgall/boeda341/downloads/ant20130183_supplement.pdf.

Borrell, Brendan. "From The Trenches: Bon Voyage, Caveman." *Archaeology: A Publication of the Archaeological Institute of America* 63, no.3 (May/June 2010). http://archive.archaeology.org/1005/trenches/voyage.html.

Bower, Bruce. "Stone Age Siberians May Have Rarely Hunted Mammoths." *The Archaeology News Network* (June 12, 2013). http://archaeologynewsnetwork.blogspot.ca/2013/06/stone-age-siberians-may-have-rarely.html#.VE7gx4WkBNQ.

Bradley, Bruce, and Dennis Stanford. "The North Atlantic ice-edge corridor: A possible Palaeolithic route to the New World." *World Archaeology Special Issue "Debates in World Archaeology"* 36, no. 4 (2004): 459–78, doi:10.1080/0043824042000303656.

Brandt, Jonathan. "Paper demand stacks up." *HSbc News and Insight* (August 11, 2014). http://www.hsbc.com/news-and-insight/insight-archive/2014/paper-demand-stacks-up.

Breton, Catherine, Jean-Frédéric Terral, Christian Pinatel, Frédéric Médail, François Bonhomme, and André Bervillé. "The origins of the domestication of the olive tree" *C. R. Biologies* 332 (2009): 1059–64.

Breunig, P. "The 8000-year-old dugout canoe from Dufuna (NE Nigeria)." In *Aspects of African Archaeology*, edited by G. Pwiti and R. Soper, 461–8. Harare: University of Zimbabwe Publications, 1994.

Butler, Virginia L., and Jim E. O'Connor. "9,000 years of salmon fishing on the Columbia River, North America." *Quaternary Research* 62, no. 1 (July 2004): 1–8. doi:10.1016/j.yqres.2004.03.002.

Chaucer, Geoffrey. *The Works of Geoffrey Chaucer*, ed. F. N. Robinson. Boston: Houghton Mifflin Company, 1957.

Chatters, James C., Douglas J. Kennett, Yemane Asmerom, Brian M. Kemp, Victor Polyak, Alberto Nava Blank, Patricia A. Beddows, et al. "Late Pleistocene Human Skeleton and mtDNA Link Paleoamericans and Modern Native Americans." *Science* 344, no. 6185 (May 16, 2014): 750–54. doi:10.1126/science.1252619.

Christian, David. "Silk Roads or Steppe Roads? The Silk Roads in World History." *Journal of World History* 11, no. 1 (2000): 1–26. http://www.medievalists.net/2011/12/18/silk-roads-or-steppe-roads-the-silk-roads-in-world-history/.

Churchill, Winston. *My African Journey*. Toronto: William Briggs, 1909.

Cinq-Mars, Jacques, and Richard E. Morlan. "Bluefish Caves and Old Crow Basin: A New Rapport." In *Ice Age Peoples of North America. Environments, Origins, and Adaptations of the First Americans*, edited by Robson Bonnichsen and Karen L. Turnmire, 200–12. Corvallis: Oregon State University Press for the Center for the Study of the First Americans, 1999.

Clark, John E., and Dennis Gosser. "Reinventing Mesoamerica's First Pottery." In *The Emergence of Pottery: Technology and Innovation in Ancient Societies*, edited by William Barnett and John W. Hoopes, 209–21. Washington: Smithsonian Institution Press, 1995.

Cline, Eric H. *1177 BC: The Year Civilization Collapsed*. Princeton: Princeton University Press, 2014.

Colapinto, John. "Strange Fruit: The rise and fall of açaí." *New Yorker,* May 30, 2011. http://www.newyorker.com/magazine/2011/05/30/strange-fruit-john-colapinto.

Connolly, Thomas J. "Fort Rock Cave." *The Oregon Encyclopedia, a project of the Oregon Historical Society*. www.oregonencyclopedia.org/articles/fort_rock_cave/pdf/.

Conover, Ted. "Peru's Long Haul: Highway to Riches or Ruin?" *National Geographic*, June 2003. http://ngm.nationalgeographic.com/ngm/0306/feature5/.

Conrad, Joseph. *Heart of Darkness*. New York: Dover Editions, 1991.

Cortés, Hernando. "Second Letter to Charles V." *Hernán Cortés, The Dispatches of Hernando Cortés, The Conqueror of Mexico, addressed to the Emperor Charles V, written during the conquest, and containing a narrative of its events.*

New York: Wiley and Putnam, 1843. Accessed at Early Americas Digital Archive, University of Maryland, http://mith.umd.edu/eada/html/display. php?docs=cortez_letter2.xml.

Cox, Jessica. "Trade and Power: The Role of Naqada as a Trading Centre in Predynastic Egypt." *Monash University Publications*, 2012. https://www. academia.edu/2980599/Trade_and_Power_The_Role_of_Naqada_as_a_ Trading_Centre_in_Predynastic_Egypt

Crawford, Medorem. *Journal of Medorem Crawford: an account of his trip across the plains with the Oregon Pioneers of 1842*. Edited by F. G. Young. Eugene, OR: Star Job Office, 1897. http://www.sos.wa.gov/legacy/publications_detail. aspx?p=11.

Darwin, Charles. *Journal of Researches into the Natural History and Geology of the countries visited during the voyage of HMS Beagle round the world*, 2d ed. London: John Murray, 1845. See also http://charles-darwin.classic-literature.co.uk/the-voyage-of-the-beagle/ebook-page-157.asp

Davydova, Angelina. "Why Russia's Forests Must Be Protected." *World Economic Forum*, January 16, 2015. https://www.weforum.org/agenda/2015/01/ why-russias-forests-must-be-protected/.

De Decker, Kris. "Medieval smokestacks: fossil fuels in pre-industrial times." *Low-Tech Magazine*, September 2011. http://www.lowtechmagazine.com/2011/09/ peat-and-coal-fossil-fuels-in-pre-industrial-times.html.

d'Errico, Francesco, Marian Vanhaeren, Nick Barton, Abdeljalil Bouzouggar, Henk Mienis, Daniel Richter, Jean-Jacques Hublin, Shannon P. McPherron, and Pierre Lozouet. "Additional evidence on the use of personal ornaments in the Middle Paleolithic of North Africa." *Proceedings of the National Academy of Sciences of the United States of America* (PNAS) 106, no. 38 August 28, 2009: 16051–56. doi:10.1073/pnas.0903532106.

Denevan, William M. "The Pristine Myth: The Landscape of the Americas in 1492." http://jan.ucc.nau.edu/~alcoze/for398/class/pristinemyth.html.

Deshpande, Omkar, Serafim Batzoglou, Marcus W. Feldman, and L. Luca Cavalli-Sforza. "A serial founder effect model for human settlement out of Africa." *Proceedings of the Royal Society B: Biological Sciences* 276, no. 1655 (September 2008): 291–300. doi:10.1098/rspb.2008.0750.

de Navarro, J. M. "Prehistoric Routes between Northern Europe and Italy Defined by the Amber Trade." *The Geographical Journal* 66, no. 6 (December 1925): 481–503. doi:10.2307/1783003.

Devitt, James. "Finding Showing Human Ancestor Older than Previously Thought Offers New Insights into Evolution." *New York University*. http://www.nyu. edu/about/news-publications/news/2011/06/29/finding-showing-human-ancestor-older-than-previously-thought-offers-new-insights-into-evolution.html.

Diamond, Jared. *Guns, Germs, and Steel: The Fates of Human Societies*. New York: W. W. Norton & Company, 1999.

Diamond, Jared, and James A. Robinson, eds. *Natural Experiments of History*. Cambridge, MA: Harvard University Press, 2010.

Dick, W., and A. Lichtenberg. "The myth of Hitler's role in building the autobahn." *Deutsche Welle*, August 4, 2012. http://www.dw.de/the-myth-of-hitlers-role-in-building-the-autobahn/a-16144981.

Dickinson. H. W., and Arthur Titley. *Richard Trevithick: The Engineer and the Man*. Cambridge: Cambridge University Press, 2010.

Discover Firemaking: An Introductory Guide, compiled by Ollie Douglas (Oxford, UK: Pitts River Museum of Anthropology and Archeology, 2010), https://www.prm.ox.ac.uk/sites/default/files/imported/basic/pdf/Fire_Making_fs.pdf.

Dorey, Fran. "The spread of people to Australia," *Australia Museum*, October 30, 2015, http://australianmuseum.net.au/The-spread-of-people-to-Australia/#sthash.7Rxcs8sQ.dpuf.

Drake, Brandon L. "The influence of climatic change on the Late Bronze Age Collapse and the Greek Dark Ages." *Journal of Archaeological Science* 39, no. 6 (May 2012): 1862-70. doi:10.1016/j.jas.2012.01.029.

Dunham, Will. "Easter Island's ancient inhabitants weren't so lonely after all." *Reuters*, October 23, 2014. http://www.reuters.com/article/2014/10/23/us-science-easterisland-idUSKCN0IC28C20141023.

Eaton, Joseph W. and Albert J. Mayer, *Man's Capacity to Reproduce: The Demography of a Unique Population* (Glencoe, IL.: The Free Press, 1954).

Elvin, Mark. *The Retreat of the Elephants: An Environmental History of China*. New Haven and London: Yale University Press, 2004.

Evans, Kate. "Martyr of the Amazon: The legacy of Chico Mendes." December 20, 2013 http://www.trust.org/item/20131220074605-dgjmi?view=print.

Flint, Henry M. *The railroads of the United States: their history and statistics comprising the progress and present condition of the various lines with their earnings and expenses; to which are added a synopsis of the railroad laws of the United States and an article on the comparative merits of iron and steel rails*. Philadelphia: John E. Potter and Company, 1868. https://ia600404.us.archive.org/23/items/railroadsunitedooflingoog/railroadsunitedooflingoog.pdf.

French, David. "Pre- and Early-Roman Roads of Asia Minor. The Persian Royal Road." *Iran* 36 (1998): 15–43. doi:10.2307/4299973.

Gadgil, Madhav, and Ramachandra Guha. *This Fissured Land: An Ecological History of India*. Berkeley and Los Angeles: University of California Press, 1992.

Giedion, Sigfried. *Space, Time and Architecture: The Growth of a New Tradition*. Cambridge, MA: Harvard University Press, 1941.

Gilgamesh, *The Epic of Gilgamesh*, tr. N.K. Sanders, Assyrian International News Agency, Books Online http://www.aina.org/books/eog/eog.pdf

Gladwell, Malcolm. *Outliers: The Story of Success.* New York: Little, Brown and Company, 2008.

Gracie, Carrie. "Qin Shi Huang: The ruthless emperor who burned books." *Bbc News,* October 15, 2012. http://www.bbc.com/news/magazine-19922863.

Graf, Kelly E., Caroline V. Ketron, and Michael R. Waters, editors. *Paleoamerican Odyssey.* College Station, TX: Texas A&M University Press, 2014. http://www.tamupress.com/product/Paleoamerican-Odyssey,7924.aspx.

Greenspan, Jesse. "The Charge of the Light Brigade, 160 Years Ago." *History in the Headlines,* October 24, 2014. http://www.history.com/news/the-charge-of-the-light-brigade-160-years-ago.

Harrison, Robert Pogue. *Forests: The Shadow of Civilization.* Chicago: The University of Chicago Press, 1992.

Hart, Diccon, with contributions by Lucy Allot, Mike Bamfort, Martin Bates, Sarah Davies, Gemma Driver, Sarah Jones, Peter Marshall, and John Whittaker. "Archaeological Investigations at Belmarsh West, London Borough of Greenwich Post-Excavation Assessment and Project Design for Publication." ASE Project Report: 2009056, Project No. 3541, March 2009.

Heaney, Lawrence R. "A Synopsis of Climatic and Vegetational Change in Southeast Asia." *Climatic Change* 19, no. 1 (January 1991): 53–61. doi:10.1007/BF00142213.

Heerwagen, J. H., and G. H. Orians. "Humans, Habitats and Aesthetics." In *The Biophilia Hypothesis,* edited by S. R. Kellert and E. O. Wilson. Washington, DC: Island Press, 1995.

Henn, Brenna M., L. L. Cavalli-Sforza, and Marcus W. Feldman. "The great human expansion." PNAS 109, no. 44 (October 2013): 17758–64. doi:10.1073/pnas.1212380109.

Herodotus, *The Histories.* Translated by Aubrey de Sélincourt. London: Penguin Classics, 1972.

Hillam, J., C. M. Groves, D. M. Brown, M. G. L. Baillie, J. M. Coles, and B. J. Coles. "Dendrochronology of the English Neolithic." *Antiquity* 64, no. 243 (June 1990): 210–20. doi:http://dx.doi.org/10.1017/S0003598X00077826.

Holen, Steven R. "Taphonomy of two last glacial maximum mammoth sites in the central Great Plains of North America: A preliminary report on La Sena and Lovewell." *Quaternary International* 142–143 (January 2006): 30–43. doi:10.1016/j.quaint.2005.03.003.

Holloway, April. "The 9,500-year-old honeycomb city of Çatalhöyük." *Ancient Origins,* September 19, 2013. http://www.ancient-origins.net/ancient-places-asia/9500-year-old-honeycomb-city-atalh-y-k-00840#!boPUoE.

Hopkin, Michael. "Ethiopia is top choice for cradle of *Homo sapiens*: Radioactive dating finds that fossil skulls are 195,000 years old." *Nature*, February 16, 2005. doi:10.1038/news050214-10.

Hochschild, Adam. *King Leopold's Ghost: A Story of Greed, Terror, and Heroism in Colonial Africa.* London: Pan Macmillan, 1999.

Hulbert, Lloyd C. "Causes of Fire Effects in Tallgrass Prairie." *Ecology* 69, no. 1 (February 1988): 46–58. doi:10.2307/1943159.

Hume, Mark. "Underwater discovery near Haida Gwaii could rewrite human history." *Globe and Mail*, September 23, 2014. http://www.theglobeandmail.com/news/british-columbia/bc-researchers-may-have-found-earliest-site-of-human-habitation-in-canada/article20737278/.

Huysecom, E., M. Rasse, L. Lespez, K. Neumann, A. Fahmy, A. Ballouche, S. Ozainne, M. Maggetti, Ch. Tribolo, and S. Soriano. "The emergence of pottery in Africa during the 10th millennium calbc: new evidence from Ounjougou (Mali)." *Antiquity* 83, no. 322 (2009): 905–17. https://doc.rero.ch/record/19037/files/mag_epa_2.pdf.

Hyslop, John. *The Inka Road System.* Orlando: Academic Press, 1984.

Jackson Jr., Lionel E., and Michael C. Wilson. "The Ice-Free Corridor Revisited." *Geotimes*, February 2004. http://www.geotimes.org/feb04/feature_Revisited.html#links.

James, Simon. "The Roman galley slave: *Ben-Hur* and the birth of a factoid." *Public Archaeology* 2, no. 1 (2001): 35–49. doi.org/10.1179/pua.2001.2.1.35.

Jefferson, Thomas. *The Papers of Thomas Jefferson Digital Edition*, ed. James P. McClure and J. Jefferson Looney. Charlottesville: University of Virginia Press, Rotunda, 2008–2015. Canonic URL: http://rotunda.upress.virginia.edu/founders/TSJN-01-38-02-0514

Original source: Main Series, Volume 38 (1 July–12 November 1802)

Johnston, Wesley. "Prelude to Famine 4: Demographics." http://www.wesleyjohnston.com/users/ireland/past/famine/demographics_pre.html

Joyce, James. *Ulysses.* ed. Jeri Johnson. London: Oxford's World Classics, 2011. See also: "Episode 15 – Circe," http://www.online-literature.com/james_joyce/ulysses/15/.

Kerouac, Jack. *On the Road: The Original Scroll.* Edited by Howard Cunnell. New York: Viking, 2007.

———. "Jack Kerouac, The Art of Fiction No. 41." Interview by Ted Berrigan. *The Paris Review*, no. 43 (Summer 1968). http://www.theparisreview.org/interviews/4260/the-art-of-fiction-no-41-jack-kerouac.

Kessler, David, and Peter Temin. "The organization of the grain trade in the early Roman Empire." *The Economic History Review* 60, no. 2 (2007): 313–32. doi:10.1111/j.1468-0289.2006.00360.x.

King, Anna. "Lessons from Japan: Is Hanford Ready to Withstand a Big
    Earthquake?" *Seattle Magazine*, August 2011. http://www.seattlemag.com/
    article/lessons-japan-hanford-ready-withstand-big-earthquake.

Kistler, Logan, Álvaro Montenegro, Bruce D. Smith, John A. Gifford, Richard
    E. Greene, Lee A. Newsom, and Beth Shapiro. "Transoceanic drift and the
    domestication of African bottle gourds in the Americas." PNAS 111, no. 8
    (January 10, 2014): 2937–41. doi:10.1073/pnas.1318678111. http://www.
    pnas.org/content/111/8/2937.short.

Kolbert, Elizabeth. "Ice Memory: Does a glacier hold the secret of how civilization
    began—and how it may end?" *New Yorker*, January 7, 2002. http://www.
    newyorker.com/magazine/2002/01/07/ice-memory.

Kuhn, Thomas. *The Structure of Scientific Revolutions*. Chicago: University of
    Chicago Press, 1962.

Kuzmina, E. E. *The Prehistory of the Silk Road*. Edited by Victor H. Mair.
    Philadelphia: University of Pennsylvania Press, 2008.

Kuzmin, Yaroslav V., Robert J. Speakman, Michael D. Glascock, Vladimir K.
    Popov, Andrei V. Grebennikov, Margarita A. Dikova, and Andrei V. Ptashinsky.
    "Obsidian use at the Ushki Lake complex, Kamchatka Peninsula (Northeastern
    Siberia): implications for terminal Pleistocene and early Holocene human
    migrations in Beringia." *Journal of Archaeological Science* 35, no. 8 (August
    2008): 2179–87. doi:10.1016/j.jas.2008.02.001.

Kuzmin, Yaroslav V. "Long-Distance Obsidian Transport in Prehistoric Northeast
    Asia." *Bulletin of the Indo-Pacific Prehistory Association* 32 (2012): 1–5. doi:
    http://dx.doi.org/10.7152/bippa.v32i0.9997. http://journals.lib.washington.
    edu/index.php/BIPPA/article/view/9997.

Lancy, David F., and M. Annette Grove. "'Getting Noticed': Middle Childhood
    in Cross-Cultural Perspective." *Human Nature* 22, no. 3 (September 2011):
    281–302.

Laporte Nadine T., Jared A. Stabach, Robert Grosch, Tiffany S. Lin, and Scott J.
    Goetz "Expansion of Industrial Logging in Central Africa." *Science* 316, no. 5830
    (June 8, 2007): 1451. doi:10.1126/science.1141057.

Laurance, William. "As Roads Spread in Rainforests, The Environmental Toll
    Grows," *Environment 360*, January 19, 2012, http://e360.yale.edu/feature/
    as_roads_spread_in_tropical_rain_forests_environmental_toll_grows/2485/.

Leakey, Richard, and Roger Lewin. *Origins Reconsidered: In Search of What Makes
    Us Human*. New York: Anchor Books, 1993.

Le Corbusier. *The City of To-morrow and Its Planning*. Translated by Fredrerick
    Etchells. New York: Dover Publications, Inc, 1987.

Legge, James. trans. and ed., *A Record of Buddhistic Kingdoms Being an Account
    by the Chinese Monk Fa-Hien of His Travels in India and Ceylon (AD 399-414)*

in Search of the Buddhist Books of Discipline (Oxford: Clarendon Press, 1886), 9–36, quoted in Daniel C. Waugh, "The Journey of Faxian to India," https://depts.washington.edu/silkroad/texts/faxian.html.

Lewis, M. J. T. "Railways in the Greek and Roman World." In *Early Railways. A Selection of Papers from the First International Early Railways Conference.* Edited by Andy Guy and Jim Rees. http://www.yieldopedia.com/paneladmin/reports/fb8f151d1ee5d60af0482d429fd27c10.pdf

Li, Heng, and Richard Durbin. "Inference of human population history from individual whole-genome sequences." *Nature* 475 (July 28, 2011): 493–96. doi:10.1038/nature10231.

Licciardi, Joseph M. "Chronology of latest Pleistocene lake-level fluctuations in the pluvial Lake Chewaucan basin, Oregon, USA." *Journal of Quaternary Science* 16, no. 6 (2001): 545–53. doi:10.1002/jqs.619.

Linklater, Andro. *Measuring America: How an Untamed Wilderness Shaped the United States and Fulfilled the Promise of Democracy.* New York: Walker and Company, 2002.

Liu, Li, Gyoung-Ah Lee, Leping Jiang, and Juzhong Zhang. "The earliest rice domestication in China." *Antiquity* 81, no. 313 (September 2007). http://antiquity.ac.uk/projgall/liu1/.

Liu, Wu, María Martinón-Torres, Yan-jun Cai, Song Xing, Hao-wen Tong, Shu-wen Pei, Mark Jan Sier, Xiao-hong Wu, R. Lawrence Edwards, Hai Cheng, Yi-yuan Li, Xiong-xin Yang, José María Bermúdez de Castro and Xiu-jie Wu. "The earliest unequivocally modern humans in southern China," *Nature,* October 14, 2015, doi: 10.1038/nature15696.

Maddison, Angus. *Contours of the World Economy, 1-2030 AD: Essays in Macro-Economic History.* Oxford: Oxford University Press, 2007.

———. "The Contours of World Development." *The World Economy: Volume 1: A Millennial Perspective and Volume 2: Historical Statistics,* 29–50. Paris: OECD Publishing, 2006. http://dx.doi.org/10.1787/9789264022621-3-en.

Malthus, Thomas Robert. *An Essay on the Principle of Population.* London: J. Johnson, 1798. http://www.econlib.org/library/Malthus/malPop.html.

Mann, Charles C. *1491: New Revelations of the Americas Before Columbus.* New York: Vintage Books, 2005.

Marcum, Diana. "Bea Kozera dies at 92; 'On the Road' character was based on her." *Los Angeles Times,* August 24, 2013. http://www.latimes.com/obituaries/la-me-beatrice-kozera-20130825,0,7434438,full.story.

McAuliffe, Kathleen. "Human evolution kicks into high gear." *Nbc News,* February 10, 2009. http://www.nbcnews.com/id/29123062/ns/technology_and_science-science/t/human-evolution-kicks-high-gear/#.UdjFH4WkBNQ.

Metspalu, Mait, Irene Gallego Romero, Bayazit Yunusbayev, Gyaneshwer Chaubey, Chandana Basu Mallick, Georgi Hudjashov, Mari Nelis, et al. "Shared and Unique Components of Human Population Structure and Genome-Wide Signals of Positive Selection in South Asia." *The American Journal of Human Genetics* 89, no. 6 (December 9, 2011): 731–44. doi:10.1016/j.ajhg.2011.11.010.

Mendelson, Marcy. "Warrior Graduation Ceremony Reveals Kenya at a Crossroads." *National Geographic,* September 22, 2013. http://news.nationalgeographic.com/news/2013/09/130921-samburu-moran-warrior-graduation-ceremony-kenya-culture/.

Miller, Kenneth. "Archaeologists Find Earliest Evidence of Humans Cooking With Fire." *Discover Magazine,* May 9, 2013. http://discovermagazine.com/2013/may/09-archaeologists-find-earliest-evidence-of-humans-cooking-with-fire.

Monbiot, George. "Indonesia is burning. So why is the world looking away?" *The Guardian,* October 30, 2015. http://www.theguardian.com/commentisfree/2015/oct/30/indonesia-fires-disaster-21st-century-world-media.

Montenegro, Álvaro, Reneé Hetherington, Michael Eby, and Andrew J. Weaver. "Modelling pre-historic transoceanic crossings into the Americas." *Quaternary Science Reviews* 25, nos. 11–12 (June 2006): 1323–38. doi:10.1016/j.quascirev.2005.11.008.

Mukherjee, Anna J., Elisa Rossberger, Matthew A. James, Peter Pfälzner, Catherine L. Higgitt, Raymond White, David A. Peggie, Dany Azar, and Richard P. Evershed. "The Qatna lion: scientific confirmation of Baltic amber in late Bronze Age Syria." *Antiquity* 82 (2008): 49–59. http://archiv.ub.uni-heidelberg.de/propylaeumdok/volltexte/2011/892.

Nelson, George. *Diaries.* Manuscript, Baldwin Collection, Toronto Public Library.

Opie, Kit, and Camilla Power. "Grandmothering and Female Coalitions: A Basis for Matrilineal Priority?" In *Early Human Kinship: From Sex to Social Reproduction,* edited by Nicholas J. Allen, Hilary Callan, Robin Dunbar, and Wendy James, 168–86. Malden, MA: Blackwell, 2008. http://www.academia.edu/177474/Grandmothering_and_Female_Coalitions_A_Basis_for_Matrilineal_Priority.

Owsley, Douglas W., and Richard L. Jantz, editors. *Kennewick Man: The Scientific Investigation of an Ancient American Skeleton.* College Station, TX: Texas A&M University Press, 2014.

Parker, Geoffrey. "The Spanish Road to the Netherlands." MHQ: *The Quarterly Journal of Military History,* September 28, 2012. http://www.historynet.com/the-spanish-road-to-the-netherlands.htm.

Pegler, Edward. "A primer on old-world metals before the Copper age (revised)." Armchair Prehistory, August 30, 2015. http://armchairprehistory.com/2015/08/30/a-primer-on-old-world-metals-before-the-copper-age/.

Pétrequin, P., S. Cassen, M. Errera, L. Klassen, A. Sheridan, and A. M. Pétrequin. "Jade. Grandes haches alpines du Néolithique européen. Ve et IVe Millénaires av. J.-C." Presses Universitaires de Franche-Comté, Besançon.

Pitblado, Bonnie L. "A Tale of Two Migrations: Reconciling Recent Biological and Archaeological Evidence for the Pleistocene Peopling of the Americas," *Journal of Archaeological Research* 19, no. 4 (December 2011): 327–75.

Pitulkoa. Vladimir V., Elena Y. Pavlova, Pavel A. Nikolskiy, and Varvara V. Ivanova. "The oldest art of the Eurasian Arctic: personal ornaments and symbolic objects from Yana RHS, Arctic Siberia." *Antiquity* 86, no. 333 (January 2012): 642–59. doi:http://dx.doi.org/10.1017/S0003598X00047827.

Pongratz, Julia, Ken Caldeira, Christian H. Reick, and Martin Claussen. "Coupled climate–carbon simulations indicate minor global effects of wars and epidemics on atmospheric CO_2 between AD 800 and 1850." *The Holocene* 21 no. 5 (August 2011): 843–51. doi:10.1177/0959683610386981. http://hol.sagepub.com/content/21/5/843.

Reel, Monte. "Traveling From Ocean to Ocean Across South America." *New York Times,* February 19, 2014. http://www.nytimes.com/2014/02/23/magazine/south-america-road-trip.html.

Roberts, Benjamin W., Christopher P. Thornton, and Vincent C. Pigott. "Development of metallurgy in Eurasia." *Antiquity* 83, no. 322 (December 2009): 1012–22. doi:http://dx.doi.org/10.1017/S0003598X00099312.

Romero, Simon. "Once Hidden by Forest, Carvings in Land Attest to Amazon's Lost World." *New York Times,* January 14, 2012. http://www.nytimes.com/2012/01/15/world/americas/land-carvings-attest-to-amazons-lost-world.html.

———. "Taps Start to Run Dry in Brazil's Largest City." *New York Times,* February 16, 2015. http://www.nytimes.com/2015/02/17/world/americas/drought-pushes-sao-paulo-brazil-toward-water-crisis.html.

Roosevelt, A. C., R. A. Housley, M. Imazio Da Silveira, S. Maranca, and R. Johnson. "Eighth Millennium Pottery from a Prehistoric Shell Midden in the Brazilian Amazon." *Science* 254, no. 5038 (January 1992):1621–24. doi:10.1126/science.254.5038.1621.

Sanft, Charles. *Communication and Cooperation in Early Imperial China: Publicizing the Qin Dynasty.* Albany, NY: SUNY Press, 2014.

Schivelbusch, Wolfgang. *The Railway Journey: The Industrialization of Time and Space in the Nineteenth Century.* Berkeley and Los Angeles: University of California Press, 2014.

Schobinger, Juan. "200.000 años del hombre en América: ¿qué pensar?" *Espacio, Tiempo y Forma, Serie I, Prehistoria y Arqueología* 1 (1988): 375–95. doi:http://dx.doi.org/10.5944/etfi.1.1988.4500.

Schwartz, John. "As Fires Grow, a New Landscape Appears in the West." *New York Times,* September 21, 2015. http://www.nytimes.com/2015/09/22/science/as-fires-grow-a-new-landscape-appears-in-the-west.html.

Severin, Tim. *In Search of Genghis Khan.* Sydney, Aukland, Johannesburg: Hutchison, 1991.

Shelach, Gideon. "*On the Invention of Pottery.*" *Science* 336, no. 6089 (June 2012): 1644–45. doi:10.1126/science.1224119.

Sherratt, Andrew. "The Obsidian Trade in the Near East, 14,000 to 6500 BC." *ArchAtlas,* Version 4.1 2005. http://www.archatlas.org/ObsidianRoutes/obsidian.php.

Soderstrom, Mary. *Green City: People, Nature and Urban Places.* Montreal: Véhicule Press, 2006.

———. *Making Waves: The Continuing Portuguese Adventure.* Montreal: Véhicule Press, 2010.

———. *Recreating Eden: A Natural History of Botanical Gardens.* Montreal: Véhicule Press, 2001.

———. *The Walkable City: From Haussmann's Boulevards to Jane Jacobs' Streets and Beyond.* Montreal: Véhicule Press, 2008.

Soffer, O., J. M. Adovasio, and D. C. Hyland. "The 'Venus' Figurines: Textiles, Basketry, Gender, and Status in the Upper Paleolithic." *Current Anthropology* 41, no.4 (August–October 2000): 511–37.

Stang, John. "Skull found on shore of Columbia." *Tri-City Herald,* July 29, 1996.

Stiner, Mary C., Natalie D. Munro, and Todd A. Surovell. "The Tortoise and the Hare: Small-Game Use, the Broad-Spectrum Revolution, and Paleolithic Demography." *Current Anthropology* 41, no. 1 (February 2000): 39–73.

Strasser, Thomas F., Eleni Panagopoulou, Curtis N. Runnels, Priscilla M. Murray, Nicholas Thompson, Panayiotis Karkanas, Floyd W. McCoy, and Karl W. Wegmann. "Stone Age Seafaring in the Mediterranean: Evidence from the Plakias Region for Lower Palaeolithic and Mesolithic Habitation of Crete." *Hesperia: The Journal of the American School of Classical Studies at Athens* 79, no. 2 (April-June 2010): 145–90. http://www.jstor.org/stable/40835484.

Sturdevant, Jay T. "Still an Open Book: Analysis of the Current Pre-Clovis vs. Clovis Debate from the Site of Meadowcroft Rockshelter, Pennsylvania and Monte Verde, Chile." *Nebraska Anthropologist* 15, Paper 125 (1999). http://digitalcommons.unl.edu/nebanthro/125.

Tamm, Erika, Toomas Kivisild, Maere Reidla, Mait Metspalu, David Glenn Smith, Connie J. Mulligan, Claudio M. Bravi, et al. "Beringian Standstill and Spread of Native American Founders." PLOS (September 2007). doi:10.1371/journal.pone.0000829.

Taylor, Timothy. *The Artificial Ape: How Technology Changed the Course of Human Evolution.* London: Palgrave Macmillan Trade, 2010.

Tegel, Willy, Rengert Elburg, Dietrich Hakelberg, Harald Stäuble, and Ulf Büntgen. "Early Neolithic Water Wells Reveal the World's Oldest Wood Architecture." PLOS (December 19, 2012). doi:10.1371/journal.pone.0051374.

Tennyson, Alfred Lord. "Charge of the Light Brigade." The Examiner, December 9, 1854. Accessed on the Poetry Foundation website at https://www. poetryfoundation.org/poems-and-poets/poems/detail/45319.

Thomas, Dylan. "The Force that through the Green Fuse Drives the Flower," The Poems of Dylan Thomas. New York: New Directions, 1952. Accessed September 20, 2015 at https://www.poets.org/poetsorg/poem force-through-green-fuse-drives-flower.

Thompson, Jennifer L., and Andrew J. Nelson "Middle Childhood and Modern Human Origins." Human Nature 22 (2011):249–80. doi:10.1007/s12110-011-9119-3.

Thompson, Logan. "Roman Roads." History Today 47, no. 2 (1997). http://www. historytoday.com/logan-thompson/roman-roads.

Thoreau, Henry David. "Sounds," chap. 4, paragraph 8, in Walden; or, Life in the Woods. Boston: Ticknor and Fields, 1854. Accessed at "The Thoreau Reader: Annotated works of Henry David Thoreau," ed. Richard Lenat, http://thoreau. eserver.org/walden04.html.

Thornton, Russell. "Population History of Native North Americans." In A Population History of North America, edited by Michael R. Haines and Richard H. Steckel, 9–50. Cambridge, UK: Cambridge University Press, 2000.

Torrent, Danielle. "UF study of lice DNA shows humans first wore clothes 170,000 years ago." News: University of Florida, January 6, 2011. http://news.ufl.edu/ archive/2011/01/uf-study-of-lice-dna-shows-humans-first-wore-clothes-170000-years-ago.php.

Twain, Mark. The Adventures of Huckleberry Finn. Berkeley, Los Angeles, London: University of California Press, 1985.

Vasconcellos, Eduardo A., and Michael Sivak. Road Safety in Brazil: Challenges and Opportunities. Report No. UMTRI-2009-29. Ann Arbor, MI: The University of Michigan Transportation Research Institute, August 2009. https://deepblue.lib. umich.edu/bitstream/handle/2027.42/63586/102260.pdf .

Vidal, John. "Modern cargo ships slow to the speed of the sailing clippers." The Guardian, July 25, 2010. http://www.theguardian.com/environment/2010/ jul/25/slow-ships-cut-greenhouse-emissions.

Wade, Nicholas. "Phonetic Clues Hint Language Is Africa-Born." New York Times, April 14, 2011. http://www.nytimes.com/2011/04/15/science/15language.html.

———. "Why Humans and Their Fur Parted Ways." New York Times, August 19, 2003. http://www.nytimes.com/2003/08/19/science/why-humans-and-their-fur-parted-ways.html?pagewanted=all&src=pm.

Wadley, Lyn, Christine Sievers, Marion Bamford, Paul Goldberg, Francesco Berna, and Christopher Miller. "Middle Stone Age Bedding Construction and Settlement Patterns at Sibudu, South Africa." *Science* 334, no. 6061 (December 9, 2011): 1388–91. doi:10.1126/science.1213317.

Walsh, Bryan. "The 10 Most Air-Polluted Cities in the World." *Time*, September 27, 2011. http://science.time.com/2011/09/27 the-10-most-air-polluted-cities-in-the-world/.

Weatherford, Jack. *Genghis Khan and the Making of the Modern World*. New York: Crown Publishers, 2004.

Webb, Steve, Matthew L. Cupper, and Richard Robins. "Pleistocene human footprints from the Willandra Lakes, southeastern Australia." *Journal of Human Evolution* 50, no. 4 (2005): 405–13. http://epublications.bond.edu.au/hss_pubs/40.

Weiler, Nicholas. "Menopausal killer whales are family leaders." *Science*, March 5, 2015. http://news.sciencemag.org/biology/2015/03/menopausal-killer-whales-are-family-leaders. doi: 10.1126/science.aab0277.

Wilford, John Noble. "World's Oldest Paved Road Found in Egypt." *New York Times*, May 8, 1994. http://www.nytimes.com/1994/05/08/world/world-s-oldest-paved-road-found-in-egypt.html.

Young, Rodney S. "Gordion on the Royal Road." *Proceedings of the American Philosophical Society* 107, no. 4 (August 15, 1963): 348–64.

Tatiana Zerjal et al., "The Genetic Legacy of the Mongols," *The American Journal of Human Genetics* 72, no. 3 (March 2003): 717–721, doi: http://dx.doi.org/10.1086/367774

Zimmer, Carl. "New DNA Results Show Kennewick Man Was Native American." *New York Times*, June 18, 2015. http://www.nytimes.com/2015/06/19/science/new-dna-results-show-kennewick-man-was-native-american.hotml?_r=0.

———. "A Single Migration from Africa Populated the World, Studies Find." *New York Times*, September 21, 2016. http://www.nytimes.com/2016/09/22/science/ancient-dna-human-history.html?_r=0.

INDEX

ABOUT THE AUTHOR

Mary Soderstrom is the author of four previous works of non-fiction, including *Green City: People, Nature and Urban Places*, a *Globe and Mail* best book of 2007; *The Walkable City: From Haussmann's Boulevards to Jane Jacobs' Streets* (2008); *Recreating Eden: A Natural History of Botanical Gardens* (2001); and *Making Waves: The Continuing Portuguese Adventure* (2010.) As well, she is the author of six novels and three short story collections. Originally from Washington State, she grew up in San Diego and was educated at the University of California at Berkeley. She has made Montreal her home for decades.